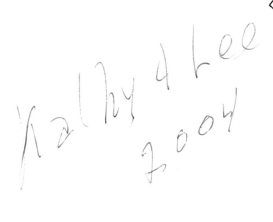

Kathy & Lee
2004

ST. LOUIS
Sports Folks

Tom Wheatley

Sports Publishing L.L.C.
www.SportsPublishingLLC.com

Direction of production: Susan M. Moyer
Project manager: Greg Hickman
Developmental editor: Doug Hoepker
Copy editor: Cynthia L. McNew
Dust jacket design: Christine Mohrbacher

ISBN: 1-58261-661-2

Printed in the United States.

SPORTS PUBLISHING L.L.C.
www.SportsPublishingLLC.com

ACKNOWLEDGEMENTS

These stories are reprinted by permission of the St. Louis *Post-Dispatch*. Most appeared between 2001 and 2003.

Freelance photographers Don Adams, Dave Kennedy, Erik Lunsford and Trisha Siddens graciously allowed their work to be reproduced, much to the reader's advantage.

Three editors at the *Post-Dispatch* rate special mention: Cameron Hollway for encouraging the pursuit of these profiles, Larry Starks for encouraging the pursuit of this book and Carolyn Kingcade for her encouragement, period.

These stories wound up between hard covers only because of three conspirators who have never actually met or even spoken to each other.

Buck Smith is the can-do leader of the Challenger Baseball kids. He got the project airborne over the inertia of a certain Doubting Thomas.

Mike Pearson of Sports Publishing in Champaign, Illinois, convinced his colleagues to take a shot at a book by someone they never heard of, about people they never heard of, doing things they never heard of.

Most of all, Jerry Stack of the *Post-Dispatch* went to acrobatic lengths to fit such lengthy pieces into the paper. As an editor, Stacko is a throwback to the golden age of newspapers, when content dictated design and not vice versa.

Finally, thanks to my favorite sports folks for bearing with me and my wacky work schedule: My wife Suzanne (swimming), son Tommy (basketball), daughters Katie (figure skating) and Carrie (volleyball), and dog Punky (sleeping).

TOM WHEATLEY
St. Louis, Missouri
April 15, 2003

THE LINEUP

FOREWORD

I am just fascinated with *St. Louis Sports Folks.*

I've lived in St. Louis for 33 years now, but I never realized how much I don't know about my own town. I failed to realize how many interesting people live in this community and how many of them I've never met.

You think the whole world is contained in your own small corner. A book like this helps you see how far from the truth that is.

I've been reading Tom Wheatley for nearly 20 years in the *Post-Dispatch.* He doesn't just look for the facts and the figures, the superficial things in the world of sports. He has the curiosity to get to know the people.

He knows that regardless of how famous you are or how obscure you are, everyone has an intriguing story. To get that story, to ferret it out, there has to be someone like Tom.

People think of him as a friend first and a writer second. These are not the kinds of stories that come from a 15-minute phone call.

Tom helps you see that the richness of life isn't necessarily sitting on the 50-yard line at the Super Bowl. Sometimes it comes from sitting in a folding chair on The Hill with your friends, reliving a life well lived.

And I love the diverse field of subjects in this book. From those who played professional sports for a living to those who have to put a ball on a tee to be able to hit, Tom shows us that a great story doesn't always revolve around a standing ovation from 50,000 people.

Hand in hand with that, we live in a *SportsCenter* universe where everything is "me, me, me." It's really enjoyable to read about people who are the antithesis of that.

There's not a doubt in my mind that this book will enrich you. It'll leave you feeling good about people in general. You'll want to meet every person in it.

And here's the real payoff: You'll feel good to know that you live in a town with so many quality human beings.

DAN DIERDORF
CBS Sports

INTRODUCTION

I'm a refugee from Pittsburgh, which I always thought was the cultural hub of the universe. Until I joined the Marine Corps and met my first St. Louis sports folks.

There was Don Todaro, son of a Florissant barber who ran track at Westminster College with Bake McBride. As a college grad, Donny could have gone straight to Officer Candidate School, as I did. Instead, just for the heck of it, he started as a private in boot camp before eventually being commissioned.

Then there was Gunnery Sergeant Michael P. Casey, a former South St. Louis soccer player. He was the most leathery leatherneck I ever met. His sarcasm could stop a tank. Once in the Philippines, a stray dog bit one of our marines, who had to find it or undergo rabies shots.

"Bring back that dog," Gunny Casey barked at the trooper, "or I'll bite you and you *will* die."

Another time, I goofed up and left our troops stranded in blistering heat.

"Don't worry, Lieutenant," snapped the Gunny. "That's good training. It'll teach 'em to hate!"

But my two favorite St. Louisans in the Corps were stationed together at Camp Lejeune, N.C. They were Lieutenant S.J. Stockhausen, a former swimmer and Southwest High grad, and Corporal Leon Spinks, another city kid who boxed a little. In November of 1976, Lt. Stockhausen was the administrative officer at Headquarters Company. Cpl. Spinks had just won his gold medal at the Montreal Olympics. I had just been discharged, honorably I might add, and was in the area, as the marines say.

Lt. Stockhausen, a friend of mine since we first were commissioned two and a half years before, picks up the story from there.

"Leon was in my company," said the lieutenant. "He was in charge of fighting and folding towels in the gym. None of us knew who he was until the Olympics. He was a private first class, but his rank was so unimpressive that we promoted him to corporal because of the Olympics.

"Several other things happened in his status after he won the gold medal, such as he was UA coming back from the Olympics."

UA means Unauthorized Absence.

"My CO [commanding officer] told us to hurry up and make leave papers for him," said the lieutenant, "so we could pretend he was on leave until we could find him." He was about a week late. We didn't want to have to court-martial him right after the Olympics.

"Then someone made the unbelievably dumb mistake of sending him—unescorted—up to Washington, D.C., to see the Commandant of the Marine Corps. When my CO found that out, he started yelling, 'What idiot was in charge of this? Why would anybody let him try to get to Headquarters Marine Corps by himself?' Naturally, Leon got lost and was late to see the Commandant. Then he went UA again on the way back, and we had to make up more retroactive leave papers for him. He finally made a dramatic return.

"He drove into, and knocked down, the huge billboard that welcomed poor unfortunate souls to Camp Lejeune. At this point, my superiors wanted to get him out before he became an embarrassment to the Marine Corps.

"He was fabulous public relations for awhile: The Fighting Marine from Camp Lejeune. So they felt they owed him a decent discharge and a chance to begin his pro career...plus get rid of him.

"He had about a year left, but papers were drawn up to give him a hardship discharge. There's a list of maybe 10 criteria for a hardship. Leon met one: that he could make more money outside of the Marine Corps.

"We tried to get him to qualify under another one, that his family needed him to fight professionally to provide financial assistance. But even though his family needed the money, his mother would not sign the papers. Leon called her from my office phone and begged her to sign. The only words he got in were, 'But Momma . . . *Momma!*' I never talked to her, but I had a magazine article where she said she wanted Leon to stay in the Marine Corps. She knew he needed that disciplining force in his life. And she never signed the papers for him, ever. So I told my CO that Leon didn't qualify."

The Marine Corps decided to go ahead with Leon's discharge board anyway. The brass figured that was better than court-martialing their gap-toothed recruiting poster for his unmilitary behavior.

"I was the recorder for the discharge board," said Lieutenant Stockhausen, "which means I presented the government's case. I had to show whether Leon qualified to get out with a hardship discharge.

"It was weird. The government wanted him out, but the guidelines did not support that. There were six or seven officers on the board, and they all sat there like a bunch of puppets. They all had the word that Leon was supposed to get this discharge. I pointed out that he didn't qualify, but they all voted for it anyway. I had the only dissenting vote. I recorded that and wrote a dissenting opinion. I had my company clerks type it up, because I knew the board would change it if they typed it up. Then I got everybody on the board to sign the report, and I turned it in.

"A few days later, they called me up to sign the new copy they'd typed up anyway. It didn't lie, but it didn't mention my dissenting vote. I felt like an ant that was ready to be stepped on, so I signed it.

"It seemed kind of futile to make any more noise. But I'd gone through so many cases of marines who had real hardships and could have gone back to help their families, but who didn't qualify. We held those people, who really had a need, to the guidelines. And we let Leon go when he didn't have a need."

The lieutenant always admired Mrs. Spinks for trying to put her son's welfare ahead of any quick riches in pro boxing.

"She obviously made the right decision by not signing the papers," Lt. Stockhausen said. "She was farsighted enough to know what would happen."

What happened is that Leon quickly numbed the world by winning the world heavyweight title from Muhammad Ali. Then he continued to numb the world with his immature antics, such as driving the wrong way on one-way streets and partying away his title, money and future. But would Leon have been better served by serving out his Marine Corps hitch?

"Well, I don't think we could have changed his attitude," said the lieutenant. "After the Olympics there weren't any other goals for him to attain in the Corps. He'd gone as far as he could in amateur boxing in the service. And he'd folded all the towels at Camp Lejeune."

What the lieutenant left out were the veiled threats received from certain superiors who wanted a quick and unanimous discharge verdict. It wasn't easy for a junior officer to stand on principle over policy in the face of that pressure. I always admired my friend's gutsy stance.

Anyway, we all moved on.

Eight years later, I became a South St. Louisan myself when I was hired by the *Post-Dispatch*. Among other things, I covered boxing. Among other boxers, I covered Leon's three sons in the amateur ranks. When their wayward dad finally showed up to watch a bout, I introduced myself and mentioned the discharge caper. Leon, a man of few words, had none to spare on the subject.

Along the way, I never lost touch with my favorite lieutenant, Suzanne J. Stockhausen. As a matter of fact, I married her. We eventually moved with our three kids into her old South St. Louis neighborhood, within walking distance of Ted Drewes Frozen Custard Stand.

For the record, I'm not related to any other St. Louis sports folks that you'll meet here. But be advised that I do salute all of them as meritorious characters with character. Even the ones who aren't ex-marines.

MICKEY GARAGIOLA

The Hot Stove League on The Hill

Traditionally, the baseball Hot Stove League operates in winter, during the off season, when fans warm themselves with speculation. Then baseball kept expanding its season until it slopped into nearly all of nature's seasons. Other sports followed suit. So when a group of self-styled experts on The Hill began gathering year-round to debate the issues of the day, it seemed only logical.

Logical, by the way, is a word not always associated with the repartee at "The Home." That's what Mickey Garagiola, one of the retired regulars, calls their home base at Fairmount Service, an auto repair shop at the corner of Marconi and Bischoff, across from Vitale's Bakery and the Italia-America Bocce Club. The soiree meets on weekdays at lunchtime for a couple of hours, or until tongues become too tired to wag.

Hot-stove was a fitting term when the grizzled experts grilled themselves, in more ways than one, on a July scorcher on the pavement in front of the shop. As each expert arrives, he picks out a chair from the stock inside the garage, places it in or out of the shade, as his constitution requires, and starts to yak. Or as Mickey, former voice of wrestling at The Chase, likes to say, "Just throw another log on the fire."

The lineup changes daily and by the minute. Experts come and go, tossing opinions and wisecracks and needles as needed. Here is the roster for a recent pow-wow, with ages and former professions included: Les Garanzini, who says he is "81.5 years old," bartender; Freddie Regalia, 81, a union tile setter; Mickey Garagiola, 80, waiter; Gene "Cookie" Cucchi, 68, supervisor for Laclede Gas; Charlie Gualdoni, 68, barber; Bob "House" Garavaglia, 67, carpenter; John Beltram, 65, teamster/contractor; Joe Bova, 65, city employee, mainly in the street department; and Brian "Booger" Vangel, 39, self-employed.

All were raised on The Hill and still live there, except for Booger, who is in Lemay, and Mickey, who settled nearby in the city nearly 50 years ago, explaining that housing prices were too high in his old neighborhood.

"I was a busboy at Ruggeri's when Mickey waited tables there," said Cookie. "Survey all the busboys around, and he was Number One. That's the cheapest! He never gave us busboys nothing."

Booger, the youngest by almost 30 years, seems like a gate crasher.

"Yeah," he says, "but I was here before almost every one of these geezers. Me, Lester and Cookie used to barbecue back here in '85, '86. When the geezers saw the food down here, they all piled in. Never pass up free food, right?"

He smiles and looks straight at the visiting sports writer as he says that. Booger is the only group member still working. He says he's "in the coin-activated amusement industry," meaning pinball and video games. He spends two days per week checking his machines, draining off their quarters and bending his itinerary around sessions at The Home. Still, his elders are dubious about his employment.

"He's a bug sprayer," says Joe.

On this day, the group invited three ringers to sit in: Cookie's grandaughter, Molly, 10, a smiling rose in this thornfield; Mickey's son, John, 47, frittering his day off from Schnucks; and a pen-wielding interloper, 50, feeling sprightly among the geezers but somewhat inadequate, being foreign-born—in Pittsburgh—and only one-fourth Italian.

Occasionally, a customer runs the gauntlet of chairs with a vehicle for Harry Berra, Fairmount's owner and voice of reason, to examine. Less occasionally, Harry leaves the garage to comment on something he's overheard. Even when business is slow, he refuses to pull up a chair.

"They stay out here," he barks, "and I stay in here. That's the only way it works."

Harry is no relation to Yogi Berra, the legendary New York Yankees philosopher-catcher who was raised on The Hill.

"We didn't play baseball," Harry says. "We're the poor Berras."

Yogi is in the Baseball Hall of Fame. So is Mickey's older brother, Joe Garagiola, a former big-league catcher now living in Phoenix who was enshrined for his work as a broadcaster. In the group, the only actual athlete is Cookie, inducted into the St. Louis Soccer Hall of Fame as a halfback. Joe claims special stature, having umpired for the Catholic Youth Council. His real distinction lies elsewhere.

"He's the only Sicilian in the bunch," Mickey says. "We're all northern Italians."

Because he is outnumbered, or a former ump, or just plain ornery, Joe loudly takes the offensive.

"All these guys are Cardinal rooters," he snorts, adjusting his Yankees cap. "They think Tony La Russa's the greatest manager in the world."

Joe then scalds La Russa for not knowing the tag-up rule on a fly ball, citing an example from a recent game. The group gnaws on this bone for several minutes, Joe against the world. Since nobody saw the play, or heard about the play, or has a rulebook handy, the matter finally dies unresolved.

Joe returns to his general theme.

"I don't like the Cardinals and La Russa," he says. "I don't like the way he manages. They say he's so great, but has he ever had a bad team to work with?"

"Yeah," says Mickey. "The Cardinals."

Joe switches gears to the recent demise of Ted Williams.

"These guys think that Stan Musial is the greatest hitter of all time," he says. "It's Williams, no contest."

Les enters the fray to say, "The Pope and I and Musial are all born in the same year—1920."

"Who the hell did he marry?" Joe asks the group, referring to Les.

"A Sicilian," says Les.

"What does that tell you?" says Joe, forgetting about Musial as he scores against the northerners.

Almost on cue, a car rolls through the four-way stop on the corner.

Hot Stove Hill toppers: from left, Cookie Cucchi, Cookie's granddaughter Molly—a rose among the thorns—John Beltram, John Garagiola, Joe Bova and Mickey Garagiola.
(Photo by David Kennedy)

The driver leans out the window and yells, "Hey, Joe! Make sure you put your teeth in!" After the chortling subsides, Mickey starts grumbling about the big-league All-Star Game, which ended in a draw after 11 innings when the teams ran through their rosters.

"You got nine innings," says House. "Then you got two more. What more do you want?"

"How can you run out of players?" Mickey says.

"You want to hurt the ballplayers?" House snaps.

"I have to agree with that one," says Freddie, to murmurs of agreement.

The interloper butts in to ask how long the group has been meeting.

"Almost since Harry's been here," Mickey says.

And when was that? The panel can't remember. Harry is summoned and asked how long he's owned the garage.

"Twenty-three years," he says.

And how long has the group been squatting on the premises?

"Too long," he says, turning away before the laugh track kicks in.

Meanwhile, Les finally notices that Mickey is in Bermuda shorts.

"Mick," he says, "if I was you, I'd cover up those legs."

"You wish you had legs like these," said Mickey, flexing both pale toothpicks.

Talk turns to how the social order on The Hill once arranged itself around sports.

"There used to be 24 athletic clubs up here," Charlie says.

"Each block almost had a club," Cookie says.

"And we played street ball all the time," Freddie says.

"We don't know how the heck Yogi and Joe's brother ever played big-league baseball," Cookie says. "Everyone around here played soccer and fastpitch softball.

"Yeah, we played softball," Mickey says, inspiring sneers that he never played anything. "Hey, I played left field."

With no one to talk to out there, what did he do?

"I played the ball on one hop and threw it to second," Mickey says. "What'd you think I did?"

At which point Harry re-emerges from the garage, spots a passing lad and yells, "Get an education, kid, or you'll end up like this!"

As he returns to work Joe says, "It's all in fun. If these guys weren't here, they'd be home with their wives."

Doing what?

"Nothing," Joe says. "Hey, let's get back to your man, Stan."

Musial is a common subject. But he runs a distant third to The Hill's two famous graduates, Yogi and Mickey's brother Joe.

"Yogi never comes back," someone grumps. "But Joe does."

John Beltram, showing up belatedly, says, "I was born in Yogi Berra's house. And I got a picture of Mickey's brother, with a full head of hair, in my back yard. Joe's babysitting me and I'm in diapers."

"You're still in diapers," somebody huffs.

Charlie says, "I've got a picture of Yogi Berra when he's about 16 years old, and his sister and my cousin and my brother and myself. His parents and my parents were very close. They came here from the same town in northern Italy."

Joe, the Sicilian, is not impressed—despite Yogi's affiliation with his beloved Yankees.

"The only thing I agree with Yogi on," Joe intones, "is he did have Jackie Robinson out at the plate. Remember when Jackie stole home that time in the World Series? Yogi had the plate blocked and he had the glove down."

The World Series reminds Mickey of the current champs, the Arizona Diamondbacks. His nephew, Joe Garagiola Jr., is general manager.

"Joe Jr.'s the one who gave me this cap," says Mickey, pointing to the big A on the front.

Did his nephew invite him to the World Series in Phoenix?

"We would have gone," Mickey says, "but Booger couldn't get the limousine."

At this point, a few hard-boiled experts move their chairs out of the sun and under the carport, where the station's gas pumps once stood.

"They call it the veranda," says Harry, blowing his gruff image by appearing with soft drinks for the squatters.

A huge pot with a flowering plant graces the veranda. Cookie gets up to water it.

"We want to put in a pool," Booger says, "but Harry won't go for it. We're working on a screened-in porch and a ceiling fan."

In the winter, Harry invites the group inside where it's warm without benefit of a hot stove.

"You wonder why Harry lets us stay here?" Cookie says. "Look at all the chairs, and our cars parked here in front, it looks like he's busy, right?"

So you scare off customers so Harry doesn't have to work as much?

"You got him pegged exactly!" Cookie says.

Harry, having heard that, says, "I'm working all the time. Except I took a vacation to Kodiak, Alaska. I lock everything up. And I leave. And I call my wife back here to see if everything's okay.

"And she says, 'About six of 'em are still out in front, sitting there. They brought their own chairs.' "

But on this afternoon, the experts start to drift off at about 2:30 . . . to do what?

"Take a nap," John Beltram says. "Then go play bocce. Go cruising. There's always something to do."

"And I'm never in a hurry," Les says. "By the way, what are you calling your story?"

How about Day of the Living Dead?

"That's a good one," Les says. "Another good title would be: It Pays to Be Retired."

"Call it the Pigeon Coop," John says. "That's what they call northern Italians, pigeons."

This is actually the third shift of pigeons since Harry "bought the corner," as he put it, in 1980. Since then, the first two shifts of geezers have moved to an even more heavenly perch. Sadly, shortly after this memorable day like any other, Lester died from a bout with cancer. His wife had passed several years before, and he was at peace with himself and his fellow debaters. They got one last smile when they paid their last respects at the funeral home.

"Lester was laid out in a tuxedo," said Mickey. "That's how he wanted to be buried, because he always told us, 'That night, I'll be dancing with my wife.' "

Lester, of course, is not forgotten when the lawn chairs come out now at Fairmount.

"His name is brought up every day," Mickey says. "Somewhere in the conversation, someone says, 'Well, Lester would have said . . .' "

For the record, how does Harry, the host, refer to his opinionated guests?

"Roundees," he says. "When the first group started coming around, another old guy said to me, 'Why do you put up with those Roundees?'

"I said, 'Roundees? Where do you get that?' And he said, 'Because they just sit around and hang around.' "

All day. Every day. As long as there's a breath of hot air left in them.

2

CHALLENGER BASEBALL

Can-Do Kids Know All About Winning

t's the aptly named Challenger Baseball League, a chance for youngsters with mental or physical disabilities to don a uniform, hit the ball and run—or wheel, if need be. Not away from their challenges. Toward them.

That was the noble motive in 1994, when Buck Smith of Kirkwood read about Challenger ball in a magazine. Something else appealed to Buck, a graphic designer at Fleishman Hillard who is divorced with no children.

"It seemed like a lot of fun," he said. "For everyone. Kids. Parents. Coaches."

So he declared himself commissioner, put an ad in the paper, reserved a field at Tilles Park in West County and awaited developments.

"The field was kind of muddy," he said. "We had about 15 kids and their parents and we're all standing here like, 'What do we do now?' Then a van pulled up. It was Gene LaVigne and his two daughters and their girls' softball team. Gene saw the ad and he just showed up. His players jumped out of the van and got everything organized."

Debbie Carter of Pattonville brought her son Chris, who is autistic, to play that first day.

"We were the outfield, the parents," said Debbie. "We didn't have enough kids. Now it's eight teams."

Eight teams and 120 players just at Tilles. Joe Torressi, brother-in-law of Mayor Francis Slay, leads another 60 kids on four teams at Gallaudet School in South St. Louis. And two new teams have cranked up in Franklin County.

"We want to start teams in Illinois, St. Charles and South County," Buck said.

The Challenger game plan is magnetic. Every player gets to bat every inning—and hit the ball, either off a tee or as pitched by a grownup.

Nobody is ever out, so there are no umpires or arguments. Since every batter becomes a runner who eventually winds up safe at home, there are no scores and no losers.

Ironically, this no-fail, all-fun concept was spun off 15 years ago by Little League Baseball, which holds its own high-pressure, high-stakes World Series.

But the Challenger program lets the kids revel in what they *can* do, not what they *can't*. It has done wonders for the local players, as advertised.

Dan Heffington, a Delta Airlines pilot and boyhood friend of Buck's, is awed by the view from the pitcher's mound.

"One little guy came out and just screamed his entire first day," said Dan, who calls himself the Grand Exalted Pooh-Bah. "He wouldn't wear his hat. He wouldn't get out in the field.

"His name is David. I don't want to embarrass him by saying his last name. But he's out there today with his buddies, fielding the ball, throwing the ball, running the bases. And his dad's elated.

"We have another guy, Brady Kedge, in a mechanized wheelchair. I'm pitching to him, and he says, 'I'm taking you downtown.' I said, 'Oh, yeah? Where's downtown?'

And he points. And of course he tagged one. Is that confidence? He's out here trash-talking. I love it."

The transformation starts with the wardrobe. To put it another way, clothes make the kids.

"The big thing is the uniform," Buck said. "On Opening Day, they all get a full uniform. Hat, shirt, pants and socks. And they're so excited. Once they get that uniform, they're part of a team, like their brothers and sisters.

"And now, *they're* the heroes. Now, their brothers and sisters are cheering for *them*. The self-esteem level, their confidence, is higher. And they have teammates.

"That's important to these kids."

Teammates are important to any kid, with or without disabilities. And Challenger kids, it turns out, are more typical than strangers would ever suspect.

"I had never spent any time with disabled kids," Buck said. "I thought, 'They're disabled. How do I talk to them? How do I deal with them?' "

Answer: The same as with any other boy or girl.

"Exactly!" Buck said. "I never feel sorry for these kids. Ever. All they need is a chance. And once they get a chance, it's a whole new world.

"Every Saturday it's something. There's always a kid who always had to hit off a tee, who hasn't gotten a hit with a pitched ball in two years, and all of sudden he'll get one.

"We have a kid, Cory McMahon, who has cerebral palsy and he's blind. And he hits a pitched ball. He's amazing. Everybody has a story."

Buck expected wonderful things to happen with the players. What he didn't expect was the wondrous effect the Challenger kids had on him, the coaches like Dan and the "buddies," or helpers, aged 10 to 18.

This is no Saturday penance in the park for do-gooders.

"We have a ton of fun, I'll tell you," Buck said.

Beyond that, the buddies are having their lives changed by the kids they set out to help. Meg LaVigne of Town and Country was 12 on that 1994 Opening Day when she hopped out of her dad's van to pitch in. Now 20, she is the anchorwoman of the purple-shirted buddies.

"I was actually supposed to stay up at school this summer," said Meg, who attends the University of Dayton, "but I wanted to come home for this."

The Challenger kids actually altered her schedule for life. She decided to major in music therapy, a new way to help the disabled stretch their limitations.

"I had no experience with this population when we started here," said Meg. "That first day was intimidating at first. But if you spend five minutes with these kids, they win you over forever."

Her sister, Nellie, 16, was also present at the creation in '94.

"It's just been wonderful," said Nellie, who attends Nerinx Hall High. "My friends love it, too. They come by every week. If they come out once, they just keep coming back."

Face of a winner: Megan Ferranto thinks Challenger Baseball is No. 1.
(Photo courtesy of Dan Heffington/Challenger Baseball)

The Challenger kids have that magic pull on people.

Kids like Bryan Wheatley of Chesterfield, who just turned 16 and will be a freshman at Parkway Central.

"Bryan is non-verbal, mentally retarded," said his mom, Barbara. "He can't talk and he also has attention deficit. There's no medical diagnosis for what he has.

"But he likes social stuff. He likes to swim and is a good skater, but he won't play hockey. Bryan doesn't like anything mean. He thinks hockey is too mean."

So Challenger ball is a perfect fit.

"Bryan was off the tee at first," said his mom, "but now he hits a pitched ball. He just likes to be out there with the people. He really liked it when the Hazelwood Central baseball team came out one day to be buddies. He thought that was just the most wonderful thing."

Bryan can form sounds that only a practiced ear like his mom's can decipher. But when he hustles over to her after another successful at-bat, he doesn't need a translator for his ear-to-ear smile.

"These kids are used to working for everything they get," said Barb. "If my other son, Andrew, worked as hard as Bryan, he'd be at Harvard one day. Bryan's made everything happen. If he was a quitter, he wouldn't have made it through the first week of this.

"People think Bryan is my hardest son, but he's cheerful and he keeps working at everything. Bryan's going all the time. He'll do yard work for all the neighbors.

"Andrew's the one who's hard. He'll get frustrated at something and give up, but Andrew is great with Bryan.

"Bryan doesn't know a stranger. Everyone's his friend. Everyone looks out for him. It's amazing: The kids who look out for him the most tend to be bullies with other kids."

Barb was sitting with Meena Laks, who is from Chesterfield by way of India. Her son, Deepak, 23, is a Challenger player with Down Syndrome.

"They're just like anyone else, just slower," said Meena. "They like to get out of the house and see their friends every Saturday. But they take it seriously. They follow the rules. They know the game. They watch the Cardinals on TV. They want to slide and imitate real baseball players. See what they do with their hats?"

She nodded toward Nate Mangold of Fenton. His cap was tucked smartly into his rear waistband while he wore his batting helmet. Nate, 16, attends Southview School. He has Down Syndrome.

"He was hooked from the minute he got here," said Lisa Suda, Nate's mom. "There's not too many sports he can play. He's got a pacemaker, too. At school, they do a Special Olympics, but he never had a full uniform."

Nate is a natural athlete. He needed just two swings in his Challenger debut to jump to the most advanced group.

"His first time up, he hit a ball onto this field from the other diamond," Lisa said. "The second time, he hit another one. The coach said, 'I think you need to be on a different team.'

"Nate was worried. He said, 'What did I do? What did I do?' I said, 'You hit the ball so far you get to go to another team.' "

Nate caught on quickly. He now describes his move this way: "I hit two home runs for the Eagles, then I got traded to the Stars."

Even more impressively, he caught a fly ball.

"They let the kid keep running," said Lisa, "and Nate goes, 'Hey, I caught the ball!' And his teammates are all yelling, 'He caught the ball, he caught the ball!'"

Nate is all business at all times, bearing down in the field and sliding head first into bases.

"Put that down: I had two slides," said Nate. "My coach said that it's okay if I get dirty. Write down that I got a home run. I've got 15 of them. Put down that I'm the greatest All-Star, Number 29."

"Not!" yelled a voice from down the bench.

Nate grinned and said, "I like this team. But I think boys can hit home runs better than girls."

That shot did not faze Allison Murray, 19, of Richmond Heights, another agile athlete with learning disabilities. Allison is in a career training program and said, "I'd like to be a certified nurse." She is certainly off the tender-loving-care charts, based on the way she cradled and soothed a kitten that a spectator brought. Then, realizing that the show was going on, Allison sprinted out to play right center field, not bothering to find her cap or glove.

What she most enjoys about her second season is, "I get to be with my friends, Lindsey and my other two friends who aren't here today."

She smiled at Lindsey Goldenhersh of Clayton, who is also 19.

The feminine foursome created quite a hubbub the other weekend.

"They had their prom," said Lisa Suda, "and they brought their photos. They were all in their formal dresses, and they looked so cute."

Challenger parents are drawn to all of the players.

"All we ask the parents to do," said Buck, "is to bring their kids and yell their lungs out. And they do. Every week, a parent brings treats for all the kids on that team, and we have a little party."

When the season ends, all 200 players will be chosen for the All-Star Game at Berra Park on The Hill. Every All-Star is introduced over the loudspeaker for one at-bat, which will produce the usual hit and run. After the game comes a season-ending picnic.

Debbie Carter can hardly believe the growth—in her son Chris and in the program—since that first Opening Day nine years ago.

"Eight," corrected Chris, and he's technically right.

It's been nine seasons but eight calendar years since that autistic boy first suited up. Now, tall and trim at 18, Chris looks as natural in a baseball uniform as fellow St. Louisan Kerry Robinson of the Cardinals. He remains a big backer of Challenger Baseball.

"It gets kids with disabilities involved," he said. "It gives us a chance to bond with our buddies who help us. There are no umpires in this league. It's more important to have fun."

Hearing Chris speak, it's hard to imagine him lost inside the self-absorbed autistic world. Or to imagine his main disability when he became a Challenger kid.

"Communication," said Debbie, grinning at a stranger's disbelief. "He didn't start talking till he was six. I had kept talking to him, but he still wasn't saying much when he came here. Now he's real, real self-sufficient. This has helped a lot. It's programs like this that give him the confidence to keep going."

Chris also plays in the concert band at Pattonville. And he has a summer job.

"He works for the Maryland Heights Park and Rec Department," his mom said. "He's a junior camp counselor."

Talk about coming full circle. Every time a Challenger kid gets a hit, he or she hears the buddies yelling encouragement and starts down the basepath, and a little miracle is in progress.

And, remember, every Challenger kid gets a hit at every at-bat.

3

REINHOLD HENNINGSEN

Shooting Pool and the Bull with Minnesota Fats

R einhold Henningsen plays pool for relaxation. Nothing unusual there for a retiree of 71. A pool table is the centerpiece of his basement, which is decorated in neoclassical flea market style. A life-size poster of Marilyn Monroe. Political yard signs. Old tools. Neon advertising lights. A photo of a man with a cue stick.

Hardly unusual décor for a basement rec room. Except that the man in the photo is Minnesota Fats, wielding his cue stick in this very basement in Crestwood, playing this very table, which he personally picked out for his host.

How did the late, great hustler find his way to this South County basement . . . and return a dozen times over 20 years? Now that's an unusual story. And so is the friendship that Rein shared with this legendary character.

They met aboard a TWA flight in the summer of 1972, a decade after Jackie Gleason played a supposedly fictional character named Minnesota Fats in the movie *The Hustler.* Rein was returning from Los Angeles on a business trip for the Crane Company. He ran the naval-nuclear division, providing the main steam line for carriers and submarines.

"We always rode in first class on business," Rein said. "I sat down, and this fella next to me said, 'I'm Minnesota Fats. Want my autograph?' I said, 'Fats, I don't need your autograph. I know who you are.' "

They traveled in silence until the meal was served.

"TWA had these big cloth napkins in first class," Rein said. "I always brought this big six-inch safety pin, they call it a horse-blanket pin, to hold my napkin to my shirt.

"Fats said, 'Boy, I love that big old pin. You ought to give it to me.' I said, 'Oh, no, I can't do that.' He said, 'Why not?' I said, 'If I did that, my napkin would fall down.'"

At this point, Fats sensed he was in the presence of a fellow character, albeit one much taller and trimmer.

"He told me, 'Well, I'll buy that pin from you,' " Rein said. "I told him, 'Oh, no, you don't have enough money to buy this.' So he reaches in his pocket and hands me a wad of bills with a rubber band on it. I took off the rubber band and the first two bills were 500s. And then there were 11 one-thousand dollar bills. So I put the rubber band back on and gave them back.

"I said, 'Fats, if you ever get any real money instead of just that 12 grand, you come see me and I'll sell you that pin.' "

Fats grinned and the friendship was on. They—actually, Fats—jabbered for the rest of the flight.

"He never stopped talking," said Rein. "That's how he shot pool, too. He'd try to talk you out of a shot."

Fats, who was then in his late 50s, explained why he carried such a wad. He was just a young pool shark when a man wanted to play him for $10,000. After an hour of frantic phoning, Fats rounded up the stake, won the match and made a promise to himself.

"Ever since then," Rein said, "he never left the house with less than 10 grand in his pocket. And he said he never played pool for less than a thousand dollars a game."

Fats also revealed that his real name was Rudolph Wanderone, and that he got his nickname as a portly young newcomer at a tournament in St. Paul, Minnesota.

After they deplaned in St. Louis, Minnesota Fats was miffed.

"His limousine wasn't there," Rein said. "He said he kept a white Cadillac limo in eight cities that he went to a lot. That way, he'd always have a ride if he needed it. They all had license plates that read MF-1,

MF-2, and he always had a girl driver. For some reason, the St. Louis girl wasn't there with the car."

Rein offered him a lift.

"He said he was going home," Rein said, "and he lived about two hours away in Southern Illinois, in Dowell, over by Du Quoin. I said that's okay, that I'd still take him."

When they pulled up to the house, one mystery about Fats solved itself.

"I had noticed he had these scratches and cuts on his forearms," Rein said. "Well, when we drove up to his house, I couldn't even get in the driveway. All these dogs came running out. He said he had 50 but there were at least 75. He got out of the car, and they all started jumping up on him and scratching him.

Inside the house, Fats introduced his wife, Evelyn.

"He called her Eva-line," Rein said. "She was a nice woman, very normal. He had told me he met her in Montrose, Illinois. He was driving down from Chicago and his car hit a telephone pole. While they were fixing his car, he asked where there was a good place to eat.

"He went to the restaurant and Evelyn was working there. It took them three days to fix the car, and when he left he asked her to come with him. She did. They were married for 44 years and then she divorced him.

"When they asked her why, she said, 'I couldn't stand that man any longer. Talk, talk, talk! He'd talk your leg off.' "

The house itself was another curiosity.

"I figured he lived in some mansion," Rein said, "and it *was* a big house. But it was like a bunch of houses pushed together. None of the floors were level. Some were like six inches off. It was one story, no basement, and he had a great big pool room."

Rein got to shoot pool with the host. More precisely, he got to watch the host shoot pool.

"He told me, 'You rack and I'll break,' " Rein said. "He sank a solid color on the break. Then he made all the solids, and then he made all the stripes, and then he made the eight ball. I didn't even get a shot."

Eventually, the visitor got to try the table. He left with a bowl of chicken soup from Evelyn—"she thanked me for bringing him home"— and a promise from Fats.

"I invited him to a party we were having in a couple weeks," Rein said. "He said, 'I'll be there.' I tried to give him directions but he said, 'Oh, no, I'll get there.' I figured that meant he wasn't really coming."

Reinhold Henningsen (under the lampshade) and Minnesota Fats (left) try out the table that Fats recommended.
(Photo courtesy of Reihnhold Henningsen)

Weeks passed. On the night of the party, with the basement full of guests, Rein heard a heavy tread down the stairs. Fats walked in, sat down and held court. He told stories. He "signed" autographs using a stamp. And he shot pool, letting the youngsters win and giving tips to the adults. Rein presented him with the coveted safety pin, plus two money clips—one for the 500s and the other for the 1,000s—plus an invitation to another basement party before Christmas. Fats showed up for that shindig as well. He visited a dozen times over the next two decades, personally supervising Rein's purchase of a new table and balls at Schmidt's former store in the city.

Rein learned that Fats never smoked or drank alcohol. But he was as fastidious as the Gleason portrayal in *The Hustler.*

"When he was here," Rein said, "he'd be in the bathroom a half hour. He said, 'I take a lot of time to clean up.' He'd come out and say, 'Let's play pool.' That was in the movie."

Fats believed that pool players were born, not taught, and that it was foolish to labor over a shot.

"He'd just walk over and shoot," Rein said. "He very rarely missed, and if he did he never made an issue of it. He'd always say, 'Don't mean nuttin'!' That's how he said it, nuttin' instead of nothing."

Their get-togethers were not always pool related.

"I took him to Grant's Farm once," Rein said, "and he didn't take the tour. He just went and sat in the beer garden. He loved it, even though he didn't drink. People brought these little paper plates for him to autograph. He'd take out his stamp and start stamping them."

Fats enjoyed hobnobbing with celebrities as well. When here he roomed at the Chase Park Plaza, where the showbiz crowd stayed while playing St. Louis.

"He'd call me up and say, 'Who's in town? Look it up, and we'll have breakfast with them,' " said Rein. "I'd look in the paper to see who was at the Muny or the Fox. And he'd call them up and we'd go to breakfast. I met all kinds of people, like Carol Channing and Frank Gifford and Ruth Buzzi."

Eating was another adventure, even though Fats had lost 100 pounds due to a urinary problem by the time Rein knew him.

"He loved my homemade cheesecake," said Jackie, Rein's wife. "He'd always eat the whole thing. He called once and asked us to bring one over to the Chase. He wanted to see if mine was better than theirs. And he said it was."

"One time," Rein said, "he took my wife and me to dinner at the Peveley Playhouse. He ordered a turkey and the waiter brought him a turkey sandwich. Fats said, 'No, no, when I order a turkey, I want the whole turkey.' So they brought one out. He ate a lot of it, and then he took the rest home in a doggie bag."

Along the way, Rein learned that *The Hustler* was not a documentary. "Paul Newman plays Fast Eddie in the movie," Rein said, "but there were five or six Fast Eddies. Fats would introduce me to a guy and say, 'Here's so-and-so, alias Fast Eddie.' The next time I saw him, he'd have a different Fast Eddie with him."

Rudolph Wanderone Jr., alias Minnesota Fats, died on January 18, 1996 in Nashville, just before his 83rd birthday. Obituaries noted that he took his famous nickname from the "The Hustler," not the other way around, and that before the movie he went by New York Fats. There was no mention of any christening at a tourney in St. Paul.

When Rein heard about the true naming rights, he laughed and said, "I never knew what to believe with him."

With one exception. On one of the last visits to the Crestwood basement, the legendary hustler set aside his stick and his schtick and said, "Rein, you touched my life."

That story and others are recounted three nights a week, when Rein invites rotating foursomes to his basement to play 8-ball, 25 cents a game. Someone will miss an easy shot, and Rein will say, 'Don't mean nuttin'!" Someone will stall over a shot, and Rein will hold forth on the virtues of fast play.

A newcomer will spot the photo and ask if Rein really knew Minnesota Fats. The proof sits on the card table that holds the snacks, inside a paperback copy of *Minnesota Fats on Pool.* The inscription reads, "To Rein. Minnesota Fats." And the autograph is signed, not stamped.

4

FRED BUCHHOLZ

Batboy for a Big-League Midget

I t was August 19, 1951, a day that began like any other at Sportsman's Park. The home team had a Sunday doubleheader with the Detroit Tigers. The chores were the same for Browns batboy Fred Buchholz— with one exception, as he would find to his astonishment.

This was the debut of the tiniest big-leaguer in baseball history. This was the day that a midget, Eddie Gaedel, went to bat. When the tiny pinch hitter strode to home plate, almost everyone at the park was stunned. But not Fred, then 13 years old. He was among the few with advance warning.

On the stunt's 51st anniversary, the grown-up batboy took a break from his bustling Fred Buchholz Insurance Agency in Florissant to deliver his take on that comedy-drama.

On that historic day, young Fred was already a veteran of the ballyard at Grand and Dodier, where the Browns shared lodgings with the Cardinals. With three older brothers working at the park, Fred started tagging along in 1943 at age five. He made himself useful at first by shagging balls in the outfield and doing odd jobs. His duties gradually expanded.

In 1950, he became batboy for the National League visitors who played the Cardinals. In 1951, he added the job of home batboy for the Browns in their American League games.

"The day the midget batted I probably got there at 8:30 in the morning," said Fred over breakfast at the Missouri Athletic Club. "I had to get the clothes out of the dryer from the day before, put new sweatsocks in all the lockers, put white sanitary socks and clean towels in the lockers, stuff like that.

"Then the players would start coming in. You'd get 'em sodas or whatever they wanted. Then I had to go out and get the bats out for the pitchers. They'd take batting practice first, then the reserves and then the regulars. After the pitchers hit, I'd hurry up and get my other stuff done—the soda bottles cleaned up, tidy up the clubhouse—and then get my uniform and get dressed and go out and shag flies. I came back in when they had infield practice. Then they played the first game."

So far, so routine. Things perked up during the break between the games. The doubleheader drew a throng—by Brownie standards—of 18,369 customers, the largest crowd in nearly four years. They came to see Browns owner Bill Veeck, baseball's master showman, throw a 50th birthday party.

"I forget whose birthday it was," Fred said.

Not who... what. The American League had been hatched in 1901, and its team owners planned individual celebrations. Naturally, Veeck overdid it and outdid them all. Fans received free birthday cake and ice cream when they entered the park, plus souvenir salt and pepper shakers from broadcast sponsor Falstaff beer, which was also marking its 50th birthday.

Max Patkin, the clown prince of baseball, coached first base for part of the opener, dancing with a female fan and joining the half-hour intermission show. Two bands played, a wandering eight-piece Gay Nineties outfit and a Brownie quartet of Satchel Paige (drums), Ed Redys (accordion), Al Widmar (bull fiddle) and Johnny Berardino (maracas) at home plate. Antique cars toured the field. Fireworks exploded overhead and miniature flags fluttered to the field. Circus acts—other than the futile Brownies—performed at each base: An acrobat at first, trampoliners at second, a juggler at third.

Veeck directed these proceedings from the press box roof, without aid of microphone for his booming voice.

"Behind third base, by the Browns' dugout, they had a huge birthday cake," Fred said. "And here comes Eddie Gaedel out of the cake. He had a batboy uniform on with number 1/8. I never had a number, just a blank on the back of my uniform."

Standing small: Eddie Gaedel, baseball's most celebrated pinch hitter, steps to the plate for the St. Louis Browns on August 19, 1951.
(AP/WWP)

Gaedel weighed 65 pounds and stood three foot seven, more than two feet shorter than the teenaged batboy.

"I was big for my age," said Fred, who stands 6'4" now. "At 13 I was probably five-eight, five-ten at least, and about 120 pounds."

Gaedel's sudden jack-in-the-box appearance was a hit with the crowd. But nobody expected an encore.

"The midget went to the dugout," said Fred, "and the manager, Zack Taylor, had him on his lap. He was sitting on Zack's knee like a little kid. I'm sitting on the bench next to him because Zack had called me over. The three of us were the only ones there. The midget was older-looking, but he was the size of a five-year-old. I think he was 40-something years old, because he looked a lot older than the players."

Gaedel, it turned out, was only 26.

"He had spikes on," Fred said, "and he was holding this little souvenir bat. If he ever hit a pitch with that bat, the ball would have knocked it out of his hands."

As it was, a feather might have done the job.

"The midget was shaking," Fred said. "Zack Taylor put him on his lap to relax him, because he was having second thoughts about standing up there with that hard baseball coming at him. He said, 'If he hits me with the ball, I'm gonna hit him with the bat.' Zack said, 'Don't worry, he ain't gonna hit you. Just stand there. Don't swing.' "

Young Fred realized that he was the only witness to history's most bizarre batting tip.

"Veeck wasn't even in the dugout at that time," he said. "The midget was getting his instructions from Taylor. He said, 'They're gonna walk you. Just go down to first base and we'll take it from there.' "

In fact, Veeck had briefed Gaedel at his secret contract signing, threatening—in jest, presumably—to shoot the little rookie from the stadium roof if he swung at a pitch.

"Now it was getting close to game time," Fred said. "And then Zack gave me the instructions to stay in the dugout when the midget went out there."

Taylor's exact orders to his batboy were: "Don't get on the field. This is ridiculous enough."

Even before that, young Fred had sensed that something was brewing.

"The Browns signed a ballplayer who was a bonus baby, Frank Saucier," Fred said. "He finally signed about a month before, and they worked his butt off at the park, getting him ready. His hands were all blistered from all that batting practice, but he had never played a game with the Browns. And now they had him playing right field in the second game."

And batting leadoff.

When the Browns retired the Tigers to start the first inning, Saucier hustled in to the dugout for his first big-league at-bat. Instead, he became the first, and only, big-leaguer to have a midget pinch hit for him.

"Saucier was so mad, he went to the back of the dugout and broke his bat against a wall," Fred said. "He broke it in two. Oh, he was hot! He started yelling, 'I got blisters all over my hands, and they put a midget in for me! It's a joke!' I got out of there, because he was so hot."

Saucier, by the way, bitterly disputes Fred's memory, saying his hands were too sore and blistered to smash anything. He did not explain how he planned to smack a baseball with those tender hands if he had batted as scheduled. At any rate, Saucier may have been the only person in the park not fixated on the miniature tableau at home plate.

As frozen forever in a famous photo, the gun-shy Gaedel leans back in a deep crouch. Umpire Ed Hurley leans forward for a better look at the shrunken strike zone. Detroit catcher Bob Swift, on his knees but still towering over the batter, gloves a high toss from Bob Cain, the unseen pitcher.

"The fans were laughing," Fred said, "but no one said nothing in our dugout. They were just shocked. Nothing like that had ever happened before. Usually the guys would yell for someone to get a hit. Here, nothing."

Fred didn't hear it, but a few Tigers found their tongues in time to bark advice at Gaedel, such as, "Get outta that hole!"

No protest came from Detroit manager Red Rolfe, who had been alerted beforehand by the Browns. But umpire Hurley was left in the dark.

"When the midget went out," Fred said, "Hurley came over and Zack Taylor brought this contract out. And they were looking at it, and it was a real contract. They got that over with pretty quick."

Ditto for Gaedel's at-bat.

"Bob Swift sat on his heels," Fred said, "and four balls came in, eye level or higher. None of 'em were close. And the midget walked. I think he just took that little bat down with him. And when he got down to first base, Jimmy Delsing went out to run for him. The midget went back to the dugout and went down underneath to the ramp to the clubhouse. His job was done. And nobody saw him again. He didn't appear in the clubhouse or nothing after the game. The only thing I ever said to him was just 'Hi' or something before the game."

Afterward, Bob Broeg of the *Post-Dispatch* caught up with Gaedel, who blurted, "For a minute, I felt like Babe Ruth. I never thought I'd live to see the day I'd be a major leaguer."

After his leadoff walk, the Browns loaded the bases. Typically, they failed to score. They wound up losing 6-2 after dropping the first game 5-2.

That night, Gaedel was whisked back home to Chicago. He and Veeck hoped for return engagements, preferably with the bases loaded. But Major League Baseball quickly banned the use of midget players.

Ten years later, Gaedel's life ended just as abruptly and far more tragically. He died of injuries from a saloon beating at age 36. The crime was never solved.

Except for Delsing and Saucier, the other principals from that historic game have also left the stage. Delsing, the father of pro golfer Jay Delsing, hit .255 in a solid 10-year career with five teams. At 76, he lives in Chesterfield and is a fixture at the Browns Fan Club Banquet here each May.

After giving way to Gaedel, Saucier played only 17 more big-league games, all with the Browns in '51. A native of Washington, Missouri, he is 76 and living in Amarillo, Texas, having made a fortune in the oil business.

Also surviving is Gaedel's uniform with the No. 1/8 on the back. It belonged then, as it does now, to Bill DeWitt Jr., the lead owner of the Cardinals. DeWitt's father had preceded Veeck as Browns owner.

"They say that was Billy's uniform from when he was a batboy," Fred said with a smile, "but he was never the batboy when I was there. Maybe he wore it in spring training or something. But most of the games here were at night, and he went to Country Day. His dad wanted him studying, not batboying at the ballpark."

As for Fred, 1951 was his only season as Browns batboy. As a publicity stunt, Veeck used rotating guest batboys for the team's last two years here. Fred remained as a clubhouse boy through 1953, when the Browns left to become the Baltimore Orioles. He stayed on as visiting team batboy at Cardinals games through 1955. Two years later, after graduating from Beaumont High, he started his own insurance business. After 45 years it now includes 1,000 clients, many of them ex-ballplayers. He and his wife, Sharyn, have been married for 38 years. They have two children, Brian and Beth, and four grandchildren.

Fred has been active in his beloved Florissant, serving as past president of the Chamber of Commerce and the Rotary Club and on the board of the North County Chamber of Commerce. Drawing from his baseball contacts and his own vast memorabilia cache, he has donated items that have brought about $50,000 for local charities, he said.

In short, the ex-batboy has done well in the world. What he treasures is the lasting friendship of the ballplayers he once served. He remains especially close to the handful of ex-Brownies in town, such as Roy Sievers.

"I see the old ballplayers now," Fred said, "and I can still see the resemblance. It just seems like when I'm there at the banquets, nothing's changed. They were always nice, and they're still nice. They're just older. It's sort of sad, in a way."

So is his absence from baseball's most memorable photo. Following orders, the young batboy stayed in the dugout when the midget walked into history. In the center of the famous photo, the on-deck circle is clearly visible in the background. The on-deck batter is obscured by Swift's up-raised arm and catcher's mitt.

"Bobby Young, the next hitter, is out there by himself," Fred said. "But if I was allowed out there like I normally was, you'd see me right beside Bobby Young in the on-deck circle."

5

MANNIE JACKSON

Globetrotters Owner Learned from No-Jokes Coach

Just after the 2003 New Year, Mannie Jackson brought his revived Harlem Globetrotters back to his hometown. Mannie, a former Trotter, was in his 10th tour as owner. In this capacity he has hobnobbed with the likes of Pope John Paul II, Nelson Mandela, Prince Charles and Fidel Castro.

The afternoon before his team put on a show at Savvis Center, Mannie trotted them over for a crisp practice at Edwardsville High School. Jackson, a former Tiger, had helped the newly intergrated Edwardsville High to a runner-up finish in the Illinois one-class basketball tournament in 1956. In that capacity, he hobnobbed with the likes of Harold Patton, Govoner Vaughn, Bob Wetzel, Bill Penelton and Herman Shaw. All were on hand for the afternoon workout except Vaughn, who works for the Globetrotters as director of alumni relations at their home office in Phoenix.

This was no reunion. The old Edwardsville teammates—Shaw actually graduated just before Jackson started high school—have remained close through the years. Most went on to play college sports, and all were successful in life. The team also included Don Ohl, who played in the NBA after teaming again with Mannie and Vaughn at the University of

*Mannie Jackson is spanning the globe with 'Trotters like Herbert Lang (left) and
Matt Jackson.*
(Kevin Manning/St. Louis Post-Dispatch)

Illinois, and Ken "Buzz" Shaw, now president of Syracuse University. Their
common link is the late Joe Lucco, their tough little coach at Edwardsville.
He taught them the importance of education and discipline with a vengeance.

Mannie, who is African-American, had a career of run-ins with Lucco,
who is Caucasian. The issue wasn't race. It was the age-old battle of will
between headstrong teenager and unbending adult authority.

"Joe Lucco was a disciplinarian," said Patton, 64, who played at
Washington U. and is now vice president and general counsel of Medtronic
in Minneapolis. "He was an extreme disciplinarian. We weren't allowed to
date. All of our hair was cut the same way. But we won ballgames."

As a sophomore in '54, Mannie Jackson was the second man off the
bench for a team that placed fourth at state.

" 'Jack' was confident," said Penelton, 65, who worked 30 years at a
local refinery lab after playing football at Illinois State. "He was really
confident. When he got to high school, he thought he should be playing
right away."

"Mannie was just like everybody else," said Wetzel, an Edwardsville banker who was a senior the year between the two state runs. "Obviously, he did have a flair about him."

Too much flair to suit the coach.

"Lucco would get on 'Jack' because he'd be too flashy at times," Penelton said.

"Manny would be dunking and throwing behind-the-back passes," Shaw said.

"Lucco was in control," said Patton, "and he let you know it, too."

As Penelton put it, "He'd yell at you so bad you'd be crying. But 'Jack' didn't back down."

Not that Mannie won any of those showdowns.

"I had this fedora and liked to dress real flamboyantly," he said. "One time, we were going to a game and Lucco sent me home because he didn't like what I had on. When I came back, the bus was gone. I had to take a cab. When I got to Wood River or wherever we were playing, I said, 'Coach, the cab cost nine bucks.' And he said, 'If we win and you score 30 points, I'll pay for it.' "

Edwardsville did, and Jackson did, so Lucco did.

The team was united in survival against the coach, which is only partly why there were no racial rifts in those early years of integration.

"We all came from blue-collar families," Patton said. "We were from cornfields and coal mines. When we went to the state tournament in Champaign, the kids from the Chicago schools had scalped their extra tickets and were shooting craps in the hall. That was the most money any of us had ever seen."

Mannie—"he was always a good student," Patton said—then became the first African-American basketball player and team captain at Illinois. After a three-year stint playing for the Globetrotters, he got down to business. Mannie picked up some business tricks from Abe Saperstein, the Globetrotters' late founder.

"He was a genius," Mannie said. "He got me into marketing."

By the late '80s, Mannie was working as a senior vice president for Honeywell in Minneapolis, in charge of mergers and acquisitions, when he heard the Globetrotters were for sale. They were a national treasure in disrepair. Mannie gobbled up the team in two gulps for under $10 million, or 10 times less than their worth now, he said. He rebuilt that famous asset using lessons learned half a century ago.

"We brought discipline to all departments," said Mannie, the former flamboyant kid. "I got turned around!"

Lucco would be proud of this spit-and-polish operation. When Mannie's 'Trotters practice, shirts are tucked into shorts, everybody bears down and nobody cusses. Order is also in order at the home base in Phoenix.

"People get to work on time," Mannie said. "Their work gets done on time. I've got people who are committed to me and are passionate."

On the court, the team is still up to its old tricks, but Mannie has added real games to the familiar schedule of exhibitions.

"The Globetrotters started as a barnstorming team from 1935 to 1955," he said, "and that's what we are."

Every fall, his reborn 'Trotters cut the clowning, pay homage to their past and play bona fide preseason games against top college teams.

"And when we go on our international tour every year," Mannie said, "we play the top teams overseas."

In his first nine years as owner, his Globetrotters have given $10 million to charity. And it begins at home. Jackson has given $100,000—plus another $50,000 in personal fundraising—to the Lincoln School Foundation. It helps disadvantaged Edwardsville kids go on to college.

Lincoln was Edwardsville's pre-integration black school, kindergarten through 12th grade. That's where Mannie, Penelton and Herman Shaw started their education.

Harman Shaw, a former assistant principal at University City, presides over the foundation. He urged Mannie to put his own name on the scholarship grant. "I told Mannie that African-American kids need to see him as role model," Shaw said.

Mannie agreed, but only in addition to the name he wanted to honor: Joe Lucco.

"The significance," said Mannie, "is the really hidden messages about how relationships can happen across barriers."

6

RODNEY & RONALD LEWIS

Hoop Twins (Plus One) in Their Own Worlds

In one sense, Rodney Lewis is an original. The sophomore at Meramec Community College is headed to Barry College near Miami to play Division II basketball.

"I got a scholarship," said Rodney, "and the coach never even saw me play."

Well, yes he did.

"No, he didn't," Rodney insisted.

Well, yes he did. Because in another sense, Rodney Lewis is a carbon copy. His twin brother, Ronald, played this season for Barry College coach Cesar Odio. And if you've seen Ronald in action—on the court, in class, on the street—you've seen Rodney. And vice versa. The Lewises are six-foot-five duplicates in looks, playing style, hobbies and personality. They were inseparable growing up in their St. Louis neighborhood near the Wohl Center, commuting to Lafayette High and causing double trouble for opponents on the basketball court.

They call each other "Twin" and talk by phone at least once a day. And their similarities go far beyond looks. The twins are linked in unconscious ways that are almost spooky. Call it the "twin thing" or "twin ESP" or the "Twin Twilight Zone," but Rodney and Ronald share double occupancy on the same wavelength.

"I called him up the other day," said Ronald, the younger twin by 10 minutes, "and I asked him what he was doing. He was playing a basketball video game. I was playing a basketball video game."

Rodney chimed in and said, "We both shaved our heads, and I called him the other day and asked if he was growing any hair. He said, 'Just this little thing on my chin.' I said, 'Whoa, I've got this little thing on my chin, too.'

"A couple of weeks ago, I was thinking about this CD, *Ready to Die*, by Notorious B.I.G. I called my twin up and mentioned it to him, and he said, 'I'm listening to it right now.'"

Their rapport goes beyond the psychic to their physiques. In the 2001-2002 season, Ronald sprained his knee on December 8 during a game in Florida. Rodney broke his foot on December 19 in St. Louis.

Meramec coach Randy Albrecht said, "Their mother told me, 'I knew when Ronald got hurt, pretty soon the other one would be on crutches, too. If one of them starts getting the flu, I might as well get the chicken soup ready for the second one.'"

What about that time lapse between their December injuries?

"My foot had been bothering me for a week or two," Rodney said, "but I kept playing through the pain. Then it just finally gave out. So we really got hurt about the same time."

This brother act is actually a three-part harmony. Their sister, Angie, is a year younger but just as similar.

"We call her The Third Twin," Rodney said. "Everybody thinks we're triplets. We figure it would have been too hard on our mom to have all three of us at once, so she just waited a year for Angie to come out."

"I was chillin'!" Angie explained, playfully palming the shaved skulls of her bookend brothers.

She is also dialed into their twin frequency.

"When Ron called and told me he hurt his knee," said Angie, "I was like, 'Whoa! My knee's been hurting, too.' I got scared. Then when Rodney hurt his foot and had to sit out, too, I got really scared. I thought I'd be next."

Angie, a six-foot-one sophomore, survived the season at St. Louis University, where she made third-team All-Conference USA for the Lady Billikens. The brothers happily defer to their kid sister.

Angie Lewis, the "third twin," with brothers Rodney and Ronald—or is it Ronald and Rodney?
(Sam Leone/St. Louis Post-Dispatch)

"Rodney's handsome," Ronald said. "I'm very handsome. But Angie's gorgeous."

"She's the best player in the family," said Rodney. "She's going all the way, baby, All-America and WNBA."

"She's smarter than us, too," said Ronald, "but that's just because we taught her everything we knew."

"That's right," said Rodney. "We'd come home from kindergarten and tell her everything we learned. Reading, numbers. So she was a year ahead of everyone else in her class."

The twins also took charge of her basketball instruction.

"My parents had a basketball in the back yard," Angie said, "and my brothers would make me play. I hated it. They'd actually say, 'You *love* basketball. Now *say* it!' So I'd say, "I…love…bas-ket-ball.' I didn't at first, but then I really did.'

In turn, the twins were not happy when Angie and her boyfriend began dating four years before in high school.

"We didn't like the guy," said Ronald. "But now we do. He's been around so long, he's like family, too."

"As long as our sister's happy," said Rodney, "we're happy. If she's crying, we're mad."

Angie is also the only person in the universe—at least in this dimension of it—who can tell the twins apart.

"Day, night, in person, on the phone, we can't get past her," said Rodney. "She knows us really well."

Take away their numbered jerseys, and the twins have an identity crisis themselves.

"Look at this," said Rodney, flashing two photos of the same image shooting a jump shot in Lafayette warmup jackets. "That's both of us, but who's who? I can't tell. Maybe you can tell."

Don't ask their parents—dad Sylvester, a chef, and mom Leona, a factory worker.

"Our dad's the general of the house," said Rodney. "He's got a great sense of humor, but he always mixes us up. So he just calls us 'Boy.' The other day he said, 'Ronald, can you turn that light off?' I said, 'Ron's in Florida.'

"He said, 'Just turn the light off, Boy.' I said, 'My name's not Boy.' And he said, 'You're a boy, right? Turn the light off!'"

The three siblings cackled at the general's frustration.

"And our mom would never admit it," said Angie, "but she can't tell them apart, either. On the phone, she has no clue."

Rodney said, "I played this trick on my mom where I called her and was emulating this person from the church she goes to."

She fell for the gag even though—in a stunning show of twin-thing power—Ronald had played the same phone prank on her a couple of weeks before.

"I didn't know he did that when I called," Rodney said.

Since the twins turned 21 in January 2002, their mom apparently declared surrender in her losing battle to differentiate them before adulthood. Ronald called her from Miami to say when his flight home for spring break would arrive here. When his mom heard a twin's voice on the phone, she wearily asked, "Which is it?" Naturally, Ronald identified himself as Rodney.

"She asked, 'When are you picking your brother up from the airport?'" said Ronald, who then ad-libbed a detailed retrieval plan.

His mom never did catch on. He finally had to reveal that he was the twin who needed a ride, not the twin who was the chauffeur.

Rodney and Ronald's geographic split happened the year before, in a major breakdown of the twin-thing force. Both were starting as sophomores at Meramec when Rodney hurt his knee early in the season. He could have returned for the last few games, but that would have counted as a whole year of NCAA eligibility. Instead, Rodney took a medical redshirt, got the whole season as a do-over and returned to Meramec the next fall as a third-year sophomore. Meanwhile, Ronald enrolled at Barry for his junior season. He had somehow dodged his twin's destiny last year at Meramec, escaped injury and made the junior college All-Region team. While Rodney nursed his bum knee, Ronald caught the eye of Barry coach Cesar Odio during Meramec's annual Florida trip.

"I was scouting another kid at their game down here," said Odio by phone from Barry, "and I kept seeing Ronald. I said to my assistant, 'What's up with this kid?' He was yelling and enthusiastic and all over the court. I loved the kid.

"I know Randy Albrecht, and his players are always disciplined and good students. But Ronald works so hard. He comes to play every play, in practice and in games. Those kids are hard to find.

"You've got to compliment the mom and dad for their coaching at home. I told Rodney if his brother is anything close to him, we can't go wrong.'"

In fact, their mom made sure The Twins Plus One got along with each other.

"When we were little," said Angie, "I'd have a fight with one of them, and our mom would say, 'Go hug your brother and make up.' I'd say, 'Awwww,' and she'd say, 'Go ahead, hug your brother.' And I'd say, 'Ohhhh, okay.'"

The twins grew to be close but not clones.

"Ronald's a little more vocal leader," said Albrecht. "Rodney's more reserved. Rodney has a little quicker feet and can use his off hand better, but Ronald's a better three-point shooter. And Rodney might be a little taller."

"I think I am taller," Rodney said. "I think I'm almost six-six."

"No way!" shrieked Ronald.

In the classroom, both are communications majors.

"I'm killing him on the grades," said Rodney. "I've got a 3.7 grade point average. He had a 2.8 down there at Barry."

But what about last year when both were at Meramec?

"He had a 2.6," Rodney said. "I had a 2.7."

They have one clear difference: Ronald likes being called Ron, while Rodney hates being called Rod. And Rodney is more outgoing, although Rodney is hardly shy.

"I never had to make friends," Rodney said. "My brother always made them for me. His friends became my friends, because we're so much alike and we're always together.

"Same thing with enemies. He ticks some people off because he talks so much, and they're always mad at me, too. Now he's making friends for me at Barry. They're all waiting for me down there."

Their year apart has been rough but rewarding.

"Just to see if we could do it without each other," Rodney said. "We know we made the transition, but we're a better team together."

"In life and in basketball," Ronald said.

"I can be in a slump one day," Rodney said, "just a bad mood, and my twin will turn that atmosphere around."

Albrecht got a kick out of coaching the twins, although he never really knew who was wearing No. 40 (supposedly Ronald) and No. 50 (supposedly Rodney).

"The only good thing about Rodney getting hurt," Albrecht said, "was at least I knew I was talking to Ronald during games."

The twins deny ever pulling a switcheroo, in games or in class. Except for Senior Day at Lafayette, when Ronald took Rodney's seat in Spanish class. Odio doesn't expect to tell them apart when Rodney shows up at Barry.

"Halfway through the season," the coach said, "I started calling Ronald 'Rodney.' I said, 'I'll be getting you mixed up next year, so you might as well start getting used to it.'"

The Lewis twins don't understand the fuss. As Rodney—or maybe it was Ronald—put it:

"People ask me, 'What's it like being a twin?' I turn it around and say, 'I don't know. This is all I know. What's it like being you?'"

7

JAMES CLABON

Mizzou's Cookie Monster is Hungry to Help Kids

The Cookie Monster has completed a 30-year circuit in life and is back at the start of a new lap. James Clabon, known as the Cookie Monster during his basketball days at Mizzou, is trying to help youngsters overcome poverty. James, 48, runs JA's Sports Fitness Club in the spacious gym at St. Nicholas Church, downtown on 18th and Lucas, near Union Station. That's also not far from the corner of Jefferson and Stoddard, where he grew up across from the old Pruitt-Igoe housing project.

JA's stands for James and his wife, Angela, a corporate financial officer. The program serves 30 to 40 inner-city kids three nights a week. James also runs summer basketball camps for boys and girls, drawing mostly from nearby neighborhoods.

James has no children of his own—he is stepfather to Angela's son—but can identify with the inner-city youngsters in his club and camps. He understands their hunger for discipline, attention, and improvement. And just plain hunger.

"I really, really want to help out," James said. "If I can share what I've learned with these kids, if the kids give me a chance, I believe I can help them. I don't think anybody was poorer than us when I was growing up."

His mother, Lillie Ann, raised six sons and a daughter by herself. James was sibling No. 3.

"My dad saw too many kids," he said, "and he just left."

His mother tried to work when possible, but with seven children, she often relied on a slim welfare check.

"I will never eat another bean in my life," James said. "Or greens. When we ate greens, it was a whole week of greens. When we had beans, it was a whole week of beans. We'd get to playing with it, and see how thin we could slice each bean, and then eat each little slice. We'd say to my mom, 'We know that there is something called meat in this world. Will you ever cook us some meat?' And she would say, 'You better appreciate what you've got, because you might not have it next week.'"

Unlike most kids, James preferred the school year over summer break.

"During school," he said, "you got that little lunch bag from those government programs. In summer, you were on your own. I was one of those kids walking around, not eating hardly anything for four days, getting light-headed. When we'd get really hungry, my mom would say, 'Drink some water until you get full, and then go take a nap. Otherwise, you'll use up too much energy.'"

Even running on the fumes, James had energy to burn. Bored and hungry and competitive, he invented an inexpensive summer game: Trying to outrun a Bi-State bus.

"When I was 12, 13, I'd walk outside and see the bus going to the Wellston loop," he said. "So when it came by, I'd take off running. That must have been four or five miles. I know where I got that from, when Jesse Owens raced that horse. And my brothers thought I was crazy.

"They'd say, 'It's too hot. You go ahead. We'll see you when you get home.' In my life, I took off at least 50 times. And I beat it three times. If it hit a red light a few times, I thought I had it. It was something to do, and we were so hungry."

For all of that, he has fond memories of his mother and her strong but loving touch.

"She had seven kids," James said, "and we never had any of these tragedies you read about. None of us got killed or shot or any of that. I mean, there was no swearing in our house. You couldn't even say doo-doo. You had to say BM, for bowel movement. She was very strict like that. My mother would pray over us, and she always said we needed to pray together."

James did some praying of his own the summer before his senior year at Vashon High.

"I said, 'Please, God, in the name of Jesus, if you'll let me play this game, basketball, I'll do anything you want me to.'"

From age 11 to 17, James had concentrated on boxing at the Gamble Rec Center. Then two things happened. He grew to be six foot five, and older kids started punching harder. As James put it, who wants to have that pain inflicted on them?

Ron Coleman, the ex-Mizzou star, was the Vashon coach in the early '70s. He put the rookie on the varsity as a junior but didn't play him. James understood why.

"I could always rebound," said James, "but I didn't know how to play. I didn't know what goaltending was. I didn't know what three seconds meant. Ron said, 'Sit down, son. You don't have a clue.'"

But he was willing to learn. And he had a couple of mentors in Andrew and Aaron Reid.

"Andrew started me out," James said. "He played at Beaumont and he played college ball, and he worked with me. He'd say, 'If you play defense and rebound, you'll be valuable to any team, and you can go somewhere with this.'"

Aaron Reid went to what is now North Central Missouri, a community college in Trenton.

As James recalled, "He saw me play and said, 'Look how he shoots a jump shot. He jumps up to the sky!' Not that I could score when I was up there. I had a shot that could bust the backboard."

Aaron put in a word for James with Trenton coach Gary Garner, onetime assistant to Mizzou coach Norm Stewart. So James headed off for two years at Trenton, near the Iowa border, before spending his last two years at Mizzou from 1975-77.

"With Ron Coleman and Gary Garner, it was like I was programmed to go to Mizzou," James said. "Both of them ran the same offense as Mizzou, and when I got there I fit right in. I became known for my defense, and Gary Garner brought that out. "

James, by then almost 6'8", became known as the Cookie Monster after a team dinner at Stewart's house. As the gathering broke up, James asked Stewart's wife, Virginia, if he could take along some of her homemade cookies.

"She said help yourself," James said. "I used to wear this big hat, and I started filling it up. It looked like a 10-gallon hat when I got through."

He set the bulging lid carefully on his head and started for the door.

"Norm looked at me and said, 'What the hell's wrong with your hat?'" James said. "He tapped it and it fell off and all the cookies fell out. It was like an avalanche. His wife was in tears, she was laughing so hard.

"We beat Kansas right after that, and the headline in the *Post-Dispatch* said: Cookie Monster Makes KU Crumble. I still have the article at home."

On subjects other than cookies, Stewart was notoriously demanding, to say the least.

"It was rough," James said, "but coming from where I did, I could adapt to anything and anybody. And I will tell you this: He was a smart coach."

Mizzou went 48-13 in Cookie Monster's two seasons, advancing as far as the NCAA Midwest Regional. He was a role player alongside stars like Willie Smith, Kim Anderson and Larry Drew. And when James left Mizzou in '77, Stewart gave him a good reference to a European scout who placed him with a French team. After averaging three baskets per game at Mizzou, James was suddenly cast as an offensive player.

"When I first went over, the mentality was the American is a do-it-all player," James said. "If you won, it was 'We won.' If you lost, it was 'the American lost.' They expect you to score. It was hard for me. I never shot in high school or college. But, believe me, I was jacking it up over there.

"That's when I understood why shooters didn't play defense. I was bone dead. I shot so much my arm was actually cramping up. I told my coach one game that I had to come out, and he wouldn't let me. I had to start shooting jump hooks with my left hand."

James spent most of his time with teams in Alnoye in the north of France, Troye and Lyons—a sister city of St. Louis— in the central region and Hyeres in the south. He spoke no French when he arrived.

"The kids in town would come by my house every morning," James said. "I'd learn French from them. Little bit by little bit, they helped me. I learned to pronounce the alphabet."

He watched TV. He read the comic section, moving on to the basketball stories in the sports pages and then the rest of the newspaper. He was still playing at age 44 when he abruptly walked away.

Late in 1997, his mother became gravely ill, and he left his team in midseason to be with her. When she improved, he rejoined his team. But when her health deteriorated that February, he asked the team president for another leave of absence.

"He wouldn't let me go," James said. "He said, 'That's not my problem.' I said, 'It is now,' and I quit. I sold everything I had—my car, my furniture—for whatever anyone would give me. And I came home."

He was able to see his mother before she died and then decided to stay home. He met Angela, a freelance chief financial officer, and decided to dig in here with her and her son, now 13.

James opened his first basketball camp at St. Nick's in the summer of '98. He had never seen a camp until he worked Stewart's at Mizzou, but he ran camps every year in France. He then formed JA's Fitness Club at St. Nick's, where the parquet gym floor still doubles as a roller skating rink. The focus is on fitness, not sports.

The Rev. Stephan Brown, pastor at St. Nick's, said, "In our area in downtown St. Louis, there isn't any other comprehensive program like the one being headed up here by James. There's a need for fitness, nutrition and tutorial services for our kids, who are at risk for getting into trouble with crime.

"James also started a basketball program for older teens and young adults that goes at 10:30 at night. He's doing a fantastic job."

Youngsters of all backgrounds are welcome.

"When they come through that door, there's a lot to do," James said. "But the first thing they do is, they pair up and they have to run their laps or walk their laps, whatever they're capable of. Then they do a certain number of pushups and situps. You don't hear any griping. Kids want that structure. And they really start to take pride in the weight-loss program."

James, who never had enough to eat at home, was not a choosy eater when he hit Mizzou…as his Cookie Monster name implies.

"I was the junk food king," he said. "But I was a phys ed major, and we had to study nutrition. And when we ate at training table, I would watch the football players and the healthy stuff they ate."

Now nutrition is a staple of the Fitness Club program, which offers a healthy meal each day to members. James practices what he eats, looking as lean as in his Mizzou days.

"Kids know now that if you're out of shape, come to JA's," he said.

"If you want to improve your health, come to JA's. If you're already an athlete and want to get better in a specific sport, we have guys who can help."

Father Brown said St. Nick's takes care of expenses like utilities with the help of the Archdiocese of St. Louis and a government grant. James has begun soliciting donors to help with his frugal budget. He is paying himself no salary until funding improves. For now, program director Robert Wallace, a former Riverview Gardens basketball star, is the only full-time employee. Martial arts instructor Terrell Williams, a former Mizzou All-America wrestler, is part-time. Keith Clabon, the director's brother, handles transportation and gets paid "when I feel like it," James said with a grin.

Wallace had been teaching in the Francis Howell district before James recruited him.

"He has high aspirations to help people out," said Wallace. "And I'm a Christian myself. I want to work with people who aren't just in it for the money."

Of course, nobody is perfect.

"I still hit the cookies now and then," James said. "But I can't let those kids see that."

8

ADAM BROCKMILLER

The Outfielder Who Hacked CF

"My biggest fear is not knowing when I am going to die . . . "
—*Adam Brockmiller, high school essay, "Sweat Running Like Rain"*

Young baseball players must conquer their fear of the ball. That was never an issue for Adam Brockmiller. For all of his 17 years, he has faced up to a much darker dread.

Dane Brockmiller, Adam's dad, said, "Adam was sitting on my knee one day when he was three years old. And he looked at me and said, 'Dad, am I going to die?' I told him, 'Well, everyone's going to die.'"

For Adam, longevity was a dream to get where he is now: His senior year in high school.

"I have cystic fibrosis, a severe lung disease, which causes my mucus to be thick, my pancreas to digest my food improperly and my sinusitis to be chronic. I get deep, wet, mucus-type coughs..."

Cystic fibrosis, or CF, is the number one genetic killer of young people in this country, affecting some 30,000 youngsters. There is no known cure. When the Cystic Fibrosis Foundation was formed in 1955, CF kids did not reach age five. New treatments have stretched that baseline line farther and farther.

"When Adam was born, the average life of a CF kid was 20 years, 19 years," said his dad. "Because of people like Jack Buck helping to raise funds for research, people are living into their 30s and 40s."

Buck, the late Cardinals broadcaster, had a public-service mantra for young mothers: "Kiss your babies, taste your babies. If they're salty, have them tested."

The mucus in CF kids causes them to sweat heavily, leaving a salty film on the skin. The cause of CF itself is unknown. It stems from an abnormal gene that must be present in both parents.

"When Adam was a baby and in the hospital," said his father, "we started talking to family members. And we found out that quite a few babies through the years had died of pneumonia. They might have had CF. Nobody knew to check them."

"Most people do not know that I have this fear, because most people cannot tell that I have a disease. I do all the normal activities other people do..."

Adam, one of just two seniors on the team, has helped Union to a 5-1 start this season. He is in the lineup on merit. In fact, coach Dave Scheer knew few details of his left fielder's affliction until approached recently by a reporter.

"I just knew he coughed a lot," said Scheer, who also coached Adam last year. "He's in the outfield mainly for his defense, but he's swinging the bat better this year. He's really worked to improve his hitting."

Adam is second on the team with a .474 batting average. He had nine hits in 19 at-bats, four runs scored, three runs batted in, three steals in three tries and was flawless in left field. He had the only hit in Union's only loss, at Pacific, and has reached base six of his last seven times up. Adam was all over the field last Thursday in a 14-8 victory over rival St. Clair. He singled three times, reached base on an error his other time up, stole a base, scored two runs, drove in another and made three fine catches. Adam is scrappy and savvy, can-do and gung-ho. His attitude toward baseball doubles as his outlook on life.

"Everybody makes mistakes," he said. "I just play the best I can."

"This fear does not always scare me. This fear strengthens me because everything that I have to do, I try to do optimistically and to my full capability..."

In the basement gym next to his bedroom, Adam has worked up to 150 pounds on the bench press. That's not bad for a five-foot-seven frame

Adam Brockmiller is flying in the face of cystic fibrosis.
(Photo by Don Adams Jr.)

bound together by 135 pounds of gristle and grit. Yet digestive problems make malnutrition a constant threat for a CF kid.

"Lifting makes my muscles stronger," Adam said, "so when I do get sick, I'll have more muscle there to fight back."

The day he stops fighting is the day he stops breathing.

"I have to be a responsible person. If I am not, I get put in the dungeon known as The Hospital…"

Every week, Adam and his dad or mom, Joanne, make the hourlong drive to a St. Louis hospital for preventive maintenance. CF kids are prone to pneumonia and sinus infections. Adam was hospitalized every month until he was two, and he has had several sinus operations.

"A lot of the stuff I develop is only treatable with an IV and antibiotics," Adam said. "But if I have the IV in, I can't shower, I can't lift and I can't throw a baseball. I hate that. So I try to take every route I can to stay active and be in sports."

His normal day, such as it is, starts just after 5 a.m. He straps on his "therapy vest," with a hose running into one side and out the other. Then he flips on a compressor. For the next half hour, the vest shakes the mucus from his lungs. He undergoes the same routine at bedtime. It helps him get through the night without major interruption.

"But sometimes I have to prop myself up on an angle to sleep better," he said.

He also must ingest 10 pills at each meal, 30 per day. The effort has paid off. His once-common trips to the emergency room have faded to about one every six months.

"My fear of not being able to play basketball has come true. I am not able to be on the hardwood courts, with sweat running off me like it's raining and the rubber soles of my shoes squeaking when I go to cover my man…"

Adam played basketball in his first two years of high school in Dallas, where his family moved after his father was transferred by Southwestern Bell. When Adam was a junior, Dane took early retirement and moved the family back to Union. Adam tried out for the varsity and was cut, partly because his breathing couldn't handle the series of conditioning sprints. He refused to let his father, tying up loose ends in Texas, intervene to explain the CF factor to the basketball coach.

"I guess I didn't have what it took," he said. "It's one of those things in life you have to deal with."

"I have been through emotional battles from being in the hospital, and I can use my knowledge of overcoming them to inspire and help my friends with their problems..."

Self-pity is not an option for Adam.

"Sometimes I go through spells like, 'Why does this have to happen to me?'" he said. "I get sick of the vest. I get sick of the nebulizer, which helps my breathing. But it's all part of the game."

He hopes his story will nudge other youngsters, with CF or other afflictions, to carry on.

"To me," he said, "it's frustrating when people get sick and they don't have the drive to get better. They get down emotionally. Just keep moving on. Hey, stuff happens."

And some of it comes wrapped in silver linings.

"Through this fear, good has come. And I am getting healthier and making more friends who care about what is going on in my life. And that helps me deal with the emotional downs or pains..."

Adam's cover as a typical teen is blown several times a day.

"Lots of people don't know I have anything," he said. "Until I start coughing."

The attacks are frequent, frequently harsh and always needed. Coughing is how a CF body clears its airways of the suffocating mucus. But the attacks have no timetable. Adam can start hacking in class, on a date or playing ball.

"I give the teachers a pamphlet that explains it all," said Adam. "They should just ignore me. If it gets too bad, I'll get up and leave the class."

Happily, his peers have stood by him on the field and in class, and not stooped to ridicule.

"The first time kids see it, their faces kind of drop," Adam said. "But they're not mad. They're like, 'Why doesn't somebody help this guy?'"

The hack attacks were more awkward in his two-year interlude in Dallas.

"I've been with these guys here since fifth grade," said Adam, grinning and shaking his head. "They know me. They'll say 'Stop coughing,' just playing around. They're not ignorant about it. My friends all want to try on the vest when they come over. They think it's cool."

So far, CF has struck out on the ballfield.

"I've never started coughing when I'm at bat," Adam said. "I have started coughing in the outfield. But usually the pitcher can hear it, and he'll step off the rubber and mess around till I stop."

"My fears have brought my entire family, from grandma and grandpa to my aunt and uncle to mom and dad, closer to each other and closer to me..."

Baseball is Adam's first, but not his only, love. He is a computer nut—playing games, checking websites, chatting online with friends. He likes listening to music and playing guitar. He likes to write, with several essays such as "Sweating Like Rain" printed in school publications. He also makes time to work after school as a grocery checker.

When asked what he likes to do best, Adam said, "Watching my brother play basketball. He's really good."

Jacob, who is 15, is Adam's only sibling. Jacob does not have CF. But he does have his own medical demon. He was born with a club foot. That problem has been corrected and his leg has been lengthened. That meant sawing through the bone, inserting spacers and wearing a huge brace until new bone grew to bridge the gap in the leg.

"He's been through a lot," said Adam, with an expert's certainty.

"Some people look at fear as only a good feeling, some as only bad feeling, but I try to look at both sides and be optimistic..."

"When Adam was born," said Dane Brockmiller, "my mother told me to expect a miracle. I said, 'Come on, Mom, CF kids don't live past 19.' But we see miracles all the time with Adam."

The most obvious is on the ballfield, where Adam also played the past two years for his local American Legion team. But next fall he plans to stay home and attend East Central College, a two-year school that does not have a baseball team.

"I think I'll have too much other stuff to do," said Adam, a strong student who wants to major in electrical engineering.

His parents worry about his future beyond college, when he moves into the world. Will anyone hire Adam for a top job? Will an insurer cover his treatments? Will he find inflexible standards, as in the basketball tryouts? Will he get a chance to shine, as he did on the baseball field?

Those worries are miracles in themselves. Not so long ago, CF kids never had a chance to become college alumni. To Adam, those issues are for someone else and some other day.

He is strapping on his therapy vest for another morning jump start, inhaling the moment, breathing in today. If he wastes time worrying, he won't have a tomorrow to worry about.

"...This fear in my life makes me the person I am."
—Adam Brockmiller, *"Sweat Running Like Rain."*

9

AMANDA HOUSE

She Sees No Problem Wrestling Boys

Deke Edwards is blunt. Most high school wrestling coaches are, especially those in their 40th year at one school.

When the whistle blows, this is no sport for blowhards. Two wrestlers butt heads and the best man wins. Nothing could be more basic. Except at the Missouri School for the Blind near Tower Grove Park, where Deke is head coach. Sometimes the best woman wins, or at least tries to. For the past two years, Deke's wrestling room has been invaded by a female wrestler, 125-pound senior Amanda House from Columbia, Missouri.

"I think it's stupid," said Deke, politically incorrect as always. "I wouldn't want a daughter of mine to wrestle a boy. The girls are just not strong enough. Until they're 10 or 12, they're pretty equal physically. Then the shoulders start growing out on the boys, and they get too strong."

Amanda, 18, has heard all of this before from her crusty old coach.

"He's just concerned for me," said Amanda, who smiles a lot when she's not crossfacing someone or being crossfaced. "He's worried that I'll get hurt."

That's the only issue for Deke.

*Amanda House—going to the mat for the Missouri School for the Blind.
(Laurie Skrivan/St. Louis Post-Dispatch)*

"What really worries me," he said, "is if some guy with a macho attitude, who's really strong and not very skilled, starts slamming her around. She could break something."

"Well," snapped Amanda, "guys get their arms and legs broke, too."

Deke, 63, is not campaigning to ban females from the sport. Just the opposite.

"It'd be great if they could wrestle each other," he said. "Some states have wrestling teams for girls now. And they're talking about women's wrestling in the Olympics, which would be great.

"Amanda's wrestled four girls last year and this year, and she's beaten them all. One girl beat her early this year, and when they wrestled again Amanda pinned her. So she's 4-1 against girls. But she hasn't beaten any boys yet...except for the ones that forfeit because they won't wrestle her. There's been three of them, including one for religious reasons."

Sprinting down a hallway for conditioning, with Deke barking at each runner, is Amanda's least favorite part of wrestling. Being shunned is a close second.

"That makes me really mad," she said. "It makes me want to go over and drag them off the bench and make them wrestle. I think they're afraid of me. They just don't want to lose to a girl. I've wrestled five boys so far. I score quite a few points, but I haven't beaten any yet. Sometimes I get pinned, but mostly I hang in there.

"The most mad I got was when I was on the mat, all suited up, and I just stood there for about five minutes. Then the coach finally came out and said, 'My boy doesn't want to wrestle a girl.' He was from the Ohio School for the Deaf."

Losing to a girl is an issue that should have died in the last millennium. Religious conscientious objectors cannot be dismissed so lightly. For a boy, grappling with a girl can lead to contact that would bring a slap on any other first date. At a match, by rule, Amanda must wear a T-shirt under her wrestling singlet. That's the only concession to modesty. She wears no special protection. And sees no need for any.

"There are some moves that can be awkward," she said, "but that doesn't happen often. They don't do them because I'm a girl. If they did, I'd end up hurting them. Did you know I do judo, too?"

In Deke's wrestling room, Amanda is accepted as an equal. Volunteer coach Danny Lawrence, 31, has no qualms about Amanda. He was a three-time Missouri state qualifier in 1-A/2-A for the school at 125, 130 and 135 pounds.

"If we had a girl in the room, " said Danny with a laugh, "I don't think I'd have made it to state. Seriously, things have changed. Girls used to cheerlead and boys wrestle, and now boys cheerlead and girls wrestle. You've got to keep an open mind."

That analogy is a perfect fit to Deke's team.

Jimmy Lasley, a 98-pound junior from Scott City, is Amanda's frequent practice partner.

"It's all the same," Jimmy said. "She's really dedicated and wants to work out."

He also happens to be a gung-ho cheerleader when wrestling is out of season. "Want to see my new routine?" he asked, peeling off a series of cartwheels and backflips.

Jimmy is no slouch as a wrestler. Besides giving away five pounds at 103, the lightest weight class, he placed fourth last year in the 2001 1-A/2-A districts, went 2-2 at sectionals and just missed a trip to the state meet.

Amanda, meanwhile, said, "I didn't want to cheerlead. I wanted to do a sport. I like swimming a lot, but that's after wrestling is over. And I wanted to do this because it's physical, not because I'm a girl. That's why I do judo. It's a way to get the stress out."

At this point, it should be noted that nobody but a visitor has mentioned blindness during the team's crisp 90-minute workout. Assistant coach John Schrock, a fully sighted faculty member, is the ringmaster. He keeps both eyes on practice and snaps instructions as the wrestlers pair off for drills.

Deke has been at the school since 1951, when he enrolled at age 12 after a hunting accident stole his vision from both eyes.

"I coach by wrestling," he said.

In sweats, kneepads and wrestling shoes, he nimbly drops alongside a wrestler or a wrestling pair and works by touch. He gets cold-cocked by many a flying foot or elbow, which may be why Deke for years has claimed to be on the verge of retiring.

His wrestlers have sight ranging from dim to none. Amanda has 20-400 vision in the left eye and 20-200 in the right. Her good eye, such as it is, can make out the clock on the wall but not the hands.

"I don't use the other eye at all," she said. "I also have no peripheral vision and I'm night blind."

For all of that, she does not consider herself handicapped.

"People who say that don't know me," Amanda said. "If I want to do something, I'm going to do it."

That also goes for her male teammates. Three of them have just two losses apiece: Jimmy; Darwin May, a 152-pound sophomore from Kansas City; and Bobby Hall, a sophomore at 112 pounds from Park Hills. Adnan Gutic, 17-year-old sophomore of Affton, a Bosnian and new American citizen, is 8-4 at 160 pounds. And Tony Samson, 15, of St. Charles, is a promising freshman at 119 pounds.

They take on all comers, blind or sighted. At a recent nine-team meet, they placed third behind Soldan and Sumner while beating Gateway Tech, Vashon, Clayton's B team and schools for the blind from Indiana, Arkansas and Minnesota. Jimmy and Darwin won individual championships. Tony was third and Amanda won a match by forfeit.

Deke concedes that his team has a handicap. It's not vision, it's depth.

"We only have 10 kids," he said. "And since they went from 12 to 14 weight classes, that's four weights where we can't get points. So it's tough."

He allows no "can't-do" talk and few allowances. For safety in the wrestling room, mats cushion the walls and pillars as well as the floor. For fairness in matches, opponents touch hands with Deke's kids in the up position until the whistle blows.

By the end of the 2002 season, Amanda finally got her man. Times two.

She beat two boys, pinning them both, to place fifth in the North Central Association of Schools for the Blind, a tournament for schools in 13 states. She then ended her career with another fifth place in the Girls State Wrestling Tournament, which drew 50 contestants.

After her two victories over mankind, Amanda said, "It was sweet. I found out I can do something even if it's not usually done. I can stand up for something I believe."

That is the real purpose of all that work on the mat in Deke's wrestling room. He is training independent citizens, the school's mission since the doors opened 150 years ago. When graduates step outside onto Magnolia Street and beyond, they know how to bounce up if they stumble and fall. Confidence and enthusiasm are crucial. And so Deke encourages antics such as Darwin ambushing him in the hallways during school.

"When Darwin knows I'm coming," Deke said, "he'll single-leg me and try to take me down. Some teacher will yell at him to stop. But I always say, 'Don't criticize him…unless he's doing it wrong!'"

Deke's wrestlers have absorbed his humor as well as his instruction.

"You've got to be able to take a joke if you're in something like this," said Amanda, "or you'll never make it."

She meant living in the male-dominated wrestling world. She could have meant surviving in the sight-dominated outside world. That's why Amanda just laughed and shook her ponytail defiantly when her old coach tried one last verbal takedown.

"If she was serious about this," grumped Deke, "she'd get a haircut."

10

KEN HOLTZMAN

Coming Home to the "J"

I t may be the most over-qualified coaching staff in local Little League history.

Ken Holtzman, with five World Series rings and 174 big-league victories, is head coach of the nine- and 10-year-old baseball teams at the Jewish Community Center in Chesterfield. His assistant is his old coach from University City High, Ed Mickelson, who played 18 games in three cameo stints at first base for the Cardinals, Browns and Cubs in the early 1950s. Not that the youngsters of 2002 are overly impressed with Ken, who is 56, and Ed, 76.

"If you're below age 45," said Ken, "you probably never heard of me. And I don't want to hurt Ed's feelings, but if you're under 75 you probably never heard of Ed. I retired in 1980. That's 22 years ago. If you're a 32-year-old parent, you don't remember me. You were only 10 years old then."

Any such parents would have been newborns when Ken last lived in St. Louis. After 15 big-league seasons, he settled in Chicago, his first and last big-league stop. He actually returned to his hometown four and a half years ago. That is news to most folks because Ken works to keep his profile low. This takes some effort. That profile stands six-foot-two and carries, shall we say, a tad more heft than his 175-pound rookie playing weight.

Why St. Louis after all these years?

"My parents were getting elderly," he said, "and I wanted to see my brothers and sisters. I had just gotten divorced, so I sold my business and moved back."

And why a supervisor of health and physical education at the J?

"I wanted to work with kids," Ken said. "Originally, I wanted to teach. When I was in Chicago in '93, I went to DePaul and got a degree in PE and education. I wanted to teach in the public schools, and I student-taught in the public schools in Chicago."

That experience wasn't promising. When he moved here, someone suggested that he apply at the brand new J, as it's known.

"I said, 'Where's the new building?' I didn't know it existed," he said.

Many folks still don't know because, contrary to common belief, memberships are open to the public regardless of religious background.

"People don't realize that two-thirds of our members are non-Jewish," said Ken. "We have a lot of members from Ascension Catholic Church next door."

Ken, who is Jewish, oversees facilities and youth sports programs that are not affiliated with the pool and aquatic activities. He is a gung-ho tour guide, proudly showing off the ways a member can swim, dribble, run, jog, weight-lift or hit baseballs and softballs indoors. It's obvious that to him, the J stands for more than a job.

"The Jewish Community Center is a 120-year-old organization here in St. Louis," he said. "I grew up at the old one."

By old, he does not mean the still sparkling central facility in Creve Coeur.

"I mean the one that used to be in the city at Union and Delmar," he said. "A lot of the old Cardinals who played back in the '50s worked out there. Then, when the J in Creve Coeur was built in '62 or '63, a lot of the Cardinals would play racquetball there. That's where Bill White wrecked his Achilles tendon."

It's strictly a coincidence that the Chesterfield branch holds no racquetball courts. The batting cages were Ken's suggestion to fill some captive space in the basement. Aside from being a money maker—at just $35 an hour for individuals or teams—the cages continue the association of the Cardinals and the J.

Ken Holtzman—safe at home in the Jewish Community Center.
(Photo by Don Adams Jr.)

"In the winter, we'll have Albert Pujols and J.D. Drew and Mike Matheny down here," Ken said, "and John Mabry and Craig Paquette before they were traded. And pitchers like Gene Stechschulte come down and throw.

"They're very good ambassadors for the Cardinals. They're terrific with the little kids. Nobody bothers them, as far as autographs, because people know they're here to work. But when they're done, Pujols or Stechschulte will get in a pickup basketball game or floor hockey game with the little kids. And Pujols's family belongs to the J. His wife takes their little girl swimming here."

Ken likes the idea that toddlers and elite pros can all benefit from the facility.

"Look at Pujols," Ken said. "He had a great rookie year, and he worked out even harder in the winter. He'd get here early and take an hour of batting practice in the cage. Then he'd lift a little bit, and then go home and maybe eat something, and then come back and run the treadmill. And then hit again.

"He didn't just fall out of bed and hit like he does. He's strong as an ox. The ball just explodes off his bat. There's no secret to what he's done. It's his work ethic."

Ken freely admitted the secret to his presence at the J: His big-league pension.

"I couldn't afford to be here without it," he said. "I made a good salary when I played, but nothing like what the guys make today. I never made $250,000 a year, which is like the minimum now. We have people here with master's degrees making $25,000 a year. I have a lot of respect for them. They're here because they believe in this place and they love working with kids."

And so does Ken.

"Ed and I are obviously ex-pros who have that deep competitiveness," Ken said. "But we've learned to throttle it down. We're not in it for the money."

Money couldn't buy the credibility their backgrounds bring, even if the youngsters don't know the details.

"But the kids do know we played in the major leagues," Ken said. "They know they will be taught by a couple of guys who at least know something about the game. But we don't know all the answers."

They know a few, to be sure. Ken played for four of the craftiest and crankiest managers who ever kicked dust on home plate: Leo Durocher with the Cubs, Dick Williams with the Oakland A's, Earl Weaver with the Baltimore Orioles and Billy Martin with the New York Yankees.

"I can make a case that all should be in the Hall of Fame," said Ken. "Each one had a different style. But once the game started, they all knew how to win the game. The way they thought about it. The tactics. All were tremendously knowledgeable."

He smiled and said, "Earl liked to get up in the umpires' faces, like Leo did. And so did Billy Martin. And Dick, too."

Ken tries to avoid that example in the Kirkwood Gold League, where his teams play. "You won't see me yelling at umpires," he said, pausing afterward to smile. "Although sometimes you see some calls that are absolutely ridiculous. But I don't care. Let's just have some fun."

He took care of business with those three rings from Oakland, where he went 4-1 as the A's won three straight World Series, and two rings from the Yankees.

"I have a parents meeting," he said. "I tell them that I'm not here to win trophies. I know that the kids want trophies. I think Ed and I view our role as teachers first and coaches second.

"But even though the idea is to have fun, the focus here is the serious side of baseball. The fun is that they use their skills in the application and execution of the game."

All that fun takes serious preparation.

"We keep extensive statistics in the computer," Ken said. "I know who's hitting what and when. But that's private, not for the kids or parents. That's for me and Ed to talk about and teach with. If a kid's taking a lot of pitches, striking out a lot and walking a lot, we'll know it. And we can work with him on getting a good pitch to hit."

That's a lot of effort for beginner teams. Wouldn't the old pros be more fulfilled coaching older kids?

"It's fun working with the little guys," said Ed, who coached the U. City varsity when Ken was a sophomore and junior. "They soak up information, and they try to do what you tell them.

"You start working with the 14- and 15-year-olds, it's difficult to get them to change their hitting styles. Some of them don't want you to help them. The younger ones are more malleable, I guess."

And more sensitive.

"I've coached football and baseball with the high school kids," Ed said, "and you can get pretty gruff with them. But with these little guys, a kid strikes out and comes back with tears in his eyes. You have to tell him, 'Hey, you're okay! Get"em next time!'"

To Ken, it makes the best sense to have the best instruction for beginners. After all, the first-grade reading teacher better be good, or the whole school system breaks down.

"I like starting them off," Ken said. "And we want to start them off right. I get more satisfaction out of teaching a little kid the fundamentals of the game. Once he gets to be 11 or 12, natural ability starts to take over. But at nine and 10 years old, these are their formative years. This is where the coaching really makes a difference. And the progress is noticeable. We had a kid the other night take a ball off the chest at second base. He stayed with it and threw the kid out at first.

"You might say that's a simple play. But I told the kid, 'That's a heck of a play. That's a professional play.' And it was. It's not easy to stay down like that on a hard-hit ball."

Young minds can absorb more inside scoop than adults might think.

"We've introduced cutoff plays to our nine-year-olds," Ken said. "Next year we'll introduce pickoff plays."

To be sure, the old southpaw throws himself into all aspects of his work at the J, whether he's supervising different sports for nearly a thousand kids or cranking up the glass backboards at night. He is also an avid booster of the Maccabi Games for young Jewish athletes. He is excited that St. Louis hosted the national event in 2003, and he took a team of teenagers to the 2002 baseball event in Omaha.

Ken is not one to bask in past glory, although there are exceptions. He will do occasional autograph shows, which he dreads, but only to donate his fee to the J. And he is absolutely tickled about an upcoming appearance in Chicago. The Cubs have invited him back to Wrigley Field as guest singer of "Take Me Out to the Ballgame." His grown daughters Robyn, Stacey and Lauren will join him at the microphone.

Then it will be back to the J, his new home in his old hometown, where baseball instruction continues year-round indoors. For someone who played with Hall of Famers like Reggie Jackson, Catfish Hunter and Rollie Fingers, his roommate in Oakland, beginner baseball never grows stale. Practice enough, and a second baseman and shortstop might combine on a slick double play. It actually happened—once—this year. Then there was the lad who didn't wait to heed Ken's tip that, "When you get older, when there's nobody on base, the catcher's got to get up off his duff and back up first base on a ground ball."

The next thing Ken knew, an opposing batter hit a ground ball to shortstop.

"I happen to look up," he said, "and our catcher beat the runner down to first base. I told the kids, 'That was the best hustle play I've seen in three years out here.'

"Then I looked at Ed and said, 'That's why we're out here.'"

11

DAN FRANCIS

From Speeding Tickets to Speedboat Titles

Dan Francis of Imperial is a world champion powerboat racer. He's not the driver of the two-man water wing that he owns and sponsors. He's the throttle man. And that's a nice touch.

At age 37, a millionaire many times over—a penny or two at a time from his St. Louis Pre-Sort mailing company—he's got life by the throat. And that's a nice touch.

As an even younger man—when he was kicked out of college and joined the army by order of a local judge and blindly signed away his share of his first million-dollar company—life had him in a stranglehold.

Dan is not your typical CEO . . . unless your boss meets the press in a General Custer hair and facial do, black leather jacket, Harley Davidson T-shirt and jeans and is a regular at a neighborhood South Side eatery like Chris's Pancake and Dining.

For now, let's put the spectacular part of his story on hold and start with the blasé stuff: Doing 120 mph in a powerboat along the Atlantic Coast, careening in races from Canada to the Caribbean, with up to 275,000 fans holding their breath. In two years on the powerboat circuit, Dan has made a quick splash, as is his wont in most endeavors. He is four

Dan Francis: airborne at sea with Neil Wobbe at the wheel.
(Photo courtesy of Dan Francis)

for four in various world championships alongside veteran driver Neil Wobbe, a tanning bed salesman from St. Charles.

So which partner has the tougher role?

"I would say the throttle man is more important," Dan said with a grin. "Neil would say the driver. But it's really 50-50. It's like having your wife in the car and she has the wheel and you push the gas pedal and you have to go through traffic at 80 miles an hour."

Offshore, in traffic, careening around buoys and often airborne, a 37-foot powerboat is a handful for even two operators.

"There's too much to do," Dan said, "especially on the throttle. You've got to read the water and watch the gauges. We have two engines, one for each propeller, and you've got to adjust them when you make a turn. Or when you leave the water, which we do a lot. When you're airborne, you have to throttle back. If you hit the water too fast, you flip over backwards."

Pancaking is not a good thing in an open-canopy boat like the color-ful Zipp Express, named for Dan's local courier company. Last year, a rival racer was decapitated after tipping on edge for several seconds at top speed. Roll bars are pointless on water. A racer's best hope in a topsy-turvy boat is to be thrown clear—the opposite wish of a racecar driver. "We're not seat-belted in," Dan said. "They want us flying out of the boat."

That is changing. Boats will be fitted with a cockpit and five-point harness system. But drowning will remain a hazard for crash survivors trapped in upended boats. So racers will continue to carry mini oxygen tanks while helicopters will remain overhead, ready to drop divers to the rescue of submerged racers.

Speaking over lunch at Chris's Pancake and Dining, a favorite South Side haunt, Dan never missed a bite of his juicy burger while detailing these grisly options. After all, this is the sedate and serene portion of his life story. He *really* got up some speed when he was a kid at Fox High and, briefly, Jefferson College. Back then, working both the wheel and throttle of his sports car, he had "some ticket issues," as he put it.

Translation: By age 21, he said, he had run up 170 speeding tickets on area roads. At the same time, he had also shown a fast aptitude for commerce, even though his divorced parents had other interests. His father was a printer. His mother worked for the federal government. Yet Dan owned his first business, Lord Jim's Pizza Parlor in South County, by the time he was 19.

"I was the manager of it," Dan said, "and then I bought it from the owner, who kept the building. I always paid my rent, but the guy went belly up on the lease and I had to pack it in."

When the building was sold out from under him, he sold insurance for two years.

"That's when I got thrown out of Jeff-Co," he said, referring to the junior college in Hillsboro. "Well, I didn't really get kicked out. I got asked to leave because I threw a Frisbee through the chemistry teacher's window."

The window, it should be noted, was open.

"But the Frisbee broke a few—what do you call them?—beakers," Dan said. "It wasn't a good thing to do, but this teacher was really arro-gant. And he was always late."

Dan was only trying to be punctual when he zoomed to his last speeding ticket. While in Columbia, Illinois, he got a late-night call from a buddy who had some hot dates lined up in Festus. Dan said he was clocked at over 180 miles per hour as he shot across the Jefferson Barracks Bridge. He figured he had outrun any interested law-enforcement types until he crested a hill on Interstate 55 near Arnold and saw a fleet of police cars on the stretch below, red lights blinking furiously.

"I thought it was a wreck," Dan said.

It was a reception committee. Having not outrun the speed of sound, he was busted when a trailing traffic cop radioed ahead for help. The judge was briefed, if that's the word, on Dan's ticket history. The result was a pivotal, if stereotypical, ultimatum: Go to jail for six months or join the military.

Dan chose the army, where he responded well to the discipline and eventually impressed his superiors. "They wanted me to go to West Point," he said, "but I was too old. I missed the cutoff by six months."

So instead of training to become an officer, he was stationed near Chicago as an explosive ordnance expert. This assignment in the late 1980s led to presidential duty, sweeping public places for bombs before the Commander in Chief made an appearance.

"You wouldn't believe the stuff we found, pipe bombs and stuff like that," Dan said. "They just don't want to publicize it."

He was 24 when he left the army—"with an honorable discharge," he said pointedly—and went home to a job in asbestos removal.

"Myself and a lady in Perryville started the company," Dan said. "Everybody asks me her name, and I try to forget it. I was cleaning out asbestos from buildings and I couldn't stand it. So I quit. A few months later, she sent me $2,500 for my share as a partner. I found out later she had sold the business for $7 million. That was a drag, but what can you do? I'm the one who quit."

He sold advertising at a senior citizens newspaper before stumbling into his breakthrough in 1991. He and a buddy, Mark Winkle, enjoyed collecting metal lunch boxes and drove to a swap meet in St. Joseph, Missouri, in pursuit of their hobby.

"Some relative of his in St. Joe's had a company that had a direct mail business," Dan said. "I'd never heard of that. I went back to my hometown in Arnold and asked some people, 'Have you ever heard of this?' Nobody had. In my mind, it was either illegal or a gold mine. So I went to the post office and checked it out. And they said it was legal."

And it turned out to be a gold mine. The U.S. Postal Service gives bulk discounts to a company that pre-sorts mail—lots of mail—by ZIP code. The more being sorted, the higher the discount. Dan began asking companies like AmerenUE and Blue Cross-Blue Shield if he could process their mail through his new St. Louis Pre-Sort. He found that a penny or two per letter can add up, both in savings for his clients and in profit for his company. At a quarter of a million to two million pieces of mail per day, Francis said, Pre-Sort did $20 million in business last year.

Never one to sit still, he bought Zipp Express in 1996 because the courier dovetailed with his mail business. Zipp was another instant hit, more than doubling its sales in five years to $3.5 million.

By then, Dan was wealthy. He started branching into fun ventures, often with friends long on ideas and short of cash. Some of his concerns included River City Films, which is producing a children's musical; Archway Auto Glass and other automotive companies; U-Do-It Dog Wash in Bayless; Chimney Rock Guest House, a bed and breakfast in Imperial; Turtles Restaurant; The Note Bar; and a property management company.

His latest plunge is into the art world. He owns an 1881 oil painting by John Mullvaney titled "Custer's Last Rally." That dramatic take on Dan's look-a-like has been appraised at $3.5 million, he said. He is also hip-deep in charitable foundations, although he shuns any board position that blatantly trades status for cash. Dan is a hands-on backer of DECA, the Distributive Education Clubs of America. "It's a high school club like 4-H or Future Homemakers," he said, "but for promotions and marketing. I joined when I was a kid, and that's how I got interested in business."

He enjoys going back now to speak to youngsters, which is why he is still searching for a national sponsor to pick up the $250,000 annual tab on his powerboat.

"I don't want to be in front of an audience of high school kids and college kids and be associated with a beer or a cigarette company," he said.

By the way, Dan still keeps in touch with the judge who steered him to a responsible path. He credits his employees for giving him the free time to spend on his powerboat. And sometimes, he wonders if his life hasn't been pre-sorted in ways that go beyond understanding. Such as when he recently bought a century-old house in Imperial.

"My mom died of an aneurysm in 1982, before I got going on all this stuff," Dan said. "When I told my stepfather that I was buying this house, he said, 'You know what? Your mom used to say she always loved that place and wished she could live there.' It's weird."

It is. No matter how fast you travel, inside or outside the speed limit, the next turn may bring you right back to where you belong.

ED MACAULEY

Hall of Fame Homily Man

E d Macauley, by his own count, has two talents.

"I can organize a basketball practice," he said, "and I can organize a speech."

The first skill is indicated by his No. 50 jersey from St. Louis University, which hangs from the Savvis Center rafters. The second is not just indicated by his onetime stint as a local sportscaster. Easy Ed, as he was known at SLU and in his Hall of Fame days with the Hawks and Boston Celtics, is now an expert on homilies, or sermons, as they were once known. He is co-author of Homilies Alive, a how-to book on the subject of sermons, and its companion homiliesalive.com Web site. The book's introduction is by Joe Garagiola, the ex-catcher from St. Louis who became a national broadcasting star.

"Ed did a great job with the book and the internet site," said Garagiola by phone from his home in Phoenix. "He's been working very, very hard on that. He's very sincere about it."

Ed always had a homely love of the homily.

At age 75, his basketball days are long gone. So are his knees, replaced by two artificial joints that are less than miraculous. The pain is such that he must gingerly lower his lanky, six-foot-eight frame into a seat.

Easy Ed Macauley delivered the ball, and now Deacon Ed Macauley delivers a homily.
(Photo courtesy of Ed Macauley)

Even so, he considers himself blessed. And then some.

"I have the greatest life a person could have," said Ed. "I have a great wife, Jackie, and we had seven kids and 17 grandkids. I asked myself: Could I give something back to God?"

So a decade ago, at a stage when most famous athletes have eased into the background, Easy Ed leaped into new territory. He became a Catholic deacon in his parish, St. Genevieve du Bois in West County.

"If you want to go beyond that," he said, "you can complete the courses and pass the homily class. So I went through that."

It was a case of the student knowing as much or more than the faculty. Preaching sermons came as naturally to Ed as teaching basketball drills. Or so it seems. As with any job done well, smoothness stems from a rough plan and hard work. As with a basketball team, the secret to success is the mastering of basic skills.

"The book has 10 fundamentals on how to give a good homily," Ed said. "You're going to read them and say, 'Sure, what else could it be?'"

Obviously, based on yawns per parishioner, the basics are not so obvious.

"They have done surveys of congregations," said Ed, "where the basic question is: Do you get a lot out of the sermons? The reaction is usually: 'Just fair.' This is from the people in the pews."

This is not a knock at sermonizers. Familiarity breeds boredom, as any coach knows when hatching yet another halftime pep talk for the same players.

"If I have a speech and change my audience every time, that's easy," Ed said. "The problem with giving a homily is you do it 52 times a year, and you're doing it to the same audience every Sunday. That's tough. If you're talking to the same audience every week, you better incorporate these fundamentals."

Giving a sermon is one thing. Writing a book, at least for Ed, was quite another.

"I can speak," he said, "but I can't write. When I finished the book, I showed it to some people, and they all said, 'This is lousy!' Well, that isn't what they said. But that's what they meant."

As those wounds gaped, Ed got a healing call from Monsignor Frank Fields, president of Loras College in Dubuque, Iowa.

"He said he heard I was writing a book on homilies," Ed said. "I told him I was. He said, 'So am I.'"

Ed had no qualms about collaborating for one excellent reason: "Francis can write." When they sent their combined work to publishers, the response was unanimous.

As Ed recalled, "They all said, 'Thanks for sending it to us, but it's a terrible book. It's too long.'"

No insult was taken. The authors simply forgot Rule No. 7 in their book, which deals with long-windedness: "You must time your homilies properly."

The authors sliced their opus to 120 pages. This sleek version was snapped up by Twenty-Third Publications of Mystic, Connecticut. Since hitting the shelves in 1994, *Homilies Alive* has sold nearly 9,000 copies and is in its fourth printing. It is a blunt, breezy, paperback with tips for the sermonizer of any faith. In fact, anyone facing an audience on any topic, holy or unholy, can benefit from these tips. Ed's bottom line for sermonizers: "Preach as Jesus preached." That advice goes beyond faith to a matter of style.

"Jesus's great faculty was he could communicate his beliefs to the people," Ed said. "He told the Apostles, 'I speak differently to you, but to them I speak in parables.' And what are parables? Little stories with a moral. That was the only way he could have communicated with masses of people. Because that's all they understood. He's not knocking them. He's not putting them down. Jesus was a practical man. There is no better way to communicate with people. We can argue about other things, but that's one thing you can't argue with me about."

Ed opened his web site in July, 1999, as a resource for his over-worked target audience—the clergy. Writer's block, or speaker's block if you will, was an issue. Homiliesalive.com is a stockpile of actual sermons. And it is popular. In the first month, the site drew 634 visits. After 10 months, total visits topped 11,000. Now, the site averages between 10,000 and 12,000 hits per month—more than 220,000 all told in less than three years.

Each week, Ed posts three new homilies, two in English and one in Spanish. He recruits from a roster of over 50 bishops, monsignors, priests and deacons. They preach or have preached across the country from California to Massachusetts, and overseas from Chile to Italy. Over half have current or past ties to St. Louis.

Each is asked to contribute two homilies per year. Spanish homilies, in particular, are in demand. But recently, plagiarism charges have spun from alleged misuse of homily banks.

Ed takes a mild view of the controversy, saying, "If people can incorporate ideas from our site into their own homilies, that's what it's there for."

Others take a harsher view, charging intellectual and spiritual dishonesty. For example, a Presbyterian minister in Clayton apologized from the pulpit and then resigned after using online material without attribution.

Ed has a solution: "Most churches have some kind of Sunday bulletin or newsletter. My idea is to put in the bulletin a line that says, 'Some of the ideas for my homily were inspired by...' That covers it."

Ethics aside, a generic homily may not click with every pulpit. As Ed writes in Rule No. 4: The homily should be of interest to the congregation. The message must fit the audience. To illustrate, Ed offered a parable involving former U.S. Senator Bill Bradley, when he was a youth at Ed's summer basketball camp here.

"I told his dad, 'If Bill keeps progressing, he can have a future in the NBA,'" Ed said. "His dad looked at me like, 'What is the NBA?' He was a banker, and he didn't know sports. I said, 'He could play pro basketball and have a contract for $100,000 a year.' And his dad said, 'What!' The banker came out then when he heard that."

Finally, as mentioned earlier, longer is not better in a homily, a point driven home to Ed one blistering summer day.

"The church wasn't air-conditioned," he said. "People were wiping their brows and waiting to get out of there. The priest went to the pulpit and said, 'It's too hot for a sermon, so let's just pray.'"

Ed grinned and said, "I don't remember a whole lot of sermons in my life, but I remember that one."

BOB PAIGE

"Little Satch" Also Loves Family and the Road

Leroy Robert Paige, better known as Satchel, died in Kansas City on June 8, 1982. The seemingly ageless wonder, who pitched for the St. Louis Browns, was reputedly one month short of his 76th birthday.

In the 20 years since then, Robert Leroy Paige of St. Ann—Bob to his friends, "Bug" to his father and "Little Satch" to his father's friends—has grown even closer to the man behind the legend. Bob has seven siblings—six of them sisters. All live in Kansas City except Bob and a sister in Detroit, and all take turns representing their father at baseball functions big and small around the country. For example, Bob pinch hit for his dad at the 2002 All-Star Game in Milwaukee, hobnobbing with the likes of old pals Cal Ripken and Rickey Henderson. Bob makes three or four such appearances a year. He has a flexible job at Roadway Express, where he drives the big double-rig trailers.

"You can take your name off the board," he said, "but if you don't drive, you don't get paid."

The pay is certainly important. Bob and his wife Faye have two teenage daughters still at home—Halei, 19, who attends Missouri-Kansas City, and Ashli, 17, who attends Pattonville High. Their son, Stanley, is 24, married and working in Kansas City.

Bob inherited a love of the road from his father, who made his name and his nickname in the Negro Leagues during the segregated first half of the last century. Satch built his legend with off season barnstorming against big-league All-Star teams. He cemented it when baseball's color line finally fell in the late 1940s, baffling big-league hitters well into his 40s.

In 1948, Satch was a 42-year-old rookie with the Cleveland Indians. He won six games and lost just one. In 1953, his third season with the Browns and last full big-league season, he was 47. He worked 117 1/3 innings, gave up only 114 hits and had a career-best 11 saves for a bad team. In 1965, when he made a one-game publicity cameo for Charley Finley's Kansas City A's, he was 59. He allowed one hit and no runs in three innings. That was the only big-league game that Bob saw his father pitch. Bob, now 50, was born in Miami, the family's off season home, between his father's last two seasons with the Browns.

While the rest of the world remembers Satchel Paige as a delightful legend, Bob remembers plenty of loving fun at home in Kansas City with his father and mother, La Homa. He also remembers a strict father who was seldom home as he finished his big-league career, lingered in the minor leagues and continued to barnstorm into his 50s.

"We were not as close as I would have liked because of his travels," said Bob, born fifth among the eight children. "And then when I got in the air force, because of my travels. We were actually kind of estranged there for awhile."

That was due more to typical father-son jousting across the generation gap. And to the stubbornness that was passed down from his dad.

"He was always the disciplinarian," Bob said. "It was 'Don't do this. Do that. Be home before midnight. Stay away from those boys, they'll get you in trouble.' I didn't want to hear that."

As a boy, he bristled at chores like tending the family livestock right there in the heart of Kansas City.

"We lived at 2626 East 28th Street in the early"60s, and we had a double lot," Bob said. "It was one of the biggest lots in the neighborhood. He grew up with animals in Alabama. So we had cats and dogs and chickens and two ducks and a raccoon.

"Of course, we did all the work with those animals. The raccoon would get out, and then we'd have to throw a burlap sack over him to catch him, and he'd bite you. We called him Roy the Raccoon, and he was in a big cage in the garage."

As for Bob, his father called him Bug, which came from June Bug, which came from Junior, which came from him being the firstborn son, even though he was not a namesake, since their first and middle names were reversed.

When Bob left high school for the Air Force, he was six foot one and weighed 130 pounds. After six weeks of basic training, he sprouted to six foot four and a half, an inch taller than his father.

"It was hilarious," Bob said. "The clothes that I was issued when I got to basic didn't fit. When I went home on leave and knocked on the door, my mother actually didn't recognize me."

In 1971, Satch was inducted into the Baseball Hall of Fame in Cooperstown, N.Y. And Bob was there with the rest of his family and was included in his father's acceptance speech.

"It was great," he said, "even though he said I was in the navy instead of the air force."

When that service hitch was up after three years, the boy had grown into a man who stoodsix foot eight and a half with an aptitude for basketball. The father didn't approve.

"He had been on my case every since I started playing basketball," Bob said. "He was just a baseball fanatic."

In the mid-'70s, Bob attended three colleges on basketball scholarships, spending a year apiece at Johnson County Junior College in Kansas, University of Missouri-Kansas City and Henderson (Arkansas) College. His father swallowed his distaste for the sport to watch his son play home games at UMKC. And did not like what he saw.

"You're not rough enough," he told his son.

"And I wasn't," said Bob, who resented that critique at the time. "I was a finesse player. I was only 205 pounds and I was extremely quick. He wanted me to be a banger."

The point became moot. The son kept blowing any shot of a pro career by blowing off school. In fact, after three years of college he still remains two years short of a degree.

"I just wouldn't go to class," Bob said. "I just wanted to play basketball. I figured I'd get an NBA tryout. I used to scrimmage with the Kansas City Kings, and I did pretty well. I was just so set on 'Get to the pros, get a contract, get set for life.' That last year at Henderson, I just didn't have the desire any more when my grades kept slipping."

His father definitely did not approve of that. Or his of son's stubbornness, which, to be fair, was inherited.

"It was all 'my way or the highway,'" Bob said. "I see young guys like that now, and I say, 'If you could just remove yourself and look at it, you'd see.' But it's hard to do. People are adamant about their position on anything."

Slowly, over time, the father-son relationship began smoothing out. Bob spent four years as a driver improvement instructor for the State of Illinois, working in Springfield with people whose licenses were revoked.

"My father hooked me up," he said. "He was in public relations and sales at the minor-league team there for A. Ray Smith, before A. Ray moved on to Louisville and bought the Cardinals' minor-league team there."

Bob moved on to other jobs, some of them managerial.

"Then I took a real good personal inventory of myself," he said. "I asked myself, what do you really want to do? I always enjoyed being outside. When I worked for the State of Illinois, I had a territory I had to cover. I enjoyed that."

So he became a chip off the old suitcase, working as a Federal Express courier in Peoria, Illinois. That's where he met his wife, who worked for Ozark Airlines.

Bob also took stock of his personal habits.

"I had been smoking and drinking heavily," he said. "So I stopped that."

His relationship with his father also grew healthier.

"We were not as close as I would have liked," Bob said, "because of his travel in baseball and then my travel in the military. But we really got a lot closer as he got older and I started maturing."

Decades of smoking had caught up with the baseball immortal, who developed emphysema.

"He had resigned from cigarettes for years," Bob said, "but they had done so much damage. They had to put him on pure oxygen. When his health started deteriorating, I was the one getting the wheelchair, getting the oxygen, coming home every other weekend."

Bob went out of his way—417 miles one way, to be exact— to commute from Peoria to Kansas City.

"I used to make that little jaunt like it was clockwork," said Bob. "I've always had this knack for driving. So did my dad. They would send him airline tickets for some function, and if it was under 500 miles, he would cash them in and drive."

Now the son dwells only on the happy times at home that he experienced or heard about.

"He loved a good prank," Bob said. "He was the one who started the rumor about Cool Papa Bell being so fast that he hit a liner to second base and got hit in the head with the ball.

"When he'd barnstorm, they'd bring a rocking chair out to the mound, and he'd sit in it and a couple of the ballplayers would come out and fan him.

"He loved to play cards and dominos, and guys would always drop by. Connie Johnson, Buck O'Neill, all those guys from the Black Leagues. Cool Papa Bell, who lived in St. Louis, he'd always stop by when he was travelling this way."

Despite his distaste for basketball, Satch worked for the Harlem Globetrotters in the"60s as—fittingly—the traveling secretary.

"I'd come home from school," Bob said, "and the house would be full of Globetrotters. Meadowlark Lemon. Marcus Haynes. Jumpin' Joe Jackson."

The ballplayers would not confine their chatter to sports. But they would temper their talk while Bob and his siblings were around.

As he put it, "The conversations would change when my momma and the other women would leave the room. Then they'd say, 'Okay, Little Satch, take a hike!'"

Bob was most fascinated by talk of his father's salad days, of barnstorming and the old Negro Leagues.

"He would bring his own shortstop when he barnstormed," Bob said. "He took Jackie Robinson to several games, when Jackie still played in the Negro Leagues. My dad would say, 'I don't want to be out there any longer than I have to.' He knew Jackie could pick it and Jackie could deliver it."

He heard his father retell of the times he would walk the bases full, wave in the outfielders, tell the infielders to sit down and then strike out a slugger like Josh Gibson.

And the secret of his father's limber arm? Heat, not the false god of ice so beloved by modern sports medicine. After a game, Satch would enter the shower with a towel over his arm, then slowly turn the hot water up as high as he could stand it for as long as he could stand it.

"My dad did the same thing for his whole body," Bob said. "You'd see the steam coming up off the tub. He really took care of himself, except for the smoking."

Bob also wanted to clear up one misconception.

"He didn't die broke," Bob said. "He didn't have the money that these guys have today, but he was always buying cars and boats. He even bought a plane, a Cessna, that aided him in his barnstorming. He had a guy fly it for him.

"When he barnstormed, if his pay wasn't there when he came through the gate, he didn't pitch. My momma said he would be on the mound, holding the ball, till he could finally see her in the stands getting his money from the promoter."

Bob's mother died in 1986. He moved to St. Louis in 1989 when TWA bought Ozark and assigned his wife here. Bob is now a strict and doting parent in his own right. He steered his older daughter, Halei, away from college in Chicago to the cozier confines of Kansas City.

"She has family there if she needs anything," said Bob, who remains close to his siblings.

He is proud that Halei made the dean's list at Missouri-Kansas City, ignoring his academic footsteps there.

"I stress to my kids it's important to finish what you start," said Bob.

After 13 years in St. Louis, few insiders know him as Little Satch. This is his first interview in his adopted hometown.

"The circle I run in is small," Bob said. "I like to spend time with my family when I'm not on the road."

He is still in terrific shape, watching his food intake and playing basketball in an over-40 league.

"My dad used to say, 'It's not how old you are. It's how old you feel.'"

The Baseball Encyclopedia says Leroy Robert Paige was born in Mobile on July 7, 1906. For the record, did the father ever reveal his true birthdate to his son?

"Yes," said Bob. "He was born on July 7, 1907."

But that would make him a year *younger* than the record book shows.

"I know," said Bob with a twinkle. "But that comes from both him and my mother."

Don't Look Back…and Other Sagely Paige Advice

Tips for staying young, by Leroy Robert "Satchel" Paige, with commentary by his son, Robert Leroy Paige:

Avoid fried meats, which angry up the blood.

"He loved fried fish and fried chicken. He would keep it in moderation. But he said to avoid it before you had something stressful to do, like pitching."

******

If your stomach disputes you, lie down and pacify it with cool thoughts.

"Cool thoughts…[laughter]…*and* he took a lot of antacids and Kaopectate. We kept Pepto-Bismol and Tums and Rolaids and Maalox."

******

Keep the juices flowing by jangling around gently as you move.

"He loved to dance. My mother and he would turn on the old record player, put on the vinyl records and dance at home. All the time. He had three separate turntables. He really liked the Pair Extraordinaire. That was his favorite jazz group."

******

Go very light on the social vices, such as carrying on in society. The social ramble ain't restful.

"My mother would call over to her sisters—her family all lived within a few blocks of themselves in Kansas City—and the next thing you know, it's a party. But it was always at our house. My dad was territorial, the captain of the ship, the boss of the hot sauce. He loved total control, which he had at home. And my mother loved to cook, but not at her sisters' house, just in her own kitchen."

******

Avoid running at all times.

"He was not a fast runner, and he hated it. He would say, 'That's the reason I bought cars.' One time in spring training, the pitchers were running around the outfield, and he was just playing catch. Bill Veeck, the owner, came over and said, 'Satch, you're supposed to be running.' And he said, 'I'm a pitcher. If you wanted a runner, you should have hired Jessie Owens.'"

******

Don't look back. Something might be gaining on you.

"He said that every time he was on the basepaths and he looked back at the ball, he got tagged out. That's where this one came from. He was just a horrible base runner."

BECKY DUFFIN

Amazing (But True) Softball Legend

Becky Duffin may be the greatest St. Louis athlete you never heard of. You, as in everyone outside the windmill arc of fastpitch softball. Greatest, as in a career that defies exaggeration. Never heard of, as in women's softball's lack of media appeal. Other than publicity, there was nothing lacking in Becky Duffin, as a pitcher or a person.

"She was quite a lady," said former umpire Rich Willis, "just a real neat lady, besides being a great pitcher."

"She was quite a gal," said J.Y. Davis, her manager on the St. Louis Classics for most of the 1980s. "She was one of the most talented athletes I've ever seen. By far she's the best pitcher ever to come out of St. Louis. And she was one of the best center fielders I've ever seen."

Becky Duffin was Babe Ruth in reverse, swapping a career in the outfield for the pitcher's mound in her senior year at Southwest Missouri State. She continued to bat leadoff in college and later hit in the No.5 hole for the Classics team throughout her pitching career in the American Softball Association (ASA).

But the most amazing part of her new career was not the position shift. A physical education major, she analyzed the windmill motion and developed a new way of pushing off the pitching rubber. Her style put the stress on her legs, not her arm. That innovation is not her only amazing legacy. After making All-America at Southwest Missouri, Becky became the first St. Louis woman to play softball for her country, pitching for Team USA at the 1988 Pan American Games in Aruba. In 1989, she also made the ASA All-America first team. That established her as the country's top pitcher. She reinforced that in 1990 on her second national team, serving as lead pitcher for Team USA at the International Softball Federation World Championship in Normal, Illinois.

But her statistics are more amazing than her honors. With the Classics, Becky won 153 games and lost 24. She averaged 13 strikeouts and 0.22 earned runs per seven-inning game. She rang up more than 80 no-hitters, two dozen perfect games and 2,500 strikeouts. And those are not her most amazing numbers.

In a 1987 ASA Regional in Omaha, Becky pitched a 33-inning marathon that lasted five and a half hours. She gave up two hits and two walks, struck out 62 batters and won, 1-0. And that was not her most amazing tournament. In that 1990 world championship, Becky led Team USA to the gold medal. She went 3-0, allowing two runs overall, fanning 17 in an opening no-hitter against the Philippines and winning the clincher against New Zealand.

But her real battle in that world championship was even more amazing. Becky arrived on crutches each day, racked by pain that she traced to a family history of back trouble. In fact, her five-foot-six body was ravaged by cancers that would kill her in just five months. She died on December 29, 1990, at age 29. And the most amazing parts of her story were yet to come.

Becky was already a member of the Missouri Sports Hall of Fame. But she was never inducted into the St. Louis Softball Hall of Fame. Finally, after 11 years, that oversight was rectified. Becky was enshrined with 20 others in the class of 2002. And that happy correction is not the end of her story. Most amazingly, Becky is still a force in local softball through Duffin Fastpitch, her pitching school that is carried on by her softball-crazy family.

Becky attended Ritenour High as a freshman. Then her parents moved to Vienna, Missouri, where she completed high school. After college in Springfield, where she learned the windmill motion from John Bass, she returned to live in St. Peters. She bought the school in 1987 from local softball official George Jones.

Roger Duffin passes on Becky Duffin's technique to youngsters like Jenny Lamb. (Photo by Erik M. Lunsford)

Becky, the youngest of seven children, originally learned the game from her three brothers: Robert, a St. Louis policeman; Stan, who works at Sunnen Products; and Roger, who is with the St. Louis County Parks and Rec Department. It is Roger who runs Duffin Fastpitch at sites in Overland, where he lives, and in the Metro East in Brighton. His wife Barbara handles the paperwork. So far, more than 1,500 girls have learned Becky's special technique. "She wanted me to keep the school going to give kids an option," said Roger.

The three brothers gathered at Roger's house to brief this writer on Becky Duffin. Also on hand were Roger's daughter Tammy, 29, a teacher in Warrenton, and Stanley's daughter Katie, 25, a new instructor at Duffin Fastpitch. Both young women played college softball, as did Robert's daughter Colleen, 29, now head softball coach at Parkway Central High. The three cousins learned to pitch from their Aunt Becky, although Katie switched to catcher, playing on the boys' baseball varsity at Mary Institute-Country Day School.

Clearly, the family still adores Becky, throwing anecdotes and information faster than a stranger can absorb them.

"She was unhittable," said Roger. "Me and Robert would go and catch her…"

"…And she could be uncatchable," said Robert. "One time I was warming her up, and I said, 'You're not real fast.' And she got mad. She threw the ball so hard, if it hadn't have hit my glove, I'd have never caught it. Her control was impeccable."

"She'd throw that rise ball," said Roger, "and it'd just jump over my glove. If she wanted to kill me, she could have."

"She almost did kill me once," Stan said. "I was catching her, and she threw a pitch so hard that the pocket came out of my glove. The ball knocked me out and left a knot on my head. When I came to, she said, 'I'm warm enough.'"

A true legend does not need disciples to stretch the truth to fit the image. One yarn has Becky winning a showdown at a rural fair with a Missouri country boy named Tom Henke, the future big-league baseball pitcher. Her brothers say that if Henke lost, he must have held back. He threw a baseball over 90 miles per hour, while Becky's softball topped out in the upper 60s. And Davis, her former manager, scrupulously notes that the 33-inning siege was against a 19-and-under team, the Vess Esprit of St. Louis. That puts the 62 strikeouts and two hits in perspective. But 33 innings are still nearly five full softball games. And the feat didn't end with that last out. Becky was supposed to have the rest of the day off. But two games later, with the Classics one game from elimination, she talked Davis into letting her warm up.

"I asked how she felt," Davis recalled, "and she said, 'It's a little tired, but I think I'll be okay.' Well, she struck out two hitters in the first inning, and you could see the dobbers drop on that other team. She pitched the whole seven innings and we won. She could be very intimidating."

As Willis, the ex-umpire, well knew.

"If I called it a strike when it should have been a ball, she'd give me a dirty look," said Willis with a chuckle. "She never said anything. But she was good enough that she'd pick up my strike zone in the first inning and make me stick to it."

Willis is commissioner of the St. Louis Metro ASA, which sponsors the Hall of Fame dinner. He sounded embarrassed by the delay in Becky's induction.

"It's partly a case of out of sight, out of mind," said Willis. "That, and nobody submitted her name."

Apparently the snag in the coed group was more than just red tape.

"J.Y. Davis, he's being inducted this year, too," said Davis. "I told him if he'd been manager of a men's team, he'd have been in six or eight years ago."

The Duffin brothers don't want to pick a fight over the holdup. They're just glad and proud that their kid sister is getting her due. And it's nice that Davis is being enshrined with her. His presenter is Roanna Brazier, who lost that 33-inning marathon and later joined the Classics. Becky's presenter is Katie, who submitted the application for induction. She was about 14 when she saw her aunt for the last time.

"The day before Becky died," said Katie, "I went over to her house to say goodbye. She was in a recliner. She sat me down beside her, and she said, 'Do not let softball become your life.'"

At first, the youngster didn't know what to make of those parting words. Softball had been her Aunt Becky's life, and a happy fulfilling life it was.

"It's important to my life, too. It was an outlet for girls like me to have self-esteem," said Katie, who works for Vi-Jon Laboratories. "I got a lot out of softball. But she wanted me not to let it be the end of my life if I didn't make All-America. I got a scholarship to Country Day, but it was for my grades. You know, when you play a sport, you don't get a college scholarship at age 12. You don't peak at age 12. I think people forget that."

Even if people remember nothing else about Becky Duffin, that would be her most amazing legacy of all.

JACK GRAHAM

And His "Chariots of Fire" Hero

Young Jack Graham had never heard of the Olympics back then, when he was 12 years old and living in China as a missionary's son. The lad had never heard of the Flying Scot, also a missionary's son, who sprinted to a gold medal in 1924 after missing his best event by refusing to run on Sunday. This was nearly four decades before *Chariots of Fire* retold that inspirational tale and won the Academy Award for Best Picture.

Young Jack Graham knew none of that back in 1943 in Weihsien, a Japanese internment camp for Westerners in occupied China. What the lad did know, and right from the start, was that there was something special about Eric Liddell.

Jack, now an ex-boy of 70, came to the United States with his parents, got a degree from Northern Iowa University and eventually came to work here for the Defense Mapping Agency. He is now retired and living with his wife in Oakville.

Through the years, thanks to the stirring 1981 movie and other research, he has learned more about the middle-aged man who helped ease confinement for himself and the other captives so long ago. No details of Olympic glory could outstrip the golden memories that Jack holds of Eric Liddell.

Jack Graham and his sister Enid in China, prior to their internment by the Japanese in 1941.
(Photo courtesy of Jack Graham)

"He was a very nice, very, very pleasant person," Jack said. "One thing I remember about him was his happy disposition. I can still see him smiling and being cheerful."

They spent less than two years at Weihsien and were not especially close. After all, Liddell was 41 when they first met among the 1,500 prisoners, including 300 children.

As Jack said, "He knew me by Jack. I don't think he knew my last name. Kids that age are not dying to hang around with someone his age. But they hung around him, because he was so approachable.

"The kids actually called him Uncle Eric. He was the only one called that. Everyone else was Mister. And I can't even remember the names of some of the men we knew."

Liddell was a strong influence on the children, who needed it for several reasons. Most youngsters like Jack were separated from their parents. Jack turned 10 on December 6, 1941. The next—now infamous— day the Japanese bombed Pearl Harbor and began rounding up Western nationals in China. They swept up Jack, his younger sister Enid and others in their boarding school for missionary children in northern China. Jack's parents were 2,000 miles away at their mission in a southern province. The Graham children spent nearly four years in confinement, the last two at Weihsien (pronounced WAY-shin). Without parents, all the youngsters in the camp needed firm guidance. The mostly adult population was a varied lot, to say the least.

"There were some pretty unsavory things going on," Jack said. "Our little missionary eyes got opened up pretty quickly. There were a lot of Europeans there who were on the run from the law in their own countries. They were Caucasians, so the Japanese scooped them all up after Pearl Harbor.

"They were kind of a bad influence on us. These Russian prostitutes were there, plying their trade up against a wall in the camp in broad daylight, working for cigarette butts the Japanese guards had thrown away."

Mercifully, the Japanese treated these civilians far more civilly than military prisoners. Still, the accommodations were hardly plush in the camp, which had served as a Presbyterian mission school for the Chinese. The buildings had no utilities or plumbing. School materials were scarce. Bedding was shoulder to shoulder and tempers were often short. Strangely, security was minimal, at least for about two months after Jack arrived.

"There was a man in the camp named Arthur Hummel, who became Richard Nixon's ambassador to China," Jack said. "He was in his 20s then, and he escaped from the camp with another fellow named Tipton. We got into Weihsien in October of '43, and by November they were gone.

"They climbed over the wall and the Japanese went berserk looking for them. There was really nowhere to go, but the Japanese never found them. They were never more than 50 miles away. They joined the Chinese guerrillas and fought the Japanese for the last two years of the war."

That daring duo also smuggled news of the Allied victories into the camp under the Japanese noses—and through the nose of a Chinese coolie. The man, a day laborer, carried the handwritten notes in a tiny tube in his nostrils. He then blew out the contraband when safely past the guards. The Japanese captors never caught on, but further escape was impossible. The guards strung three fences of electrified barbed wire in front of a booby-trapped trench. One boy accidentally touched the inner wire and was electrocuted. That was the only violent death that Jack remembers. The other losses were from disease, mostly typhoid fever, and natural causes.

"People were born in that camp and died in that camp," Jack said. "I can remember seeing dead bodies. In the two years that I was there, there were probably about 40 deaths, which was very low. Statistically with the Japanese, I think one out of every three prisoners died in captivity, including civilians."

Uncle Eric, himself a missionary teacher, confined his heroics to helping the children. He had a special empathy for their plight. He had spent years at boarding school in London with his brother, while his parents and sister returned to their China mission. And he was separated from his own two daughters and pregnant wife, whom he had sent to Toronto when the China situation worsened. Uncle Eric was concerned about how the camp could affect morale and morality of the children there.

"My first recollections of him would have been in the mess hall," Jack said. "He was like one of the cooks who took shifts. The children had jobs like swatting flies, carrying water and pumping water, which was my major job."

The youngsters attended school daily despite the almost total lack of materials. Jack and others in his class had to fill and erase their notebooks three times before qualifying for a new one from the guards.

"You could almost see the corn stalks through the paper," he said.

Uncle Eric, whose college degree was in science, taught chemistry to older teens suddenly in prison instead of college. He wrote a textbook by hand, sketched in some experiments and required the older students to conduct them in their heads, since no lab equipment existed. But Uncle Eric did not set himself up as the camp morale officer.

"He kind of exuded it, though," Jack said. "Three or four boys and I would be sitting around with him and he'd tell us stories. I don't remember if he had a good voice, but he would sing or hum when he was in the mess hall. He was just an upbeat person. It's hard to do that in a prison. The food was terrible, but he never complained about it.

"Then I'd see him in the evenings, when they'd have storytelling and games for the kids. He was a strong Christian and he tried to teach us moral values. The Japanese did permit us to have church services, and he preached several times. His favorite hymn was "Be Still My Soul," and I had never heard it. It was to the tune of 'Finlandia,' and he taught it to us."

Uncle Eric sometimes talked about his days as a sprinter, but never boastfully. It wasn't until 1981, when Jack saw *Chariots of Fire*, that he learned what a sensation Uncle Eric was in the early 1920s. He had starred in rugby and track at Edinburgh University in his family's native Scotland and made headline news across Great Britain and then the world.

"I knew he was an athlete," Jack said, "probably very soon after we'd gotten into camp. I knew that he was a fast runner."

Jack saw for himself at one camp track meet. Uncle Eric agreed to run a dash against two brothers, both fine athletes half his age. Jack remembered Uncle Eric placing third in what was nearly a triple dead heat.

"I used to hear him talking about the Olympics," Jack said. "Not about winning his gold medal, but there was a sermon he gave that life is like a race. The apostle Paul talks about running the race and finishing the race that's set before you."

Jack never heard Uncle Eric mention his most celebrated act: Turning away from the 100 meters at the '24 Olympics in Paris because the preliminaries were run on a Sunday.

"I never remember him saying anything about that," Jack said, "although I knew about it before the movie came out. It was talked about in the camp. But not by him."

Due to the Sunday schedule, Uncle Eric not only refused to run the 100 meters, where he was favored, but also walked away from probable medals in both the 100 and 400 meter relays. Instead, he ran the 200 meters, placing third, and the 400 meters, winning in world record time of 47.6 seconds—in an event he rarely entered and was in no way favored.

Little Jack thought nothing odd about a sports star who lived a never-on-Sunday life.

1924 Olympic champ Eric Liddell was "Uncle Eric" to kids like Jack Graham during WWII.
(I.O.C./Getty Images)

"If an athlete did that now at the Olympics, he'd be considered a complete nut," Jack said. "But we were taught by the missionaries to honor the Sabbath. That's the way I was brought up.

"That's still one of the commandments, although it's probably the least observed. Sunday's the big sale day now. People go out and mow the lawn."

Watching Uncle Eric in that camp race, Jack was dumbfounded by his awkward running style.

"He kind of threw his arms out, kind of flailed around," said Jack, who does not recall Uncle Eric's other quirk of looking skyward as he churned. "Running like that, you just wonder how he could have been so fast."

Or how powerful he remained so far into his dotage, as it seemed to young Jack.

"That's why it was such a surprise that Uncle Eric had died," he said. "It was a shock. We knew he was in the hospital. Most of us had intestinal problems, worms and parasitic infections. Most of the deaths in the camp were from typhoid. But he didn't have that. Here's a perfectly healthy guy otherwise."

Otherwise, meaning a fatal brain tumor. Uncle Eric had borne horrible headaches for weeks, hiding his agony from the children until the pain drove him to the camp hospital.

"My last recollection was that they just kind of came on suddenly," Jack said. "My room was up in the attic of the hospital there. And that's where he died."

Most sources list the cause of death as the tumor, although Jack remembers it as a cerebral hemorrhage. In any case, the end came on February 14, 1945. That was a month after Uncle Eric's 43rd birthday and six months before American paratroopers liberated the camp.

Two years after Jack and his sister were reunited with their parents, their father died of cancer at age 45. For Jack, life went on in America and the camp receded into the past. He and his wife had just bought a house in Washington, D.C., in 1981 when *Chariots of Fire* was released.

"I thought it was a tremendous picture," said Jack, whose favorite scene is where his hero is decked in a race but bounces up to win. "And the religious part of it, that's not exactly the kind of thing you'd think would win an Academy Award. Maybe it's too much for some people who aren't interested in it, but I thought it was great."

Jack later bought a video titled *The Story of Eric Liddell,* designed to flesh out the Olympic hero for *Chariots of Fire* viewers. To Jack, the video did just the opposite: It supplied the legend behind the man that he already knew.

A decade after its release, Jack saw *Chariots of Fire* on television. He has not seen it since. He did make a trip back to China with some military veterans two years ago, visiting his parents' mission town, but not the prison camp in Weihsin. Through the years, he has told audiences young and old about his youth in prison camp.

"I really hadn't thought of Eric Liddell in several years," he said. "But then my church, Good Shepherd Presbyterian, scheduled a showing of *Chariots of Fire* for the Sunday School kids. And then you called.

"It's quite a coincidence. And, you know, this year [2002] is the 100th anniversary year of Eric Liddell's birth."

What big Jack didn't know was the answer to one last question: Was Eric Liddell able to keep holy the Sabbath day in prison camp?

"You know," said Jack, "I never thought of that. He was in charge of one of the crews in the mess hall, and if it was his shift I guess he'd have to work. But I seldom ever remember doing anything on Sunday, any games or anything like that."

16

STAN & RED

Jabbing with the Fight Mob at South Broadway

Ring names aside, Stan "The Man" Musial and Albert "Red" Schoendienst are basically nonviolent. So why have them headline the 2000 Reunion Rumble at the South Broadway Athletic Club?

"I wouldn't bring a knife to a gunfight," organizer Myrl Taylor said, "but I'd bring both of these two to a fistfight. Because they've got more hits than the whole rest of the joint put together."

The pair of baseball greats combined for one more hit, wowing over 500 fans crammed into the 101-year-old club.

Happily, Stan reported that his new knee was working better: "I played golf the other day with my doctor at Old Warson."

As a rule, the old-timers in the crowd at South Broadway don't hob-nob with the country club set. And chances are that nobody at Stan's foursome at Old Warson ever spent the day busting shoplifters.

That's what Earl Taylor, Myrl's daddy, did at the South County sporting goods store where he works at age 92.

"The guy was in his 20s," said Earl. "He had six pairs of socks. And here's what he said to me: 'You're an old man. You better stay in an old man's place.'"

Those were fighting words for Earl, a former welterweight whose top purse was $2,000 for a 1934 bout in Paducah, Kentucky.

"I said, 'Look, buddy, don't let this mileage stop you.' I was ready. I've still got a good left hook. I still go downstairs in my basement and jump rope and hit the bag for half an hour.

"I knew I could hit him once, and if I hit him once, he'd hit the ground. Of course, I'm not saying what he'd do to me if he got up. But he gave me the socks."

For emphasis, Earl tugged at his ballcap, which passed for formal wear at this blue-collar bash. The meal involved a buffet line, paper plates and plastic forks. Stan and Red, who cleaned up nice for the affair, were grossly overdressed.

"I figured if I had a coat and tie on," said the Redhead, "I wouldn't have to fight anybody. You know, I used to come down here years ago to watch the fights."

Stan, however, was a first-time visitor.

"But being from Pittsburgh," said The Man, "I used to follow the fight game. I had an uncle who was training Mickey Walker, and I helped with the water bucket when I was 10 or 12."

That name rang a bell with John Brown, the former South Broadway fighter who managed Tommy "The Duke" Morrison from nowhere to "Rocky" fame.

"Mickey Walker was one of the top middleweights in the history of the division," said Brown, who runs his own Ringside Boxing supply firm in Kansas City.

"I used to spar with Mickey Walker in Chicago," said Earl Taylor.

Amid the fight talk, Stan and Red spent well over an hour signing autographs and posing for photos. Then Myrl Taylor began the program.

"Autographs are over," he boomed. "You wore these guys out. They already signed about 55 things for every person here. They're not spring chickens, you know."

That broke up Stan (who turned 80 the week before) and Red (who was headed for 78 in a couple months). They broke up again when Myrl introduced Don Caviecy as the club's Man of the Year.

"Don's gonna be the next president here," Taylor said. "We ain't had the election yet, but you know how that stuff goes."

Jerry Clinton of Grey Eagle Distributors, a South Broadway alum who invited and chauffeured the special guests, introduced the baseball Hall of Famers as "my boyhood heroes."

Then the Redhead led off.

"I used to fight when I was in the CCC," said Red, who figured he was 16 or 17 during that Depression Era work program. "Every Wednesday night they'd have a fight, and away we'd go.

"I always ended up spraining my thumb. I was not smart enough to keep it inside of the glove. I won a few of 'em, but I'd rather play baseball.

Then Stan was up.

"I had one fight in my life," he said, noting the unscheduled bout came in the 1940s against Brooklyn pitcher Les Webber. "He had a mediocre fastball and a mediocre curve. And I could wear him out."

The fight mob howled at that immodest zinger from the modest hero.

"The first pitch, he knocked me down," Stan said. "The second pitch, he knocked me down. The third pitch, he knocked me down. Then I got up and started out to the mound.

"I don't know what the hell I was going to do, but they broke it up."

After paying Red the ultimate compliment—"We were roommates, and he did not snore"—Stan pulled out his harmonica for three sing-a-long tunes.

The final tune was "Take Me Out to the Ballgame," not the theme from *Rocky*.

17

IZO BAJMAROVIC

Fighting Culture Shock
Without His Freedom-Fighter Dad

The story is sadly familiar. A minority athlete from the city, living in a cash-strapped, one-parent family, with no adult male at home, may be squandering an opportunity to better himself through his talent. What's different about Izudin Bajmarovic, age 17, is a foreign series of twists.

They explain, in part, how the St. Mary's senior could rattle off 99 points over four basketball games and then "separate himself from the team," as coach Ed Perniciaro Jr. put it.

Separation is the key word in the life of young Izo (EE-zo), who has just turned 17. He moved to St. Louis from Bosnia 18 months ago with his mother and three sisters. The usual stress from changing high schools was complicated by the new language, new customs and new standards of behavior. His father was absent for a grim reason. After leaving an affluent situation in Bosnia to join his country's war against the Serbs, he has been missing in action since 1995 and is presumed dead.

Given that heavy load of baggage, it's less of a wonder that Izo struggled in his first and last season at St. Mary's. He has terrific ball skills for someone standing six foot six—or 6'7" or 6'8", depending on which person holds the yardstick—and weighing 230 pounds.

"He had a complete game as far as scoring inside and outside," said Perniciaro.

Shortly after a four-game burst of 25, 26, 17 and 31 points and with the Missouri 3-A Districts just ahead, Izo quit the team. He said only that he disagreed with Perniciaro's methods. Neither party went public with details. But Izo calls his ex-coach "probably the finest man I have ever met." And Perniciaro says his ex-player "was always very respectful to me."

So what was the problem?

"Some things were going on outside in his own life," Perniciaro said. "I don't know exactly what they were, but they distracted him. As far as handling team rules, it was difficult for him because of the issues he was having outside of St. Mary's."

Absenteeism was a major problem. Not just at practice, but also in the classroom.

"His attendance is still inconsistent," Perniciaro said, "but it is much better lately."

Izo realizes that skipping school was not helpful.

"I didn't want to go because I didn't speak English so well," he said. "And I had problems at home. It's private. But that's the reason I didn't go. Then I decided no matter what it takes, I'm going to go to school."

Languages were Izo's strength back home in school near Sarajevo, the Bosnian capital.

"My best subjects were Italian, French and English," he said, "but we study British English. It's a lot different. That's why I have a lot of problems. I know how to speak and how to read, but not how to write."

His father, Ohran, had moved the family to Sarajevo when the war threatened their home in the outlying town of Vogosca.

"It was a big house," Izo said. "My dad, he worked something like construction, like a supervisor. He worked in other countries like Algeria and Iraq and England. They build like huge buildings.

"In '92, something like that, he was in the army, like a soldier. When the enemy of our country, the Serbs, started to take our country, he took us close to the capital city. It was too dangerous near our house."

The house eventually was destroyed in the war. But Sarajevo was not a sanctuary.

"Bad stuff," Izo said matter-of-factly. "Bombs were falling. I was like seven or eight. People were dying. One time a bomb hit a couple meters

Izo Bajmarovic (in the white jersey) moved from an uncertain present in Bosnia to an uncertain future in America.
(Photo by David Kennedy)

from where we were living. You heard it coming. There was like a whistle, and you'd run in the basement.

"And when it hit, no more windows. I saw people dead, not dying but already dead. My mom tried to hide me from seeing it, but sometimes you couldn't do it."

He stopped to translate for his mother, Sefika, who was monitoring the interview in their South St. Louis apartment.

Izo last saw his father in 1993, after the relocation to Sarajevo.

"He sent us, a lot of times, letters," Izo said. "When the"95 year start, that's the last time we heard from him. I don't know exactly where he was. He just disappeared. That's all."

Izo translated that for his mother, who nodded solemnly.

"It's okay," Izo said, "but we really miss him. Especially when you go to somebody else's country."

At first, the family made do in Sarajevo.

"The war ended in like the end of the"95 year," Izo said. "Then like maybe a half-year after that, a lot of kids start to do like amazing stuff, use the drugs and stuff. Because I don't want to do that, because I know I'm going to have trouble late if I do, I want to find something more interesting."

That something was the local basketball club.

"People tried to help me out," he said. "I was like 10 years old. I wasn't that tall. It was a real old gym, not clean. They a little bit fixed it up. It was hard when you don't know how to do anything, but from '95 to 2000 I played with that club.

"They had a league and we played teams from other cities. Then they had national tournaments for like the junior teams. I was a pretty good shooter. And I'm still a pretty good shooter."

Meanwhile, the family was scuffling to get by without its breadwinner.

"After the war, the economy goes down and you could not find a job," said Izo. "My two sisters, the older was going to be a doctor and the other one wanted to be an economist. But we didn't have a choice. We have to leave the country to have a better future.

"We decided to come to America. Lot of good stuff here. My one grandmother and the rest of the family is all over the world, Germany and other places. We heard a lot of people were coming to this city, St. Louis. We didn't want to go someplace and be all alone, because we didn't speak English very good."

His sisters Azreta, 22, and Hajreta, 20, support the family here with office jobs. Baby sister Irma, eight, is the most Americanized of the family. Izo waited almost a year to start high school here because he wanted to pitch in financially. He took eight months of language courses and sought work. The culture shock was, in fact, shocking.

"Ooh, really hard," Izo said. "Big problems if I go somewhere and try to speak with somebody. I tried to work a little bit, but with my age, which was 15, I couldn't work much. That's when I decided to go to school. When you finish, you can get a good job."

He also decided to start as a senior at St. Mary's, even though he did not turn 17 until Christmastime. In hindsight, that was too ambitious. But his oldest sister was engaged to be married and his second sister was taking classes at Forest Park Community College.

"If I stay in high school another year," Izo said, "I won't be able to work and take care of my mom and my little sister."

Playing catch-up from his absenteeism, he is no cinch to graduate this spring. He figures, wisely, that his best plan is to attend a junior college while he polishes his English. Izo hopes to stay close to home at either Meramec or Forest Park. He picked up a strong ally along the way in Easy Ed Macauley, the former St. Louis University and NBA star. Macauley helped arrange tryouts at both Meramec and schools, as permitted by junior college rules.

Izo is not a pioneer in this department. With thousands of Bosnians resettling in St. Louis, young athletes are starting to crack local high school and college rosters, especially in soccer. In fact, a six-foot-three guard named Adanan Sabic just finished playing basketball at Forest Park.

"He's a very tough-minded player," said assistant coach Lee Winfield, "and he also played soccer here at Forest Park. He's really a conscientious kid who works hard. He plays both sports, has a work-study job on campus and another job off campus. I told him he probably does too much, and he said, 'Coach, I don't have a choice.'"

Izo wants to hoist the same workload, minus the soccer, for the same reason. That seems ambitious, given his unreliable high school record.

"He's an interesting prospect," said Meramec head coach Randy Albrecht. "He has some offensive skills, but not a lot of background in American college basketball. And he quit his team, which concerns you."

As Winfield put it, "My concern is not about his basketball. It's about his off-the-court adjustment. I have a lot of respect for these Bosnian kids and what they went through. You can't fathom what all that is about.

"But if you're talking about absenteeism, that's a problem. That's always going to affect your basketball, but it really affects your classes. No classes, no basketball."

As it turns out, Izo was headed to nearby Forest Park but never made it. He dropped out of St. Mary's. He then suffered a back injury in a traffic accident while a passenger in a truck, heading to his part-time job. With no high school diploma or its equivalent, there was no college basketball. And, maybe, no happy ending for a boy still recovering from his father's ultimate sacrifice.

18

CATHERINE HEALEY

90-Year-Old Autograph Hound

C atherine Healey is not involved in the hubbub over historic home run balls hit by Mark McGwire and Barry Bonds. Catherine, at age 90, found her niche of baseball memorabilia almost 70 years ago. She has quietly added to it without ever having to scramble in the bleachers or dive into a bay for a souvenir ball.

The longtime Soulard resident owns an autograph book. In this slim little volume, which she bought at a dime store in 1933, are autographs. Many, many autographs. From many, many players. Many of them in the Hall of Fame. Catherine, who doesn't look a nanosecond over 70, brought her precious keepsake to the Cardinals' 2001 season finale at Busch Stadium, much to the delight of fans like Ted and Dottie Drewes, the frozen custard mavens sitting nearby behind home plate.

"She's even got Connie Mack!" said Ted, gushing like a youngster at one of his custard stands. "You should hear how she got him."

Catherine happily retold how she got the legendary manager to sign in, please.

"I was at the "44 World Series between the Cardinals and the Browns at Sportsman's Park," she said, "and Connie Mack was there under the ramp. He was just there as a spectator. I asked him to please sign my book and he said, 'Oh, I never sign autographs.'"

Mack was then 81, still six years from retiring as manager of the Philadelphia A's.

"Well," Catherine said, "all of a sudden Dizzy Dean came hopping down the ramp. He said to me, 'What are you doing with this young fella?' I said, 'I'm trying to get his autograph, but he won't give it to me.'

"And Dizzy said, 'Mr. Mack, I want you to sign this for this young lady.' And he did."

She opened her book to show Mack's careful penmanship. Below him is Stan Musial. And beneath Stan's familiar signature is . . . Timothy Healey?

"He's my grandson," said Catherine. "He was about 11 then and he wanted to sign the book."

Timothy has more elite company on other pages. Rogers Hornsby, while the Browns manager in '38. Hall of Fame shortstops Arky Vaughn and Joe Cronin. Rick Ferrell, the Hall of Fame catcher, plus his pitcher-brother, Wes.

"And Lefty Grove and Mel Ott and all those guys," Catherine said matter-of-factly.

And is that Hack Wilson?

"No, that's Jack Wilson. I don't have Hack. I don't have many Cubs," said Catherine, with a commendable anti-Chicago bias.

Ol' Diz is in, of course, along with Johnny Mize and Pepper Martin and Frankie Frisch and most of that Cardinals Gashouse Gang of the '30s. Catherine, born in 1910, doesn't remember her first autograph. But she knows precisely when she got her favorite. Joe "Ducky" Medwick, the Hall of Fame Cardinals outfielder, signed in on July 20, 1935. She noted that date carefully off to the side, a practice she kept for most other signees. But she permitted no lesser mortals to sign on that hallowed page.

"Joe Medwick was my idol," said Catherine, a girl of 24 when they met. "I don't know why I liked him so much. He hadn't won the Triple Crown yet. He won that in '37. He was just so good. I'm trying to get the Cardinals to retire his number."

In fact, she has written and called the ball club to argue her case. She did get back one letter—"from some guy," she said curtly—but not a reason. She is still miffed that Medwick is excluded from the pantheon of Hall of Famers in the right field upper deck at Busch.

"They've got Enos Slaughter up there," Catherine huffed, "and Enos couldn't tie Joe's shoelaces."

As for her autograph book, it does not discriminate against non-baseball notables. For example, Bill Bradley, the basketball Hall of Famer and pride of Crystal City, checked in.

"Oh, I love Bill Bradley," she said. "He was down at Ed Macauley's basketball camp when my son, Jim, was there. And I've got a son, Pat, too."

She also has a daughter, Mary Jones, who is caretaker of the book along with her husband, Bill. The volume's value, by the way, is unknown.

"Mike Shannon told me it was worth more than the whole of Busch Stadium," said Catherine, who has never had it appraised. "One time a man offered me $2,000 to tear the page out with Jimmy Foxx on it."

Bill, her son-in-law, recalled that particular offer as $400, but the amount was moot to Catherine.

"I would never sell any of the book," she said, "but it belongs to my daughter and her husband now."

Bill, escorting her to the game that day, said, "We're going to hang onto it. For now."

As word of her hobby spread, Catherine has become a mini-celebrity. A producer from Jay Leno called about a guest spot on *The Tonight Show*, which tickled Catherine even though the invitation never came. Meanwhile, the book remains a classic work in progress. While Catherine was chatting with Ted and Dottie that day in the Busch Stadium basement, Red Schoendienst strolled by.

"You know," Catherine said, "somehow I've never managed to get Red."

A bystander hailed Shoendienst and explained the situation. The Redhead smiled and called for a pen. And Catherine Healey had another Hall of Fame autograph for her baseball bible.

19

TIDBIT

Busch Stadium's No. 1 Bleacher Bummette

Cher. Madonna. Tidbit.

All are brassy, sassy, one-name women with big voices and an adoring public. The first two are rich and famous entertainers. The third lives in Florissant and is richer, at least in baseball memorabilia and relationships, and infamous, if you've been within earshot of her bleacher act in Busch Stadium by the visitors' bullpen. Earshot being anywhere inside the stadium or a block or two from it. Tidbit may be the best fan in the world's best baseball town. She is without a doubt the hardest to miss.

"She's definitely an original," said Trevor Hoffman, the All-Star reliever for the San Diego Padres. "She's definitely one of the louder fans, shall we say."

"Never met her? Don't worry," said Steve "Bulldog" Kline, the Cardinals' reliever. "When you get out there, you'll hear her."

That's not quite accurate. Because anyone with an operative eardrum does not need to reach Section 591, Row 4, Seat 1 to make audio contact with Tidbit. From that perch, her voice can peel bark off a tree in the Ozarks. When she wants to get Kline's attention during a game, she stands up and yells. Never mind that during a game, Kline is perched in the Cardinals' bullpen in right field, half a stadium away.

"We'll be in the middle of a game," Kline said, "and all of a sudden, I can hear her yell, 'Hey, Bulldog!' And I know exactly who it is."

"Sometimes a guy on the other team wants to tell him something," Tidbit explains.

Her charm is not in her loud boldness, although that is a big part of it. Mostly she endears herself with her humor, generosity and wacky passion for baseball and the people who populate it. Players. Ushers. Vendors. Groundskeepers. Other fans, especially youngsters.

As Hoffman said, "She just wants to have fun at the ballpark."

She's been doing that for 45 years, since she was a two-year-old toddler who already answered to Tidbit.

"I don't know her real name," said Kline, in a majority opinion.

Hoffman went him one better: "I just know her as the lady in the bullpen."

For the record, Tidbit was christened Jeanie Marie Carrino. She does not hide this information. It's just useless for social discourse, like expecting people to call her by her social security number.

"Nobody knows my real name," she said. "I go all over the U.S., and everybody knows me by Tidbit. When I go on the road, players leave tickets for Tidbit at the stadium and I always get them, no problem."

And Kline said, "All I ever put on the envelope is Tidbit."

Her uncle, Jack Carrino, dubbed her that even before first taking the toddler to old Sportsman's Park in 1957.

"I used to be real little and real skinny," she said. "So he just called me Tidbit."

She grew to be only four foot eight, but a more precise nickname now would be Dumpling. And, strictly speaking, she is no Bleacher Bum, since she has a fulltime job at Jalapeno Restaurant in Clayton. Fulltime is more of a figure of speech than a pay status.

"I'm a bartender," she said, "and a waitress and a bottlewasher and whatever."

So how many of the 81 home games can she get off to see?

"All of them, almost," she said. "Plus I take seven to 10 road trips a year. I've already been to Seattle and Chicago twice and Kansas City this season. And I go to spring training for a month every year."

How does she finagle her work schedule around all of that?

"I don't," she said. "They work around my schedule."

From any other waitress, bartender, bottlewasher and whatever, that would sound preposterous.

"Once you meet her," Kline said, "you'll understand."

Tidbit is unmarried—"except to this damn game," she said—and without children. She is everyone's den mother, albeit with the volume cranked far past *Leave It to Beaver* nurturing levels. Even millionaire players seem attracted to a safe harbor in a world that, especially for celebrities, keeps getting crazier. The irony of fame is that those who get it crave privacy. The irony of fandom is that clinging hero worship is the surest way for a fan to repel a hero. Tidbit understands this mysterious way of the world.

"She keeps it real," Hoffman said.

She also understands that the last thing someone at work wants to talk about is work. Even someone whose salt mine is a ball field. So she doesn't ask players about their curveballs. She teases them about their haircuts. She'd rather get a smile than a signature, although she gets plenty of both. And helps to keep kids supplied with balls and autographs.

"She just makes me laugh," said Kline, who was in the visitors' pen with Montreal when he first met Tidbit. "I get a kick out of her. She'll ask me to tailgate at a football game or here at the ballpark. She loves to tailgate. She'll say, 'Come out and have a couple sodas.'

"She's one of those people who goes out of her way. She bakes you cookies. She made me some shirts that said Bulldog and 49, my number. She made my little baby a cloth with KLINE on it that we framed. She throws me a Tootsie Pop every day.

"She's a sweetheart."

Not everyone finds her adorable.

"Hey!" barked a bleacherite in a Cardinals cap, as a scribe retreated from Tidbit's lair. "Why are you writing about a Cubs fan?"

It's true. The most celebrated fan in Busch Stadium always roots for the home team...unless the archrivals from Chicago hit town.

Even a good buddy like Kline cannot excuse this character flaw. "Well," he said grimly, "she's a Cub fan, which we don't like."

Blame heredity. Blood is thicker than Cardinal red.

"It's because of my damn Uncle Jack," Tidbit said, possibly with affection. "He was a Cubs fan, so I was a Cubs fan. The first game my uncle took me to at Sportsman's Park, the Cardinals were playing the Cubs.

"We were sitting out in the outfield pavilion, and the man sitting in front of us got a Cubs home run ball. I said to my uncle, 'I wish I caught a home run.' And that man turned around and gave me that ball.

"Oh, man, that was it. I was two years old and I fell hook, line and sinker."

That's why, when she talks about her pilgrimage to spring training for the past 19 years, she means the Cactus League in Arizona, where the Cubbies emerge from hibernation, and not the Grapefruit League in Florida, where the Cardinals migrate.

It was Uncle Jack who introduced her to memorabilia mania.

"I snagged a lot of autographs for him," Tidbit said. "I was a cute little tiny Sicilian girl with dark hair and dark eyes. He'd send me over to the railing where the players were, and the guys would pick me up and hold me and sign whatever I wanted. Then I'd take it back to my uncle and he would go, 'Scored again!'"

It's that kind of scam that causes a friendly player to turn a cold shoulder. But her uncle, now deceased, never tried to profit from the autographs that Tidbit would charm away. He sold nothing, promised everything to her and delivered. Tidbit added so much through the years to Uncle Jack's cache that she can't display it all. Or keep track of it.

"I've got close to 2,000 autographed balls," she said. "Remember, I've been doing this for 45 years."

She recently added her 319th bat, a gift from Eric Young of the Milwaukee Brewers. "He's my baby," she said.

And part of a big brood. When former Cardinal Ron Gant jogs to left field for the Padres, Tidbit screeches at him and gets a wave back.

"Ronnie's my baby," she said.

So, it turns out, is Kline. And Hoffman. And fellow Padres reliever Steve Reed. Her foster roster expands quickly when she flips through a stack of photos. All are shots of her at ballparks with player after player.

She stops at one and coos, "There's my boy, Reggie Sanders. He's just a real sweet, sweet guy. I've got a bat from every team he's been with."

She keeps flipping, stops and sighs. "There's my *bay-bee*," she says, pointing to a smiling behemoth with his arm around her. It's Barry Bonds, the undisputed curmudgeon of the baseball world. Except to Tidbit, he's a lovable home-run king, more so than Sammy Sosa of her beloved Cubbies and Mark McGwire of her second-most beloved Cardinals.

"I just didn't care for McGwire," she said confidentially. "And I think Sammy's for Sammy, even though he does like me. When we were in Chicago, Sammy threw me a ball up in right field, and he doesn't acknowledge the fans there."

Tidbit has that effect on players. She used to ask for a memento. Now she doesn't have to bother.

"I was at the All-Star Game last year, and Billy Wagner, the Houston reliever, came running over and gave me an All-Star baseball. They know I'd never sell any of this stuff. Willie McGee came all the way out here his last year to give me a bat, and this guy goes, 'I'll give you 200 bucks for it,' while I'm still talking to Willie.

"I said, 'Excuse me, Willie,' and I told the guy, 'Are you nuts?' Then he says, 'I'll give you 400!' I told him to get lost."

She stops to peer around the screen that separates the bullpen from the bleachers. She has a snack pack for Hoffman—a box of candy and homemade cookies. For everyone else, she has her a bag of her trademark Tootsie Pops, which she tosses like confetti.

"We were in Chicago," she said, "and Matt Morris stopped me on the street and asked for a Tootsie Pop."

Tidbit can't get Hoffman's attention—in itself one for the record books—so she summons Padres teammate Steve Reed. He comes dutifully over and asks where she was the night before.

"I've been in the big leagues for 11 years," he tells her, "and you're always consistent. I never saw you miss a game. Until last night."

It turns out that Tidbit had a last-minute party to work at Jalapenos.

"I thought either you got sick," Reed said, "or you just didn't like the Padres."

Reed goes back to alert Hoffman, who gives Tidbit a big hug—even before receiving his snack pack. Then the game begins. A fly ball arcs toward Albert Pujols, the Cardinals' prodigy.

"Two hands!" Tidbit screams, in harmony with the fan sitting next to her.

That sidekick is Delores Dalton of Florissant. Retired from AT&T, with her children raised, she is in her fourth year as Tidbit's trusty baseball sidekick.

"We've known each other since the '98 playoffs in Wrigley Field," Tidbit said. "We sit together at all the home games. And then I'll just call her up and say, 'Hey, Delores, let's road trip!' And we get in the car and go.'"

They travel on a budget, stay with friends when possible and, as with home games, arrive when the gates open and stay for the last out.

"Even if it's raining," Tidbit said. "I love it. I'd never leave early. I'd be scared to miss a triple play or something."

Next they were headed to Milwaukee for the 2002 All-Star Game, having bought Kline's tickets. After that was an excursion to Cooperstown, N.Y., for Ozzie Smith's Hall of Fame induction. Tidbit, though, is most at home in her bleacher seat.

"When my uncle took me to Sportsman's Park, we always sat in left field," she said. "Those were the cheap tickets. The pavilion was the only place blacks could sit, and the winos would be out with their paper sacks."

That melting pot survives today. Tidbit shares a section with characters like Carri Coffee of Webster Groves, known as The Whistler for a shrill tweet that can cut metal. Tidbit thrives in what Kline calls "the atmosphere out there." And she and her cohorts try to maintain minimum standards.

"We don't let anyone cuss around us," she said, "because there's kids out here."

Cardinals president Mark Lamping has already assured Tidbit that her season ticket will transfer to a similar seat in the proposed new stadium.

"He said I'm their secret weapon," Tidbit said. "He even invited me up to his personal suite to watch a game once. I said, 'Naw, I don't think so.' He said, 'Hey, it's free food and free beer.'"

Tidbit thought hard about that new information. In the end, the fan who never wants to miss anything decided to stay in her bleacher seat.

"It's a good thing I did," Tidbit said. "That's the game Willie McGee brought his bat out to me."

CHARLIE SHARE

The Ex-Hawk Captain and His Jaskowiak Grandkids

harlie Share is once again the captain of a championship team. In 1958, the six-foot-10 center was the glue on the Hawks when they won the National Basketball Association title. Now, at 75, Charlie is immersed in his most cherished athletic role. He is the proud grandfather of three major college athletes and scholars who made their mark at Parkway West High: Derek, Emily and Allie Jaskowiak.

Derek, 21, is six feet four and 280 pounds and started the 2002 season as a senior offensive lineman at the Naval Academy. He helped West to the football sectionals his senior year, when he placed third in the discus at the state track meet with a throw of over 164 feet, breaking a school record that stood for 31 years. He also lettered in basketball.

Emily, 20, is a second-year freshman basketball player at Tulsa who stands 6'1". She owns most of West's single-season and career scoring records. She led the team to the state finals as a senior, and she was named first-team All-State after making the second team the previous two years. She also was also All-Conference in softball for three years and lettered in volleyball.

Alli, 18, is a 5'11" senior at West. She has started in volleyball and basketball since her freshman year, played with her sister on that state runner-up basketball team and made second-team All-State last year in volleyball. She had numerous big-time offers to play either sport, or both sports, but decided to play basketball at the University of Southern California.

Charlie's heirs are also top students.

Derek, a *Post-Dispatch* scholar athlete at West, ranks 81st among over 1,000 seniors at Navy. In the spring of 2002, he was chosen Second Class—the Navy equivalent of junior class—Midshipman of the Semester.

"It's a pretty big deal," Emily said. "He got his own parking space."

After being commissioned an ensign in May 2003, he hopes to attend the elite "nuke school," train for surface nuclear warfare, and serve on an aircraft carrier.

Emily earned a 3.5 grade point average in her first year at Tulsa despite some major health hurdles. Before leaving for college, she took an elbow to the mouth in a select basketball game. She needed over a year of repair work on two front teeth and then came down with an internal illness. The ailments kept her off the basketball court but not off the dean's list.

Allie, an A student, was president of her class the first three years at West. Among other leadership posts, she is executive president of the student government.

How does one family crank out this triple-double of brains and brawn? With the Jaskowiak clan of Chesterfield, it's a happy combination of nature and nurture. And happy is the operative word. These siblings may be compulsively competitive, but they aren't rivals. They also don't crow about their victories. Better yet, the quest for success hasn't turned them into drones. They have fun along the way, poking fun at themselves and each other.

Much of this pluck and puckishness comes from Charlie, who lives in Town & Country with his wife, Rose. He is a big, jolly man with a big, jolly laugh, usually directed at himself.

As he joined the grandkids for a photo, he blurted, "My wife said to make sure to shoot me from the side, because my face is too round to shoot me head on. All these years, and now she tells me my face is too round."

Then, staring straight at the camera, he smiled and said, "But I don't do everything she tells me to do!"

Charlie takes no bows for his grandkids' success, especially in school. He points to their mother, his older daughter Cindy, who is assistant su-

The captain, Charlie Share, huddles with grandkids Emily (left), Allie and Derek Jaskowiak.
(Photo by Trisha L. Siddens)

perintendent for high school education in the Parkway district. And the kids back him up on that.

"One time I got a C in handwriting," Emily said. "When my mom saw my report card, she yelled, 'I will *not* have an average child!'"

Charlie laughed that deep laugh of his and said, "I've heard that comment. Many times."

Charlie also defers credit for the sporting bloodlines of the Jaskowiak kids. He notes that Dennis, their father, was a six-foot-three, 260-pound lineman at Mizzou from 1970 to 1974. Dennis, president of Boxtech Packaging, was a force in the family basketball games, with a surprisingly deft shot for an ex-lineman. When fair play failed him, he toughened up his brood by throwing his patriarchal weight around.

One time Allie, a precocious tyke, was making an impressive show in a home basketball shootout when her dad cried foul.

"He said, 'You're not allowed to jump doing free throws,'" said Allie, still peeved. "I said, 'What?' It was at some ridiculous age where I couldn't get the ball to the basket unless I jumped."

In defense of dad, it should be noted that by Allie's junior year, she had broken only one of Emily's school records. And it was for free-throw shooting. At any rate, Allie got no sympathy from Grandpa Charlie on the issue of no-jump shots.

"When I play," he said, "everything leaves the ground but my feet. That's my jump shot."

That applies now and in his prime in the 1950s. The kids have only seen glimpses of their young grandpa in action. Film clips of those pioneer NBA games are rare, and shots of Charlie actually launching a shot are true collector's items. In 596 NBA games over nine years, he averaged eight points per game, as well as eight rebounds. In the '57-58 championship season, he averaged 8.6 points, along with a robust 10.4 rebounds. But his tenacity, temperament and teamwork made him the perfect captain on a team with future Hall of Fame marksmen Bob Pettit, Cliff Hagan and Ed Macauley.

"Pettit and Hagan had the ball all the time," Charlie boomed, "as well they should. I set picks and rebounded. On defense, I'd pick up everybody's man who came through the middle. And since you can't jump, you foul him. And then you sit out half the game in foul trouble."

The grandkids howled. It was the first they'd heard that self-critique. Grandpa, who spent his first pro year in a now-defunct league, drowned them out with that big laugh of his.

"I had a 10-year career," he said, "but I really only played two!"

Get the kids together with their Grandpa Charlie—their parents were at work—and the zingers start flying in every direction. When Grandpa insisted, with a straight face, "I never spoiled them," the girls rolled their eyes in tandem and let out a mocking "Ohhhh, noooo!" in stereo.

Grandpa tends to get mawkish when doting about the grandkids. As he carries on, they fidget noticeably. He calls Derek "the kind of young man I wish I could have been." Emily, he says, "is Number 44 in your program, Number One in your hearts." He introduces Allie as "soon to be president of the United States." Maybe so, but around the family she still answers to "Beetle Bomb."

"They called me that because I was the youngest," Allie said. "Grandpa thought of it."

"That was something that was said when I was a youngster in Iowa," Charlie said, "indicating you were the last one in line. When we played baseball, we'd throw the ball at the bat to see who would bat first. The one closest to the bat would lead off. Whoever was farthest from the bat was Beetle Bomb and went last."

It was Derek, the eldest, who entered high school looking like the runt of the litter.

"He was actually scared of me for about four years," Emily said. "Admit it, Derek! I was taller than he was and I weighed more than him. I'd do one of these"—she brandishes a backhand—"and he'd flinch."

Derek just shook his head and smiled. He is so massive now that the point is moot, even after complications from a recent appendectomy left him at a svelte 270 pounds.

"I was five-seven, 130, when I played center on the freshman football team," Derek said. "I was little, but I had played Little League football for about five years. So I was like the crafty veteran. I knew all the tricks, like cutting people's legs. I know a million more now."

Charlie said, "I always told him he'd be taller. I grew five inches in one summer."

Grandpa knew best. "I grew five or six inches in about half a year," Derek said.

His growth was jump-started by a temporary halt to his basketball career.

"My freshman year at West, I got cut from the basketball team," Derek said. "My mom said, 'If you don't make the team, you can be my personal trainer at the YMCA.'

"So she goes approximately nine times and quits going. I kept going and lifting weights, and that's what allowed me to be big and strong."

Emily can verify that firsthand after countless family pickup games.

"I'm at the Y the other day playing basketball," she said, "and this guy was there who just put his head down and pushes. No moves. I said, 'He's a football player, right?'

"They said, 'How'd you know?' And I said, 'He plays exactly like my brother plays. I hope I don't have to guard him.'"

The midshipman made no rebuttal.

"When I was a senior in high school, I scored 13 points," Derek said, pausing for effect. "That's 13 points the entire season."

Two of them won a game at the buzzer in the prestigious Meramec Holiday Tournament. Even those heroics are cause for abuse.

"Derek's kind of a horse, like me," said Grandpa Charlie. "He got a rebound and somebody knocked him on the floor just as he was shooting the ball. And it went in."

That brought the family rooting sections out of their scattered seats.

"Dad sits with Grandma Lydia, his mom, at the very top of the bleachers," Allie said. "Grandpa usually sits in the corner near our bench."

"With his clipboard," Emily said. "He keeps stats. On everybody, not just us."

"In his own chair," Allie continued. "Oh, yeah, we bring our chairs everywhere we go. Mom and Grandma Rose sit . . . not where he is! Usually somewhere lower in the bleachers or on the side."

"I was ostracized," said Charlie. "My wife was always afraid I'd say something critical about one of the other youngsters. But I never hollered out loud. Ever."

The girls roll their eyes again, but Grandpa is not the main culprit here.

"You could hear our mother over the crowd," Derek said.

"Her voice is high-pitched and carries well," said Emily. "And she knows nothing about basketball. She'd just yell, 'Get a board!'"

"She has an uninhibited personality," Charlie said.

And Grandpa has a little more to do with the grandkids' sporting success than he lets on.

"They may have gotten some of their interest from me," he said.

May have?

"Everything I know about basketball," said USC-bound Allie, "I learned from experience. And Grandpa."

The lessons began when Charlie sold his packaging company in 1985. He spent the next decade raising horses on five acres in Chesterfield. And helping to raise the competitive spirit in three young grandkids.

"When they were three or four, they'd come out and help clean the stables," Charlie said. "After that, we'd sit down and do math and play tic-tac-toe and learn how to make change for a dollar. When the weather got better, we'd go outside and have races and throw the football. We'd have our own Olympics. Then Dennis put up a basket, and we'd play games like H-O-R-S-E. I used to put them out with left-handed layups. Now they put me out with left-handed layups."

He stopped for a long moment.

"It was the best time of my life," he said.

And it won't end when Allie goes off to Los Angeles in the fall of 2003. Charlie's younger daughter, Suzanne, has two daughters of her own: Katie, 11, and Christine, six.

"Katie is a tennis enthusiast," he said. "And Christine enjoys gymnastics."

Grandpa Charlie is excited about plunging into new competitive worlds with two more grandkids.

As he put it, "I have yet to turn my first somersault."

PAUL JEFFRIES

Super DJ Has Dual Identity as Coach Muniz

Superman. Batman. Spiderman. All of those superheroes come equipped with a mild-mannered secret identity. And so does Paul Muniz, who is somewhat lacking in other superhero qualities. He's been a pudgy, middle-aged Collinsville homebody for most of his 51 years, as well as a happy husband and father of three grown sons.

"That pretty much describes me to a T," he said with a chuckle.

During the school week, Paul Muniz teaches driver's education at Oakville High. In the spring, he comes home after school to coach the sophomore baseball team at Collinsville High. On Saturday morning and Sunday evenings, Paul Muniz changes into Paul Jeffries, high-flying deejay on "Best Country" WIL (92.3 FM). His Saturday show is often first or second in its timeslot in local radio ratings for WIL, which is often second overall to perennial leader KMOX among listeners aged 25 to 54. Paul Jeffries is just as pudgy and just as middle-aged as Paul Muniz, and just as much of a Collinsville guy. He doesn't twang when he talks on the air.

"Oh, no, no, no, *no*," said Paul. "I'm no cowboy."

By either name, he was uneasy about going public after 22 years of discretion. When a reporter surprised his secret, Paul decided to open up only after deciding the publicity would be good for his station and his two schools. After all, this is not an ironclad secret. He doesn't deny the connection between the two Pauls. He just doesn't broadcast it, so to speak.

"I don't do this for notoriety of any sort," he said during a break in his 5 to 10 a.m. Saturday show. "I do it because I enjoy it. People know that I teach and that I coach. A lot of them don't know that I'm the guy on the radio. I really separate it.

"When I'm at school, I'm Mr. Muniz. When I'm at practice, I'm Coach Muniz. On the radio, I'm Paul Jeffries. I haven't even told my team this year about Paul Jeffries. I never want people to say, 'He's thinking more of coaching,' or 'He's thinking more of radio.'"

He is most passionate about the one role that others might find least exciting. "I'm a teacher first," he said. "Education first. No question. The kids on my teams know that they're here to get an education, keep their grades up and keep their noses clean."

He laughed off the image of himself as a caped crusader. The hero in the family, he said, is Mary Lee, his wife of 29 years. She teaches Latin at Collinsville High.

"She was named to the *USA Today* All-America Teaching Team," Paul said. "She was the only foreign language teacher to make either team. She was on the second team. She is something else." He grinned and said, in his mellifluous radio voice, "My advice is: Always marry a smart woman."

That's not the only smart thing he's done. He turned down a major celebrity job—the coveted afternoon drive-time slot on WIL—to stay in the game as a major-league dad. Paul takes no bows for that. Or for the unexpected rewards that followed. As he said off-microphone, right after plugging "The Dollar Bill Game" for his listeners, "Don't tell me the Good Lord isn't looking down and taking care of us."

Actually, Paul worked for every blessing he's counted. Paul Muniz, as he was still called, was a freshman at Bellevue Area College, as it was still called, when he saw a TV commercial for the Columbia School of Broadcasting. Enrollment was no problem. All it took was a check.

"It was one of these mail-order deals," Paul said. "They had a local office in Clayton to try to recruit people. They brought you in, sat you down and did a little audition. Then they said, 'Oh, yeah, you've got talent!'"

He stuck with the program after switching to Illinois State in Bloomington, where he became a utility man on campus and local stations. He read news, did college baseball play by play and spun records, classical as well as rock.

Paul Jeffries, on his weekend break from mild-mannered Paul Muniz.
(Photo by David Kennedy)

"Hey, I could read the covers of those classical albums as well as anyone," he said.

The campus station named him program director in his junior year.

"I was a physical education major," he said, "and I had people who majored in mass communications working for me."

He did phone interviews on the morning show with Illinois State basketball star Doug Collins, who went on to the NBA and also coached Michael Jordan in Washington. Doing Illinois State baseball play by play, he learned the inside game from Duffy Bass, the team's crafty old coach.

"What a great baseball man," Paul said. "He was a lot like Whitey Herzog."

Paul, not good enough to play organized baseball, settled for softball. And a good thing he did. As a college senior, he found the basepath to life in a friendly softball game.

"I'm playing first base," Paul said. "A guy got a hit and stopped at first. He said, 'I understand you're from Collinsville and you want to be a teacher.' I said yeah. He said, 'They're opening up a new school in the Mehlville District.' So I went and applied and got hired. That was 1973."

Paul arrived as the new driver's ed teacher and sophomore baseball coach at Mehlville, which had lost some staffers to the district's new Oakville High.

"School's started," Paul recalled, "and the athletic director came up and said, 'Hey, we have an opportunity to hire a former minor-leaguer. Would you mind stepping aside as sophomore coach?'"

Paul was eager to put Duffy's lessons into play, but the softball player reluctantly stepped aside. "That was obviously best for the kids," he said.

He eventually got a master's degree in instructional technology at SIU-Edwardsville and left driver's ed to run the audio-visual aid department for both Mehlville and Oakville. After seven years he decided to fill a driver's ed opening at Oakville.

"I missed being in class with the kids," said Paul. "Kids keep you young. Being with these kids keeps you thinking young. You hear people say today, 'What's wrong with teenagers?' There's nothing wrong with teenagers. The only thing they ask is to tell them what you expect, and what are the consequences if they don't do what you expect."

Teaching is not something he does to fill the time between coaching assignments or the radio.

"It's not fun and games," he snapped. "If I allow you to sleep in my class, something you miss might save your life down the road. Automobile accidents are the number-one killers of teenagers in this country. We lose a thousand 16-year-olds a year in this country.

"That's 10,000 every decade. We lose a person, not just a teenager, every 20 minutes on the road in this country. We just accept that. It's an epidemic."

As his teaching career solidified, only his coaching career was on hold. In need of summer work in 1975, he got back into radio, latching on to weekend duty at WIBV in Belleville. Tom Calhoun, now with KTRS, was program director then and a mentor for Paul. So was Joel Meyers, who eventually moved into the Cardinals' radio booth.

"He got into doing play-by-play on our high school sports," Paul said, "and then he made his jump. I remember that I asked him one night, 'Joel, do you think I've got what it takes to make it in the St. Louis market?' He said, 'Yeah, you'll do great!'"

So in 1980, Paul jumped to another local station, KADI (1380 AM) . . . and fell through a trap door.

"Gary 'Records' Brown was program director," Paul said, "and I was there three months when they changed owners. I was out. Man, oh, man,

I needed the extra income, and here I left a secure job at WIBV. So I started calling every station in town, about 18 or 19 at that time. Nobody needed any help."

Number last on his list was WIL.

"I had no desire to play country-western music back then," Paul said. "I was a rock'n' roll guy. But I called. Mike Carta was program director then, and he said, 'Yeah, we're looking for someone to do Sunday afternoons.' So I sent him a tape and he hired me."

Paul, remember, was no cowboy. He braced himself for his first day on the job at the WIL corral.

"I thought that I'd walk in here," Paul said, "and they'll have hay in the corner and everybody'll be in cowboy hats and boots. To my surprise, everybody's in three-piece suits. It's big business, very professional."

That was only the second biggest shocker. When payday arrived, you could have knocked Paul over with his check.

"We never talked money when Mike hired me," he said. "I got my first paycheck, and I went in and told Mike, 'Instead of paying me for one shift, they paid me for a whole week.' He just laughed. That's when I found out that everything at this place is first class."

The move to WIL brought one final twist: A secret identity.

"I had always used my real name until I came here," said Paul, who is proud of his Hispanic heritage. "But Mike thought Muniz might be hard to say for some people, that it wouldn't flow."

It was just a suggestion, but Paul liked the idea of separate names for separate jobs.

"My youngest son, Jeffrey, was just born," he said. "So I chose Paul Jeffries."

The Collinsville guy who had learned to spin classical music in college fell in love with country-western.

"It is truly America's music," Paul said. "And this is a great place to work. The people here are real, and so are the listeners."

Paul filled various weekend slots until 1987. Then WIL paid him "the ultimate compliment"—the 3 p.m. to 7 p.m. weekday shift. This was a headliner gig with headliner pay. There was no time for teaching and no need to stretch his salary by moonlighting on the weekend. Naturally, Paul took the offer.

"For about four hours," he said.

He called home with the news and then floated home for a hero's welcome. Instead, Mary Lee greeted him with the news that Joe, their eldest son, was really upset. His junior high basketball games were in the afternoon, and his dad would never see him play. After much soul-searching, Paul phoned his boss.

"I said, 'My family means everything to me. We'll only have the guys around for a short period of time, and then they're gone. I've decided to stick with my old job.'"

Paul smiled. "You know who they gave the job to then? Johnny Rabbit. He's a legend. I tell him, 'Johnny, you owe me.'"

Radio gigs are fickle. Even a legend like Johnny Rabbit moves on. Who knows how long Paul Jeffries could have ridden that drive-time bronco? Paul doesn't know or care.

"I never looked back," he said. "I never regretted it. And because I didn't take that job, I got into coaching baseball."

Collinsville head coach Steve McFall, a longtime buddy, hired Paul as freshman coach 11 years ago. He had to mold his competitiveness to the situation.

"My job is not to win at this level," Paul said. "My job is to get you to make that transition to the next level. Winning's a lot more fun than losing. But I tell my kids that if they need to make a doctor's appointment, make it on a game day, not a practice day. Practice is more important than the game. You'd be surprised how many kids never miss practice after that."

Paul was able to coach not only his sons Joe, Brian and Jeffrey, but also his nephews, Kevin and Kent Muniz. All but Jeffrey played college ball. Paul was able to follow all of their careers, even when Joe went away to star at Iowa. And Paul's decision to put family ahead of fame was not lost on Paul's sons. They have all followed his footsteps down one path or another. Joe is now a math teacher at Collinsville with his mom. He also helps coach baseball with his dad, as well as basketball. Brian teaches math at Oakville with his dad and also helps coach baseball and basketball there. Jeffrey, whose name inspired his dad's radio persona, inherited the broadcast fever and is a producer-reporter for the NBC-TV affiliate in Peoria.

Fifteen years later, Joe feels a little sheepish about torpedoing his dad's dream job.

"It meant a lot having my dad's support," Joe said. "It really felt good that he could still go to every event. And when I was in college, he would do his show on Saturday morning and then drive to Iowa City or Champaign, watch me play a doubleheader and then go right back.

"To us, the greatest asset about him is that he's been a very good example as far as family goes. He showed us how to raise a family, how important it is, what priorities are. Since I was born, he's worked two jobs six or seven days every week for us. He was a teacher for us in baseball, and a teacher for us in life.

"To us, he's just our dad. Being on the radio is no big deal, even though it seems like a big deal to some people who meet him. He likes the private life. He considers himself a normal human being who doesn't do anything special and does his work the best way he can."

Secret identity aside, that sounds like a textbook definition of a superhero. By any name, secret or otherwise.

JEFF CLINTON

A Full Life at Full Throttle

Jeff Clinton, a quiet competitor, went full throttle at everything he did. Family, friends, work, charity and auto racing—his passion—got the same intense attention. Nothing was short-changed. So his death on March 1, 2002, in a crash at Homestead-Miami Speedway in Florida immediately left a series of deep holes across the St. Louis landscape.

"He's more people's best friend than anybody I've ever known," said local developer Jim Koman, who has held Jeff in that regard for 20 years. "He was the best man at countless weddings. He was there for everybody. He was generous beyond all means.

"This was a guy who packed so much into life. He touched so many lives in the short period that he had. I lost a brother years ago, and he was like that to me in so many ways I can't express. I just can't tell you what a great guy he was. He was a competitor who took everything to heart. And everything was first class with him. That's how he felt about his family, Grey Eagle, Anheuser-Busch and everything he did."

The most visible void that Jeff left was in the leadership of Grey Eagle Distributors, the Anheuser-Busch wholesaler for St. Louis County. Jeffrey M. "Jeff" Clinton was president and chief operating officer. He had succeeded his father, Jerry G. Clinton, who was said to be passing along total control of the company to Jeff. The elder Clinton, a former race car driver, was en route to Florida after the crash. He and Jeff's Grey Eagle colleagues were too stunned to make any immediate public comment.

But August A. Busch III, chairman and president of Anheuser-Busch, stepped in with a statement on behalf of the Clinton and A-B families. It read:

"We are shocked and deeply saddened by the death of Jeff Clinton. We have lost a valued friend and an important member of the Anheuser-Busch wholesaler family. Jeff grew up in the beer business.

"He and his family have had a long association with Anheuser-Busch and have a unique relationship with the company, serving as one of our wholesalers in our headquarters city.

"Jeff and his father have both ensured that Grey Eagle Distributors exemplifies the Anheuser-Busch philosophy of uncompromising quality in everything that they do. That philosophy was also reflected in Jeff's life.

"Jeff was a skilled and experienced championship driver who loved racing. We will miss Jeff. Our thoughts are with his family and we extend our deepest sympathy to them."

Along with Jeff's father, he is survived by sons Mark, five, and Nathan, three; his mother, Jo, of Sanibel Island, Florida.; and his brother, Brian, 33, who owns Café Campagnard in West County.

Jeff was divorced but continued to team with his former wife, Ellie Williams, in raising their sons.

"Most of all, he was a great father to two of the greatest boys I've ever laid eyes on," said Koman. "It's amazing. The guy runs such a big corporation, runs to so many events, and still takes his kids to school every day. And countless times, he picked them up after school, too.

"He just moved from his condo in Clayton to a new place he bought in Ladue. He wanted a big yard and pool for the boys, because they loved to swim. That was the whole reason for buying the place."

Jeff was also concerned about other children. He was vice-chairman of the board for Marygrove, a treatment center in Florissant for abused children.

"He was a friend," said Marygrove administer Sister Helen Negri. "Aside from the fact that he was always a gentleman and respectful, he had an unusual quality. He wanted to do something to make a difference in the lives of our kids.

"He was on our board for 12 years, and one time after I spoke to the board, he called me and said, 'I just want to thank you for reminding us of what we have. And what we owe.' And he meant it."

Jeff Clinton—a competitor to the end and a friend forever.
(Photo courtesy of Grey Eagle Distributors)

Jeff also inherited an interest in amateur boxing from his father, a former local Golden Gloves champ who sponsored the St. Louis Golden Gloves Championships and the annual Guns 'n' Hoses charity bash between local police and firefighters.

"Jeff was real," said local boxing organizer Myrl Taylor, a lifelong friend of Jeff and his father. "Jerry grew up with us, and he never forgot where he came from. But Jeff has no background with us. He does it because he likes what we do. He's just so sincere.

"The other day I asked Jerry for some stuff for admissions prizes for one of our fights. I went over to Grey Eagle to pick it up, and Jeff was walking out. He said, 'Hey, let me help you with that.' He runs the company, and he's out there throwing boxes into my truck. That's what I mean about being real. Everybody's just stunned by this."

Jeff was practicing for the Rolex Sports Car Club race when his car left the course entering turn one. The car repeatedly flipped over and Jeff was dead at the scene. The Grand Am circuit is a lower-level series owned by International Speedway Corp, parent company of NASCAR. Jeff was in his second year on the circuit after several years in club and professional racing. He was a two-time Sports Car Club of America national champion in 1990 in the GT-5 Class and in 2000 in the Sports 2000 Class.

"Oh, that sport of his," murmured Sister Helen. "I would tell him, 'Oh, God, we pray for you that you stay safe.' And Jeff would smile and say, 'Thank you. I need it.' "

Conrad Franey, a St. Louis businessman, was Jeff's friend and fraternity brother. They spoke just before Jeff's final drive.

"I talked to him on the phone when he was putting on his racing suit," said Franey. "He told me the car was great and running good and the weather was perfect.

"He was surrounded by his friends, and doing what he loved to do. He did so much behind the scenes for people. He'd do anything for his friends.

"About 20 of us are here together at Jim Koman's office. We're all torn up. There's a lot of tears. But we're all hoisting a Budweiser to him."

WANDA TAYLOR

Angel in the Corner of Local Boxers

They were the oddest of couples, Myrl and Wanda Taylor. He was an ex-convict, boxer and labor leader, huge and rough and rude, with a soft spot for kids and dogs, especially strays of both species. She was thin and kind and soothing, with an even softer spot for strays, especially the ornery human she took in 51 years ago. They had three kids, two grandkids, three great-grandkids, plus who knows how many other kids that were treated like family.

Myrl spent 20 years as a junior football coach and has run amateur boxing in St. Louis for 30 years. Always barking and sometimes biting, he turned St. Louis amateur boxing into a national power, before youth gangs and adult infighting crippled the program.

Wanda was his silent partner. She kept to the background and handled the paperwork. Most of all, she loved up the hardscrabble kids that her husband brought home. She never made a penny or earned a headline from that unofficial career, which ended at their Fenton home. Wanda Barrett Taylor died peacefully after a painful siege from lung ailments. She was 68 years old and a competitor to the frail end.

"She was apologizing to me till she died because she ain't here to help me no more," Myrl said. "We're buddies. She's my best friend."

Wanda Taylor with hubby Myrl, her favorite stray.
(Photo courtesy of Taylor family)

William "Sarge" Anderson, a family friend since beating Myrl in a Golden Gloves match 50 years ago, said, "She was so cordial and sweet. Myrl has a heart of gold, you know, and she was a big part of his backbone."

Her own backbone stood nicely on its own.

"The last thing she did was type up our mailing list for all my boxing officials and coaches," Myrl said. "She was so sick, but she'd say, 'Let me get my breath and I'll go do it.'"

His own breath caught for a moment and he whispered, "That's a heartbreaker."

It will be for the kids and ex-kids whose lives were eased by her touch. Many lived in areas so tough that a boxing ring was actually a refuge from violence.

"It can be 20, 25 years later," Myrl said, "but when they come back to town, they call Wanda. When she was sick, Bill Guthrie called to check on her. Ray Lathon called every day to see how she was."

Guthrie was jailed on a drug rap, got out, got right and became world light-heavyweight champ. Lathon, a pro boxing contender, was later shot dead at a city gym.

"Ray's little boy called her every day," Myrl said. "She meant so much to so many people. They called her Saint Wanda because she put up with all my stuff. But she don't get credit for all that time—I was in the joint for some of it."

She was not proud of his past as an incorrigible youth and failed thug. It was Wanda who inspired him to straighten out, with boxing as the lever. So she never balked when he spent their puny savings on his early boxing teams.

"If I didn't spend it on them kids," he said, "*she* would."

But even saintly patience has limits.

"She kind of frowned when I mortgaged our house," Myrl said. "We had the Russians coming to fight us in 1976, and Kiel Auditorium wanted five grand in case of any liability. So I guaranteed the house. She said she didn't mind giving everything away when we didn't have anything. But she thought our kids ought to have a roof over their heads at least."

The roof stayed overhead. The show netted $10,000. And every penny, as always, went back into the boxing program.

"She was talking to me the last time," Myrl said, "and I started feeling bad. She looked at me and said, 'Hey. We did good.'"

It was the only time Wanda Taylor ever took credit for anything. And it was long overdue.

KRISTIN FOLKL

Final Four Queen Hits the Real World

The year 2001 brought a string of firsts of a different kind for Kristin Folkl. She moved into her first apartment, took her first overseas trip and started her first job. Actually, the South County resident had done all of the above, but always in a sports context. Until now, her housing had always been provided by her team of the moment. Kristin had trekked to Europe, Asia and Australia to play volleyball or basketball, not sightsee. And her steady paycheck comes each summer when she hoops it up in the WNBA, lately for the Portland Fire.

That resume is a wild daydream for most young athletes. As she neared age 26 in 2001, Kristin found adventure in routine rites of passage that came earlier to her peers. Such as finding her own South County apartment and buying her first sofa and bed. And bumming solo through Central Europe to research her family tree. And, for the past three weeks, commuting to a nine to five job downtown at Ralston Purina.

"I'm a member of the Purina One brand management team," said Kristin, proud to be a marketing intern in pet food. "It's the first paid job I've ever had that was not sports-related. I could never work during school or in the summer because I was always playing sports."

She has that Jackie Joyner-Kersee knack of saying the right thing without sounding trite, phony or boastful. She easily handles the trick question that everyone tosses at her: What's tougher, playing sports or working in an office?

"One isn't harder than the other," said Kristin. "They do take different disciplines. Obviously, sports are physically harder. But I don't think getting up early and driving during rush hour and sitting there at work for nine hours and having to concentrate all day is easy.

"With basketball, I could still read a book at night. When I come home now, I don't have the energy to concentrate on reading, and I have to force myself to go work out. So it's been a shock. But I've really had fun. I'm learning stuff and the people are really nice."

The sports world and workaday world have their own challenges. At Ralston, there was the case of the runaway printer.

"I hit the wrong button," Kristin said, "and it started printing out this 100-page report that I didn't need. I had to yell for help."

Which brings up the downside of her civilian job. Namely, everybody knows her name.

"I was hoping no one would know who I was or where I came from or what my qualifications are," Kristin said. "Then if I do well, it's icing on the cake because I did it myself. And if I mess up, then nobody knows about it."

Incognito is not an option in this town. Recognition is the price she pays for not messing up in sports. In four years in the early '90s at St. Joseph Academy, Kristin helped win four state titles in volleyball, four more in basketball and was named national Female Athlete of the Year. In four years in the late '90s at Stanford University, she played in four volleyball Final Fours—winning three national titles—and two basketball Final Fours. No wonder fans here still see her frozen in her schoolgirl glory from the past decade.

The 2001 season was her fourth with the WNBA, although she sat out the first year while rehabbing a knee injury from college. Her championship magic ended in the pros. She has yet to make the playoffs with expansion teams in Minnesota and Portland. But Kristin was a frontcourt force in her first year with the Fire (11-21). She averaged 7.7 rebounds per game, seventh in the league. She also averaged 5.6 points, shooting 43 percent from the field and 83 percent from the foul line. Just six foot two and 195 pounds, she swung comfortably between center and power forward.

"I don't feel I'm overmatched against the bigger players," she said. "People my size are a dying breed, but I haven't died yet."

Except from embarrassment in the season finale. The culprit was another first: The only technical foul of her athletic life.

"The thing that absolutely killed me," said Kristin, "was that it came near the end of the last game, and it was one of our two nationally tele-vised games on ESPN. So everyone that I knew said they watched it."

She got entangled with 5'11", 205-pound Latasha Byear of Los An-geles.

"She's very nice off the court," said Kristin, "but she's one of these cagey veterans who knows how to get away with stuff. She was falling into me and I put my hands up to try to catch her. The next thing I feel is someone with a death grip on my jersey. It was her, taking me down with her. So instead of catching her, I pushed her away."

The referee, naturally, caught only this Folkl-point. It was also the part of the sequence that ESPN replayed. Again and again.

"Then the camera pans back to me," Kristin said, "and I'm laugh-ing. I mean, it was so ridiculous. I average two fouls per game and I get slapped with a T. But on ESPN, it looks like I decide to push her down and I think it's funny. My mom wanted to know how I could turn into such a ruffian."

Happily, Kristin has had no such episodes in her new job at Ralston.

"No," she said, "I haven't thrown anyone on the floor…yet."

GARY DUNAHUE

Baseball Coach for Life

Life isn't fair.

The Lafayette High baseball team thought it had grasped that concept last year. The Lancers were 20-2 but then lost by a run in the district finals. They were mostly juniors then. They are mostly seniors now, older and savvier and raring to make a run. Especially since Gary Dunahue, their beloved freshman coach, was promoted to rookie head coach at age 47.

The Lancers are attacking this season with a solemn urgency. And not just because their high school lives will soon be over. This may be the end of the line, period, for their beloved coach.

As senior Eric Klumb said grimly, "Everybody knows we're on a mission to win state because he's sick."

Their coach has cancer of the pancreas.

Unfair? The timing was cruel. Gary was promoted to head coach last May and diagnosed in October. The cancer is a nasty strain that quickly spread to areas including his liver.

Unfair? This is the meanest of deals. Gary needs potent chemotherapy, which causes blood clots in his legs, which cause cramping so painful that sleep and normal activity are impossible. Cut back on the chemo, and Gary's body is up and running, but so is the cancer. Knowing Gary, his players and friends were not shocked when he decided to dial back the dosage after several months in the hospital. When practice began on March 3, the Lancers were greeted by their little Buddha of a coach. He was bubbling as always with knowledge and his knack for sharing it.

"I don't feel sorry for myself," said Gary, who is also back teaching driver's education. "You know what? I've had a great life for 47 years. I come from a very religious background. That's helped me cope with this."

Gary, a bachelor, is living at home with his mother in Overland. "She's my nurse," he said. "She's been a real trooper through all of this."

So has Gary, a Don Zimmer look-alike.

"I do understand what's going on," he said. "My boys understand. We're going to learn something about life. And we're going to be better for it."

His boys try hard to believe that. It's not an easy concept to accept, absorbed as they are in a youthful quest for meaning in every mystery. To them, death is still a spectre. And every practice is a reunion of sorts. The team's emotions are understated but unavoidable. Things couldn't be better, and things couldn't be worse.

"When I heard about it, I was just devastated," said Chris Short, a senior pitcher. "He was the freshman coach when I came to high school, and he took care of me. But having him back, it's been everything for the whole team. He's kept his spirits up, so we have to."

"He's awesome," said Klumb, a slugging outfielder. "I don't ever think I've seen him without a smile on his face. He loves baseball and he loves everything about the team. In the summertime, I'd come up to school just to talk about baseball, just about the team and the season."

"I just know he cares about us a lot," said shortstop Dane Miller, another top player and senior leader. "That drives us, and we know we have to drive him. If we get things done on the field, that'll keep his engine pumping."

Miller, son of Lafayette athletic director Steve Miller, is on target. But the boys have a different definition of "getting things done" than their coach does. Gary cringes at their win-one-for-the-Gipper mission. This is their season, not his. He wants them to play for themselves, not him. For one thing, they don't need extra pressure weighing them down when they need a good throw or a good swing. For another, the coach is deathly allergic to any extra attention. That's why Gary fought the idea of a Walk for Cancer on his behalf at Lafayette.

"I didn't want people to think I'm trying to get their money," he said.

Steve Miller, Gary's boss and close friend, pulled rank on that one and okayed the event. It was a rousing morale boost for both the patient and his droves of supporters. They include dozens of his fellow basketball officials. Gary had officiated for years along with his brother Bob—the baseball coach at Francis Howell North—and kid brother Steve. Gary quit a couple years ago to focus on baseball, his lifelong passion. He was a star catcher at Ritenour High and briefly at Southwest Missouri State before leaving.

"Academics weren't my forte," he said wryly.

Gary umpired professionally from 1981-88, rising to the Class AA Southern League and working three All-Star Games and six championship series. He kept a notebook on managers he observed. And once, in a spring-training dugout, he got a 45-minute discourse—plus an autographed baseball—from Ted Williams.

"When I was umpiring, my goal was to get down to Busch Stadium," Gary said. "But I think goals have to be adaptable."

When his umpiring career stalled, he came home and switched to coaching. He helped Neil Fiala run summer teams here, grooming the likes of T.J. Mathews and Bill Mueller for big-league careers. Gary also managed the Wichita Broncos in the elite Jayhawk League, a summer loop in Kansas for collegians. He then became pitching coach for the power program at Missouri-St. Louis, but only after head coach Jim Brady promised to help him enroll as a student. After five years, at age 37, he got his degree from UMSL in 1994.

"I was in the 20-year program," said Gary, who was class of ca'74 at Ritenour High.

Diploma in hand, Gary moved on to Lafayette and his dream of coaching in high school.

"We grow baseball players out here," Gary said. "I feel very honored and privileged to follow in the footsteps of Rusty Ryan and Bob Swift. Swiftie was taking teams to the state tourney, and then when he left, Rusty came in and was averaging almost 20 wins a year."

Gary considers himself a teacher in a diamond-shaped classroom. His pupils are in awe of him.

Gary Dunahue is the Don Zimmer of Lafayette High.
(Photo by Don Adams Jr.)

As Klumb said, "It's ridiculous how much baseball he knows."

As some observers have said, it's ridiculous how much he expects his players to know. Complex pickoff plays. Bunt coverages. Signals. A season with Gary is an honors course in baseball.

"They love it," he said. "When they have options and they understand them, it's like a whole new world has opened up. That's when you as an educator feel really good. And it's the same on the baseball field. One thing I won't do is put limitations on these kids. We don't know their limitations. We don't know how good they can be."

On a damp day last week, he spent the whole 90-minute practice in the gym, teaching his defensive package with runners on first and third.

As a teacher, Gary is firm but funny. "Bet you lost five pounds there," he booms when a catcher's throw almost beans the runner at third.

When a pitcher stumbles while trying to execute a rundown, Gary says, "Just throw the ball to the fielder. Let him worry about it."

And when the runner at first steals second while the runner at third stays put, Gary says, "No problem. We'll just get the batter. If they had any faith in him, they wouldn't have tried to steal the run."

Later, Gary declared the drill a success, even though errant throws ricocheted around the gym like pinballs.

"A lot of coaches don't want their kids to make mistakes," he said. "I don't mind," he said, pausing to smile. "I'd just rather have them make mistakes in practice!"

Later, Gary had his fielders cool down by playing long toss. A bystander noticed two outfielders throwing curveballs and ratted them out to the coach.

"So what?" Gary said. "They're having fun. They need time to have fun out here, too."

His bedside manner helps explain a remarkable team statistic.

"I've got a very good group of 14 seniors," Gary said, "with a group of juniors right behind them. Some of the seniors I told: 'You will not see much playing time. There will be no token at-bats.'"

Nobody quit. That's how much the players love the game, their coach and his practices.

"We've got a 25-man roster," Gary said, "but that won't be a problem. I've set expectations with the boys, and they know where they stand now. They're just good kids. They're not the type of kids who sit on the bench and root against the kid ahead of them."

What they all root against is his cancer, which is a heavy favorite.

"They say there's a 17 to 20 percent chance of recovery," Gary said.

About the same odds of his first-and-third defense getting an out?

"Oh, no," Gary said with a grin. "The odds are a little bit better with my group."

He has been blunt with the team. They know that with the reduced chemo, he injects himself daily in the stomach. So far, he has missed only a couple practices. But he never misses a chance to make a point, even with his disease.

When one player moped after a bum round in the batting cage, Gary gathered the team, pulled up his T-shirt, exposed the two Band-Aids on his round tummy and snapped, "You think *you're* having a bad day?"

Needless to say, he has the team's full attention. And support.

"He's probably the nicest guy I've ever known," said young Miller. "It's easy to learn from him. There's something about him, just a glowing personality. And it's something that spreads, like an energy that just spreads."

It's the energy of life from someone staring down death. Not that the coach would mind a slightly extended warranty.

"So many people have done so much for me," Gary said. "You wish you could go around and shake everybody's hand and hug 'em and thank"em.

"I don't think the good Lord is done with me yet. I hope he lets me finish this baseball season. I think I still have a purpose in life. I hope what I'm doing is helping these young men. Hey, I'm too busy looking ahead to be looking over my shoulder."

NICKY SARACINO & CO.

Nine-Year-Olds Take Canada with Mr. MacInnis

Al MacInnis has starred in the National Hockey League more than twice as long as Nicky Saracino and Joey Horak have been alive. Yet the nine-year-olds from South County helped the All-Star Blues defenseman to one of the highlights of his hockey life. Al spent part of the 2001 off season as head coach of the St. Louis All-Stars, whose 16 players included Joey, Nicky and his own son, Carson. The summer highlight came when the team went undefeated to win the prestigious Paramount Canada's Wonderland International Tournament in Toronto.

Nicky is a defenseman from Affton. Joey, a right winger from Sappington, scored a key goal in the shootout of the finals. Both boys play their regular-season hockey for the Affton Squirt team. Al was assisted by Chris Saracino, Nicky's dad, and Scott Welch of Chesterfield, home to most of the team's 16 players.

"Chris and Joey are really good little players," said Al, "but all of the kids were unbelievable. We went 7-0 up there, and we never had a lead going into the third period."

The feeling was mutual.

"Mr. MacInnis is really nice," said Nicky, although that sentiment is not shared by NHL goalies facing Al's 100 mile-an-hour slapshot.

Al MacInnis (back row, middle), with assistants Chris Saracino (left) and Scott Welch and their tiny champions. (Left to right) Front row: Brandon Fischer, Spencer Viele. Second row: Alex Mundt, Sam Warning, Joe Horak, Kevin Walters, Andy Thurby, Eric Combs, Carson MacInnis. Third row: Nicky Saracino, Corey Briggs, Thomas Wells, Adam Welch, Tucker Long, Brett Bauza, David Goodwin. (Photo courtesy of Chris Saracino)

The tourney drew over 300 teams in different age groups. Al's team was invited after placing third in a previous tourney this summer in Toronto. St. Louis competed in a division for players born in 1992. Other entrants came from hockey hotbeds such as Toronto, Montreal, Ottawa and Boston.

Chris Saracino, who owns Chris's Pancake and Dining near The Hill, said, "Some of these teams had really long winning streaks . . . until we played them. The first team we beat, from Toronto, had won like 60 games in a row."

He ran the defense and Welch switched the forward lines for MacInnis. Late in tight games, Al got more involved in the matchups and changes.

"He had a lot of nervous energy," Chris said. "He's used to being on the ice and having some control of the situation. He said that was tough to get used to behind the bench."

And were the youngsters just as jumpy?

"I wasn't nervous at all," Nicky said. "Except for the shootout."

That fingernail-biter decided the championship game. But St. Louis almost didn't squeeze out of the semifinals, having to overtake Ottawa in the third period before sprinting to a three-goal win. Then in the finals, the Montreal Ice Storm took an early 2-0 lead before St. Louis hustled to tie at the first intermission. Montreal scored again in the second period and again St. Louis rallied to tie. The third period and overtime were scoreless. That brought on the shootout. Each team designated five shooters, with the victory going to the team with the most goals after all the players had taken one breakaway shot apiece.

"We had to write the names down for the shootout," Chris said, "but none of us had a pen. These kids were waiting by the boards to get Al to sign stuff for them after the game, so I bribed one of them. I said, 'If you give me your pen, I'll get you an autograph.'"

Montreal scored three times in the shootout. St. Louis scored four goals, including one by Joey and the clincher by Sam Warning of Chesterfield.

"The kids celebrated pretty classy," Chris said. "They didn't throw their sticks and act crazy."

In fact, the lads took the whole experience in stride, including having a future Hall of Famer as head coach.

"Other kids on other teams asked Al for autographs, but our kids never did," Chris said. "You know why? He was just like another dad to them."

This was definitely not just another tourney for Al, who won the NHL's Stanley Cup championship with Calgary.

"You'd have thought Al won another Stanley Cup, he was so excited," Chris said. "He was just so happy for the kids."

At age 38, is coaching in Al's future?

"No . . . no . . . *no!*" Al boomed. "No way. I couldn't handle it."

SAM HILL

The Punching Policeman

The fight mob expected a reverse case of police brutality. Instead, it got this headline: "What in the Sam Hill happened to David Reid?"

Reid, of Philadelphia, is a former Olympic and World Boxing Association middleweight champ who was ranked No. 2 by the WBA. What happened to him in November of 2001 was a ninth-round technical knockout by Sam Hill. Reid's only prior loss came nearly two years earlier in a title bout with Felix Trinidad. And Sam Hill? He is a policeman in the city's 7th District, working the North Patrol Division.

"That's what makes the story so dramatic," said Cory Spinks, a top welterweight contender and stablemate of Hill's at the Marquette Rec Center in the south city. "He's a full-time police officer, but he still has time to train and get up early in the morning and run."

Sam is not insulted by those who dismiss him, as Reid apparently did, as a part-time fighter. That's what he is, after all.

"When I'm on the three to 11 shift, I can't be here to spar," said Hill during a workout at the Marquette gym. "So I just run on my own. When I get off, I go to the Police Academy and work out on the bag."

Besides, the fight mob will soon be calling him something else: Top 10 contender. That's where he should vault in the next WBA rankings after disposing of Reid, who was on a wobbly, three-fight winning streak after his beating by Trinidad.

Sam, 31, started boxing out of boredom a decade ago when the army sent him to Fort Riley, Kansas. Appropriately, he fought Reid on November 11—Veterans Day. Reid, 28, came in at 17-1. Sam had won just 13 of 16 prior bouts, including a tie and two losses to fighters so bland he can't remember their names. But Sam took charge early. He won the second round decisively and scored a knockdown in the fifth. Reid was then reduced to holding and hitting low. After that, the referee repeatedly warned Reid for holding and low blows, finally stopping the fight after Sam scored a second knockdown 39 seconds into the ninth round. That bout was broadcast on Fox Sports Net from an Indiana casino. Now HBO is talking to "The Punching Policeman" about a multi-fight cable deal.

It's been quite a ride for the 160-pounder, who weighed 30 pounds more when he first laced on gloves in 1991. Sam hit the swing of things quickly as an amateur. Within six years, he had won All-Army and St. Louis Golden Gloves titles and turned pro. He came to St. Louis with his wife, Nina, a registered nurse. They met when she was a servicewoman stationed at Fort Riley and now have three children under age six.

"They actually help me," said Sam of his energetic young brood. "You have a hard day at work, and you go home and your kids help you forget all about that stuff."

What he really needs each day is a set workout time. Plus the rest of the day off to recuperate. He's not complaining, just explaining.

"My two losses were two years ago," said Sam, who sounds and looks like a junior executive. "I was on the evening shift both times when they called me on short notice for the fights. And I took them even though I wasn't in the best of shape.

"The last time, I only got to spar four rounds for an eight-round fight and I ran out of gas. So we stopped taking fights when I wasn't able to train."

That's a no-win position for most no-names. If the phone rings and you don't answer the bell, the calls go elsewhere. But Sam has an edge in getting fights. His manager-trainer is Kevin Cunningham, who has growing clout as a local promoter as well as Spinks's handler. Sam and Kevin are a tight team.

"We have basically the same background," Sam said. "He was in the service. He boxed. He was a city policeman. And now he's into professional boxing."

Sam Hill is pounding a different beat.
(Photo by David Kennedy)

Sam grinned and said, "He's the smart one. He's managing, not fighting. But boxing is kind of addictive. I went down to the gym with a buddy at Fort Riley, and once I started I couldn't stop."

Sam has no plan to quit police work. His badge always comes first.

"Our schedules at work are done a year in advance," said the seven-year patrolman, "so that helps me plan my training. I get three weeks of vacation and four designated holidays. That gives me 19 days to play with for out-of-town fights."

The St. Louis Police Department has been firmly in his corner, from Chief Joe Mokwa down to his fellow 7th District coppers.

"At the station," Sam said, "they had the Reid fight on the TV and said everyone was jumping and screaming. Some of the guys call me Champ. I know I'm not the champ, but it makes me feel good."

So far, fitness and pride are his main rewards. He earned a personal-best $10,000 against Reid, but expenses and taxes drained more than half that purse.

"To me, it's great secondary work," said Sam, whose colleagues usually do security moonlighting. "With my job, I have to stay in shape anyway.

"When I'm on the street, if anybody runs I can chase him and not worry if I can catch him. And I know I can defend myself without right away using my gun."

He said his district is bounded roughly by Kingshighway, Lindell, Skinker and Natural Bridge roads. That covers some of the nicest and nastiest turf in town.

"The guys in my area know I box," Sam said, meaning guys "who are in the business…you know, gangs, drugs. But I just do my job. They know I'm not going to mistreat them.

"The boxing, they respect me for it. It helps me out a lot. I found that if you show them respect, they'll show you respect."

Ditto for his young proteges at the Marquette Rec Center. Gym time to Sam is too precious to be wasted. The youngsters take notice, from a top pro like Spinks, 23, to top teen amateurs like Devon Alexander.

"I watched the Reid fight at my cousin's house," said Spinks. "I was yelling with Sam every step of the way. I'm so happy for him. He deserved it. He worked very hard. He stuck with it no matter what the adversity."

Sam sends that message with every drill and without saying a word.

"Try hard, that's what he shows us," said Alexander, 14. "Do your best at everything you do."

And that ends the mystery of what the Sam Hill is going on.

JODIE BAILEY

Teacher First, Then a Coaching Legend

Jodie Bailey is synonymous with local basketball. He coached for 40 years in the Public High League. He won state titles at Vashon and O'Fallon (now Gateway) Tech before finishing at old Northwest High. He co-founded a longtime summer league that bore his name.

So why is he the perfect honorary chairman for a golf tournament? Because it is the William L. Clay Scholarship and Research Foundation, which has helped send over 30 local youngsters to college. And Jodie, above all else, is an educator. Aside from teaching, he worked for years at YMCA Camp River Cliff. And even now, in his eighth decade, he teaches Sunday School at Union Memorial United Methodist Church near his home in St. Louis.

He was happy to lend his presence to the former congressman's golf tournament. It is run by Clay's son and successor in office, William "Lacey" Clay, who first met the old coach at the YMCA camp.

"Ninety percent of my athletes succeeded," said Jodie, not referring to basketball. "I maintain close contacts with them down through the years, down through college and the rest of their lives.

"I always told the boys and girls I coached that if you ever need me, I'll come running. Well, I can't run any more, but I always try to follow through on what I said."

He has a balky knee and problems with one eye. Those speed bumps have not slowed his energy, memory or conversational ability, though. It's not vanity that keeps him from telling his age for the record. He readily confirms that he graduated from Vashon in 1934.

"You can do the math if you want to," he says.

Of course, that calculation will be wrong. He was a precocious student who got his diploma well before he was 18. Why so fussy about his age? He bounces that question right back at the curious.

"I really don't see what age has got to do with it," Jodie said. "Some students make it miserable for a teacher if they find out he's old."

Not his old students. They adore and respect him. Take his connection to the tourney—Darryl Pigge, now a lawyer in Lacy Clay's office.

Pigge had no guess as to his mentor's age and had no plans to find out. With a laugh, Pigge said, "There's no way I would ask coach that question."

The golf tourney sought to raise $50,000. However, the students who will benefit from the proceeds would probably benefit as much, if not more, from a long chat with the honorary chairman. Some of his proteges did play sports for a living. Notably, the late Elston Howard, a longtime catcher for the New York Yankees, and JoJo White, a Boston Celtics guard who remains close to his old coach. Many others who played for Jodie—at Vashon from 1944-63, at O'Fallon Tech from 1963-68, at old Northwest High from 1968-84—took his advice to put education first.

"He's one of the reasons I went to Dartmouth," said Pigge, who starred at Northwest in the '70s. "I had hurt my leg, and my dad came in with the letter that I'd been accepted at Dartmouth. I could have gone other places to play basketball, but Coach said, 'You know, you could get hurt again. Maybe you should think about the Ivy League.'

"He's made a big difference in all our lives…at least the ones who paid attention. With coach, you had to write down your strengths and weaknesses, and then he'd give it back to you. He'd say, 'Son, you have a miscalculation here.' Then he'd give you the truth."

The truth about Jodie Bailey is this: He had every reason to be bitter at life. He was orphaned early. Racial segregation was the rule for his first 35 years, including his first coaching decade at Vashon.

Yet he says, "I've been in the sunshine all my life, even though my mother died when I was eight and my father died when I was 10. But what happened to me happened through the extended family watching over me."

Beyond his two brothers and sisters, that "family" extended to the people in the Iowa neighborhood of his youth and the local YMCA, where he gravitated.

Jodie clung to one steady guidepost all his life: "There is no substitute for education."

His resume reflects that creed. A degree in social studies from Lincoln University in 1938. A master's degree in physical education from Springfield (Massachussetts) College in 1942. Studies overseas at Oxford in England and the Sorbonne in France. His basketball education got a boost at Springfield from glimpses of the sport's founder, Dr. James Naismith.

"I never met him," Jodie said. "He was quite up there in years, but he would come up to the college."

Naismith created basketball to keep kids busy and fit in the winter. Jodie—with the help of St. Louis recreation official Harold Bailey, no relation—created his basketball league to keep kids busy and fit in the summer.

"There was a need for our black boys and girls to be doing this and not running the streets," said the coach.

Pigge, at Dartmouth when the league began, came back to referee. In keeping with the coach's educational bent, each morning began with an activities camp for grade school boys and girls. Then came a similar camp for high school girls at noon. Basketball for the older boys started at 3 p.m.

"College coaches from all over the country were trying to recruit these boys," Bailey said.

The black coach raised in segregation soon was drawing youngsters of all colors and zip codes to his league.

"In its day," Pigge said, "it was *the* center for competition here."

"We had 'em from everywhere," Bailey said. "That was the strength of the league. Then Harold would go to these places all over Missouri and Illinois and Indiana and Arkansas, and he'd run into guys—white guys, too—who would say, 'Is your name Mr. Bailey? Hey, I played in the Jodie Bailey League, and it was great.'"

The league dissolved a couple of years ago after the death of Harold Bailey, its day-to-day director. The league's namesake remains active for a man of whatever his age actually is.

"Coach is such a treasure," Pigge said. "He does represent a lot to the community. Hopefully people who meet him at the golf tournament or who read about him will be inspired."

The golf tourney, after all, fits nicely with Jodie Bailey's lifelong message:

"There's more to life than basketball."

JAN & KEVIN WIGGS

Her Kidney Keeps Him Whistling

After 22 years of marriage, Jan Wiggs was concerned. Her husband, Kevin, was planning to run around on her. So one night in November of 2001, she left their Bellevue home and followed him to Alton. She was determined to protect her interest. Namely, her kidney. Specifically, her right kidney, which she had donated to her husband the previous May 31. Jan trailed her husband to Alton because, for the first time since the transplant, he would be back running around on a basketball court. Kevin Wiggs is one of the top high school referees in Illinois.

"I just wanted to keep an eye on him…and it," said Jan. "That's why I figure I have a voice in all this."

As in the voice of reason.

"That's right," Jan said. "I kind of made him promise to cut back on his schedule."

Kevin, his eyes misting, has another term for his mate: "She's my hero."

Jan's response: "I don't think I'm comfortable with that."

Kevin's rebuttal: "Well, you'll just have to live with it."

And he'll just have to live with a kidney whose former owner has not quite let go. For his own good.

"When we got close to the season," Kevin said, "I told Jan I was starting off with a game on Monday, a game on Tuesday, a game on Wednesday, a game on Friday and two on Saturday.

"She didn't like that. She said, 'My kidney will be going,'"What the hell was that? What did I just go through?'"'"

The voice of reason nudged him to accept barely half his usual workload. He will work 40 prep games in his season back, compared to his usual 60 to 75 junior college, high school and junior high games. His—their—kidney breezed through that first test in Alton and every one since.

Actually, Kevin's best match for a transplant was their daughter Nicole, 19 and a sophomore at the University of Illinois in Champaign. Kevin and Jan thought she was too young. Ryan, their son, is 13 and was not tested. After Nicole, the best match was Kevin's father, but he was a little too grizzled at age 64. Blood relatives usually make the best donors, but Kevin's two brothers were not as good a fit as Jan. That closeness between this husband and wife shocked nobody who knows them. Unless the surgery had also joined them at the hip, not even a shared kidney could improve this couple's tensile strength.

"We've known each other since second grade," Kevin said. "This may be the most incredible part of this story. I've known her for 36 of my 43 years. I never had a date with anyone else. I'm serious. Hey, this is too good to make up."

So was their first encounter.

"I asked her to clean out my desk in class," Kevin said.

"Actually, I volunteered," Jan said. "I was trying to get his attention. I was seven years old. And I'm still cleaning up after him. You should see his desk at home."

They went through Abraham Lincoln Grade School together. They attended West Junior High together and had their first official date. They went to high school together at Belleville West and to college together at Eastern Illinois, where they were headed for a split as seniors. Kevin still had a semester left when Jan graduated in December. So they decided to marry in January, both of them just 21. By then, she knew that he had been openly flirting for three years with his other love, officiating.

Kevin and Jan Wiggs, sharing a grin and a kidney.
(Photo by Erik M. Lunsford)

This season back is Kevin's 25th in a striped shirt. That anniversary seemed dimly out of reach the year before, even as he whistled his way to his first Illinois State Tournament assignment. Kevin was on top of his game despite being under the weather. He had known since January of 2000 that his kidneys were failing. The tipoff had been swollen fingers, which he assumed were due to a heart or circulation problem. Instead, both kidneys were shutting down.

"They said it first started in 1982, when I had strep throat and it wasn't treated properly," Kevin said. "And they said I should start thinking about a transplant in a year or 18 months. Meantime, last basketball season I didn't miss a beat. But afterward, I can't tell you how many people said, 'We were really worried about you.'

"I guess my color was bad. But the first time anyone said anything directly to me was last January. I was working a tournament in Nashville,

Illinois, and a guy came up to me and said, 'I don't want to pry, but you don't look very good.' So I laid the whole story out for him. And then I guess the word got around."

Until then, Kevin had only confided in Tom Jackson of Belleville, his longtime officiating sidekick. Kevin, always the competitor, wanted to make sure he earned his trip to the state tourney.

"I'll never know that for sure," he said, "but the last thing I wanted was to go because someone felt sorry for me. But I think I had a very good year. I had some people tell me afterward that they didn't notice anything wrong from the way I was officiating."

As it turned out, there was plenty wrong.

"I worked a state semifinal on March 17th, which was a Saturday," Kevin said. "I went back to my doctor on Tuesday, and he said he was surprised that I didn't come in an ambulance. He gave me the impression that my life was in danger at that moment. He said, 'We have to get you ready for dialysis.'"

For two months, three days a week, four and a half hours a day, he was on the dialysis machine. He hated it.

"They have a portable television for you to watch," Kevin said, "but you can only watch *Hollywood Squares* so many times. And I'm sorry, Oprah doesn't do much for me."

Even though he is a made-for-Oprah story.

"If there's anything I hope people get out of this," Kevin said, "it's that they shouldn't be afraid of having a transplant. Some people at the clinic had been on dialysis for three, four, five, six years. Not all of them were trying to find a donor. One lady had been on it for 27 years.

"My choice was have this transplant done, or be on dialysis forever at age 42. I didn't look at it as a choice. It was something I had to do to have a life. And my wife wanted me to have a life."

A series of health hurdles popped up before the surgery. Each was an emotional obstacle. Even now, Kevin's eyes get watery as he relates them. One, a rise in Jan's blood pressure, threatened to scuttle the mission a week before liftoff.

"I'm feeling fine now," said Jan, who has just one complaint. "I found out a kidney doesn't weigh much, so giving it up wasn't like a quick weight-loss program. But we had to walk a lot after the operation, and the exercise kept me in better shape."

Kevin did not try to talk his wife out of donating.

"No. Not at all. Never," he said. "All the doctors told us there is very little risk to the donor, although the operation itself is harder on the donor. They had to cut a rib out of her to remove the kidney. But she's back to 100 percent now."

He smiled and said, "And I've built my life around taking pills, not that I object to it."

The kidney from Jan is pulling its weight. At first, the weight differential in the patients caused a complication.

"My wife's maybe five feet tall and significantly lighter than me," said Kevin, who is 5'9" and 195 pounds. "Her kidney wasn't prepared to handle a body of my size. Normally a kidney will start making urine in five minutes after a transplant. Mine took 30. Even today it's not functioning in the optimal level. You can exist with a 20 percent kidney function. Mine's 50, which is fine. It was eight percent before I went to dialysis."

Also less than optimal is their financial status. Kevin, an accountant, lost his job as an office manager because of his illness. Friends urged him to take legal action against his old company. He refused, a decision his wife supports.

"This is a new lease on life, for both of us," Kevin said. "I don't want to spend it on something like a lawsuit."

He is not yet back to full speed. When he is, he must always make time for a couple of checkups per month. Until he can land a full-time job, he has been filling in as a substitute teacher at Jan's school in nearby Swansea. She teaches second grade, a nice coincidence. And now for the nicest part of Kevin's ordeal. His financial bind mobilized three friends—Jackson, fellow referee Scott Jones of Centralia and Mark Onstott, co-owner of Locust Hills Country Club in Lebanon—to run a benefit golf tournament. The goal was to draw the maximum of two foursomes per hole. Kevin wondered if they could fill all 36 spots. They wound up turning people away. As expected, referees from all over Illinois rallied to his side. Less expected, to outsiders at least, were the many coaches happy to tee off on something other than one of Kevin's calls. Referees are known for being glib. But thinking about the solidarity at that tourney, Kevin's tongue rusted shut as his eyes kept flooding.

"Boy, I don't even know where to start," he murmured. "How can I phrase this?" Pause. "I can't find the right words to say." Longer pause.

Finally, the search ended in halting eloquence.

"Sometimes in a game," Kevin said, "coaches and referees go at it. But we're all human beings. I have a lot of respect for anyone who spends that much time with kids. And it really touched me that so many coaches thought enough of me and my family to respond the way they did."

He was just as touched when the season began, and the same coaches starting responding the way they always did. When did the first coach start barking at him?

"As soon as we threw the ball up at the first game," Kevin said. "And I wouldn't have it any other way. I won't say which coach it was, but he's a really good guy. We'd barely played a minute, and he was in my ear about some play. That showed me I was back.

"So far, a lot of people have said they didn't see a dropoff this season. One guy at the beginning of the season did say that I looked a little out of shape, which I was then. After the surgery, I couldn't train in the summer like I usually do."

Despite his job loss, Kevin has no complaints about his new life.

"Nothing's painful right now," he said.

As for his wife, she lost a kidney but gained a lever for bending Kevin to do chores. Any chore.

"I made him come to my class and help with my Halloween party," Jan said. "I tell you, those second graders don't let me rest. Sometimes I think I need to wear his referee shirt."

Her kidney for the shirt off his back? Sounds like a deal made in heaven.

BILL BOMMARITO

The Winning Formula for Youth Coaches

outh team sports don't start until the coach shows up. No coach, no team. It's that simple. Sometimes the coaches are true volunteers, anxious to donate their time and knowledge of a sport. Sometimes the coaches are volunteered, dragooned into action as a last resort. Either way, the task is not so simple, as every rookie volunteer—or "volunteered"—coach soon learns. No matter how much a coach knows about a sport, working with youngsters can be complicated. Not to mention lonesome and stressful.

Where can volunteer coaches turn for help? To one of their own: Bill Bommarito of Kirkwood. Bill, who answers to Bommer, is a telecommunications salesman by trade. By passion, he has spent the past 15 years as a dad who jumped in to coach three athletic daughters: Lauren, now at Webster University; Molly, now at Truman State; and Amy, a sophomore volleyball player at Nerinx Hall. By tireless trial and inevitable error, Bill has hatched a coaching guide for volunteers called *The Winning Formula*. This indispensable package includes a dandy handbook, a lively half-hour videotape and other helpful tools, such as surveys like the one showing that kids plays sports mainly for fun, not winning.

Warning: This is not a skills-and-drills manual for the winning-is-the-only-thing mob.

"I've redefined winning," Bill said. "My winning formula attacks that win-at-all-costs mentality."

His formula is: Self-Esteem + Fun + Individual Development = Winning. Follow that equation, he has found, and even hard-nosed trophy collectors will be tickled by the results. His method applies to recreational teams, like those in the Catholic Youth Council program, and ultra-competitive teams, such as year-round select programs.

"From the kid's point of view," Bill said, "you have to feel good about yourself, enjoy the experience and show growth. If you do that, then you're winning. It doesn't matter what the scoreboard shows.

"As volunteer coaches, we have to understand that it doesn't matter what the almighty scoreboard shows if, at the end of the day, the kids don't have fun."

Bill, 47, is basically serving as an assistant coach to all of his volunteer peers, no matter how grizzled or green. He empathizes with their plight. And he empathizes with kids—and parents—who are frustrated by the well-meaning coach armed only with a whistle and a prayer.

"We expect doctors to go to school for six or eight years after college before we send our kids to them," Bill said. "We expect teachers to have a hundred hours of education classes before we put our kids to their classrooms.

"But in a heartbeat, we'll turn over 10 or 15 kids to someone who checked a box on a form and said, 'Yes, I will volunteer to coach.'"

Bill, who also speaks for a nominal fee to local sports groups, does not want his fellow volunteers to get defensive. He does want them to grasp that fun is not an option. It's mandatory. For all concerned.

"If you're not having a good experience as a coach, I can guarantee that those 15 kids aren't having fun either. And if they're miserable, what do you think they'll do? They'll quit," he said. "Hey, if you don't feel good about yourself at work, what do you do? You end up moving on. Well, why do we expect a 10-year-old kid on a team to feel any different?"

His booklet and tape are crammed with savvy tips on how to:

Communicate better with kids and parents. Organize practice. Be consistent. Be creative. Avoid common pitfalls. Act like an adult. And, above all, focus on each youngster and not the scoreboard.

Bill's fans range from the St. Louis CYC Athletic Department to child psychologists to the University of South Alabama, which uses *The Winning Formula* in a physical education class on coaching.

So why is Bill so smitten with this topic?

"I played football for Don Heeb and Jim Farrell at Vianney," he said. "I knew even then that I wanted to do what they did. Not only did they have a big influence on me, as a kid, but I saw that they really enjoyed what they did.

"Even at 16 or 17 years old, I knew that their organizational skills were so effective. Every day when we came to school, they posted our practice schedule—by the minute—and they stuck to it.

"So every day during school, I could mentally prepare for what I had to do in practice that day. That was huge. A lot of people looked at practice as work, but I loved practice, because I was able to prepare to get the most out of it."

Bill went to Dayton University, where he played hockey, earned a business degree and got his teaching certificate. He then spent four years on what he hoped would be his life's work, coaching high school baseball and football in the Dayton area. Then his wife Margaret—they met when Bommarito coached her flag football team in college—became pregnant.

"She wanted to quit her job and stay home with the baby," Bill said. "I agreed a hundred percent. So without her income, I could either stay with my dream of teaching and coaching, or we could eat."

Foodstuffs won out over the stuff of dreams. He left teaching for higher pay in the business world.

He finally returned to the sidelines when his daughters began playing sports. And he quickly saw that, as he put it, "There was a big difference between what I did as a professional coach in high school, and what I saw happening at the volunteer level."

He began jotting down a growing list of dos and don'ts. That soon morphed into a 90-minute slide presentation for other coaches, who then clamored for something tangible to take home as a reference. That demand evolved into *The Winning Formula* program. Bill sells the whole package for $29.95, or $15.95 for the handbook alone.

It's all designed, as Bommer says in the video, "to make your time with these kids the best time of their week."

And remember, he said, "The wins come in all sizes and shapes…just like the kids themselves."

JOHN GRASS

Raking In Big Mac's 63rd Home Run Ball

Three years later, John Grass has no regrets. Well, maybe a couple after becoming the first fan to catch and not release a milestone Mark McGwire home run ball in that summer of 1998.

"If you dwell on the bad part of anything," he said, "then it'd bother you. But too many good things happened to me."

Grass, the aptly named groundskeeper for the Oakville-Mehlville School District, gloved Big Mac Home Run No. 63 on September 15, 1998, at Busch Stadium. After some on-the-spot indecision and ambitious negotiation, he decided to keep the ball to sell it at auction. Unfortunately for him, a different precedent had been set by previous members of the Big Mac home run retrieval society. Most immediately swapped their milestone balls to McGwire for autographs and memorabilia.

One week before John gloved No. 63, he was upstaged by another groundskeeper. Timmy Forneris of Collinsville, a part-time employee at Busch and a recent St. Louis University graduate, had retrieved McGwire's record 62nd homer. Forneris gave the ball to the millionaire player without asking for so much as an autograph.

Forneris, acting according to plan and not on impulse, was jeered by many fans and commentators—including *Time Magazine*—for donating what was said to be a $1 million ball to a millionaire player. John was jeered by many fans and commentators for not donating his ball, worth considerably less, to the same millionaire player. Even though John, who is about to turn 50, is an average, blue-collar guy who works with his hands for a living.

Three years later, he was still getting stained by misperceptions. He won a small settlement from a sports magazine that said he obtained the ball by foul play in the left field bleachers.

"They had an article where they said I stampeded little kids to get it," John said. "That's a lie. I caught it in the air. Then I got punched in the head and knocked down."

His buddy, Affton fireman Larry Thomas, quickly threw his body on top of John, like a teammate protecting a football player who recovered a fumble. The partnership with Thomas, now retired, led to the next misconception: That John, also an Affton resident, was selfish. After catching the ball, the two friends were taken under the stadium near the Cardinals' locker room to have the ball verified as genuine. Then Cardinals officials asked to barter for the ball right. After huddling with his buddy, John came up with a long list of autographed items and free trips to spring training.

"I didn't want all that stuff for me," he said. "Larry and I had said that if either of us got a ball, we would split whatever it was worth 50-50. And I wanted to share whatever I got with my whole family. I have six brothers and two sisters."

The Cardinals vetoed his wish list. John was then left alone to tell the press that the ball was leaving with him.

"If I had it to do over again," he said, "I'd do it differently. I'd never had a press conference before. I was just so excited. And when you're excited, you're talking and you don't really sound like that, you know?"

Then came the backlash, notably from some local talk-radio hosts. He wound up signing with a lawyer who had rounded up other ball catchers who followed John's lead and kept their relics. The group, including fans with McGwire's final No. 70 and Sammy Sosa's runner-up No. 66, went to New York City to hype their upcoming auction.

"The balls were put on display in Trump Towers," Grass said. "McGwire wouldn't come, but we met Sosa, who was as nice a person as you'd want to meet. And I got to put my feet up on Donald Trump's desk."

The ball catchers returned to New York after the New Year for the auction at Madison Square Garden. Big Mac No. 70 went for $2.7 million. No. 63 brought $50,000, which Grass duly split with Larry Thomas. And what happened to John's $25,000 cut?

"The lawyer got his share, which wasn't that much," he said. "The auction house got a share and taxes got a share. There wasn't all that much left. We did some home improvements and put the rest in the bank."

As he tends to the school grounds, he does not fret about the old criticism.

"It wasn't really that nasty," said John, "just negative. I got nice letters from all over the U.S. I got one letter from California signed, 'Supporters of John Grass.'"

That, presumably, is one piece of memorabilia he hung onto.

THE NIGHTINGALES

Go Figure Olympic Skating Judges

The figure skating flap at the 2002 Olympics hardly startled John and Helen Nightingale of Ballwin. When asked for the immediate reaction to the pairs competition in Salt Lake City, John chuckled.

"I *know* what happened," he said, as his wife nodded.

The longtime skating coaches stressed that they have no inside scoop. They cannot say exactly how the judges hoisted the Russian pairs team, despite at least four clear mistakes, to the gold medal over a flawless Canadian pair. The Russians won a 5-4 split decision in voting that fell along old Cold War lines. The Russians carried the judges from Communist China and three former Soviet satellites, with France supplying the Western Bloc swing vote. Afterward, a French judge admitted bowing to pressure to favor the Russians out of fear of retaliation against the French ice dance team.

Why were the Nightingales not shocked by the idea of unfair judging at the Olympics?

"This type of thing has been going on for 50 years," said John. "There's always been block judging—at least since I was at the Olympics."

He represented the United States in pairs skating at the 1952 Winter Games in Oslo, Norway. John, who was born and trained in St. Paul, Minnesota, placed sixth with his partner, Janet Gerhauser of Minneapolis. Helen almost joined her future husband in Oslo. She missed the U.S. team by one spot, placing fourth in women's singles at the '52 Olympic Trials. Helen is a lifelong St. Louisan who took her first skating lessons at the old Wintergarden. The couple moved here in '74, after John retired from the army as a lieutenant colonel. They began coaching together, based mainly at the Creve Coeur Figure Skating Club.

John, 73, and Helen—"She's younger than me," he said chivalrously—are known as two of the nicest people in an often cutthroat sport. The Nightingales never have a harsh word to say about anyone. Which is why their open disgust at this Olympic scandal is so telling.

"We were watching it on TV," said Helen, "and I said two or three times that night, 'This is so blatant.' And John said, 'It's nothing new.'"

His first Olympic eye opener came while competing in Oslo in '52.

"A comment was made when we were putting on our skates before a practice session in Oslo," John said. "Someone—I won't say who or from which country—said, 'We have seven judges. We're in pretty good shape.' But I have to be careful. I can't prove that anyone had any judges lined up."

He smiled and said, "The only reason I mention it is, as I said, this kind of thing has been going on for a long time."

As it turned out, he had no beef with the order of finish in Oslo.

"A West German pair won," he said, "and the Kennedys, Carol and Peter, a brother-sister team from Seattle, were second. The Nagys, another brother sister-team from Hungary, won the bronze.

"We were sixth," John said, "and that's where we should have been."

The Olympic aside that John overheard was the second dubious comment that he had heard about international judging. An exchange that was even more blunt took place at the '51 world championships in Milan, Italy.

"It was our first time at worlds," said John. "I was 22 and Janet was about 18. We finished eighth. The day after the competition, a judge ran into us. She identified us and she said, 'You skated very well last night.' And we thanked her. And then she said, 'You will do much better next time . . . because you'll be known.'"

Helen and John Nightingale: never expect smooth skating at the Olympics.
(Wendi Fitzgerald/St. Louis Post-Dispatch)

John chuckled and said, "It wasn't, 'You'll do better next time be-cause you had a year to practice.' It was, 'You'll do better because you're not a rookie any more.' You know, in any of these other sports, any of these people that you call rookies, if they score a goal or a point, they're given credit for what they've done.

"They don't say, 'Well, that's just a rookie, so it doesn't count.' I don't want to sound like I'm saying this happens at every competition. It's just that there's always that opportunity. Figure skating has always been subjective, like gymnastics and diving.

"You have no finish line, no goal, like you do in other sports. It's left up to the judges."

Helen noted that not all judges score the competition before the skaters take the ice. Even though it may have seemed that way after the Salt Lake controversy.

"It's just that this time was so blatant," Helen said. "Judging is a tough job. And the judges don't get paid. All they get is expenses. There are so many good ones. The local ones here are very good and very dedicated."

She was referring to the three top-level St. Louis judges: Bill Beck, Dennis Sveum and Jan Olesky.

"But I'm afraid all of them, everywhere, will get a bad rap now," Helen said.

The Nightingales saw no way that five Olympic judges could have lifted Elena Berezhnaya and Anton Sikharulidze of Russia over Jamie Sale and David Pelletier of Canada.

"The Canadians just looked so secure," John said. "They really enjoyed what they were doing. I didn't get that impression with the Russians, who were very good. The Russians were more classical, which would appeal to the European judges.

"But they were coarser, maybe, is the word I'm looking for. They didn't look comfortable skating, the way the Canadians did."

Helen was more emphatic: "I think the Canadians had the best performance I've ever seen by any pair. Ever. They were just so natural. Their music was 'Love Story,' and they skated beautifully to it. I think they deserved some sixes myself."

In Olympic scoring, a 6.0 equals perfection.

"And the Canadians had no mistakes," Helen said.

"The Russians had several," John said. "He fell out of a double axel on the landing. The two throws that they did, she barely kept her feet. She held on for dear life. One time, she came down on an inside edge instead of an outside edge."

Judging suspicions aside, the pairs event was much different than the '52 Olympic version.

"We didn't have a long program and a short program," John said. "We had one program. You got once chance. And we skated on an outdoor rink for our practices and the competition.

"We went over 10 days early in February and skated in every kind of weather. One day, it was so windy at practice that Janet and I skated the program in two sections, so we could always have the wind at our backs. After awhile, we just gave up and spread our jackets like sails and let it blow us around the ice.

"Some days we had what they called the Olympic thaw. The ice got softer. If it got too slushy, it could be dangerous. Your skates start digging in, so they wouldn't let us skate. We practiced at outdoor rinks, but they couldn't make ice like they do now. You didn't have Zambonis to scrape the ice."

Olympic pairs performed lifts back then, he said, "but if you did one, you were up and down. You didn't carry her very far. You see them starting their programs now across the ice from each other. We were always together.

"There were no throws. But the Canadians, who finished fourth, did this thing where she did an axel and he would catch her in the air. That was kind of a neat thing. We didn't do any triple jumps. Dick Button was the only one doing double axels then, and he did a triple loop, which was like a quad today. Nobody else could do a triple."

The competition itself was held outdoors in a stadium filled with 32,000 fans, double the seating of the indoor Delta Center in Salt Lake.

"It was just fantastic," John said. "The weather was perfect. You could see the stars overhead. The people all stood because it was too cold. That's how they kept warm, standing next to each other and leaning on these railings."

Security was far looser then, with one exception.

"The Hungarians had this armed guard with them whereever they went, so they couldn't defect," John said. "I remember the guy with a pistol in his shoulder holster. There would be a guard outside his room on the hall where we all stayed. And he'd be there at the rink when they practiced."

Needless to say, such measures are not needed at the Creve Coeur rink, where the Nightingales teach four of their eight grandchildren— Trisha (age 13), Kim (10), Karen (seven) and Michael (six). And after 50 years, the Nightingales still keep in touch with John's Olympic partner, Janet Gerhauser.

"She was a bridesmaid in our wedding," said Helen.

Janet, whose married name is Allen, stayed in the Twin Cities and also remained in skating. She is a respected world-class judge.

"We got a note from her before Christmas saying she was chosen to judge the men in Salt Lake," John said. "She worked the '88 Olympics in Calgary, and she said this is probably her swan song."

As it turned out, the men's competition at Salt Lake went off without a judging stumble.

But as John said, with a twinkle, "I know I wouldn't want her job."

MARK GARTLAND

The Cop Who Fended Off the Great Scorer

Grantland Rice, the poet laureate of the press box, captured the essence of competition in a single terse verse:

> *"When the One Great Scorer comes to write against your name*
> *"He marks—not whether you won or lost—*
> *"But how you played the game."*

That Great Scorer is now sharpening his pencil for Mark Gartland, a St. Louis County Police captain and outstanding rec athlete. Mark, 50, refuses to run out the clock in his one-on-one match with cancer, a prohibitive favorite. The surgeon who opened up Mark's abdomen took one look and stitched him back up. It was the worst form of colon cancer, rooted all along the outside of the organ instead of growing in one removable lump inside. Mark was a given a month to live, maybe two, when he was diagnosed. That was 18 months ago.

"He's the consummate competitor," said John Burke, a close friend and former St. Louis City cop. "He's what amateur sports are all about. He plays sports because he loves them, and he's able to leave it behind when the game's over.

Mark Gartland took life into overtime.
(Photo courtesy of the St. Louis County Police Department)

"But he's fearless. He never quit at anything. He just decided to treat cancer like another opponent."

Mark got a late start in soccer and basketball at old Mercy High, class of '65, arriving as a junior after a two-year detour into a seminary. As an adult, he was the kind of sandlot athlete whom everybody talks about but nobody hears about. Mark leads all county cops in medals won at the Missouri Police Olympics, where he was a charter entrant in 1977. He competed in track, soccer, softball and basketball. He also plays shortstop for the St. Louis Police Browns, an elite softball team. In 1983, while attending the FBI National Academy, Mark decided to master the obstacle course. He left with the course record time.

But Mark is most proud of his backstage work for the Budweiser Metro Boxing Showdown, alias Guns 'n' Hoses, where local cops and firefighters punch each other for charity at Savvis Center. The event benefits the Backstoppers, a support group for families of cops and firefighters killed on duty. Mark recruited county boxers and built esprit by centering workouts at the County Police Academy. The fitness center there now bears his name.

On duty, Mark has run the county's elite SWAT team and also its emergency management program. At work, at play or at home, only one crisis ever buckled him. Andy, the youngest of his three sons, was killed in a car accident two summers ago. The boy was 16, with a beaming face that could have launched a zillion Wheaties boxes. The loss of their "baby" devastated Mark and his wife, Ann.

"Three months later," Mark said, "the cancer was diagnosed. This has all been much harder on my wife than on me. But she's a trooper."

Mark could have surrendered and let the disease quickly end his misery over Andy. Instead, he got competitive and attacked back.

"I did a lot of research on what's out there for treatment," Mark said. "Conventional methods, alternative medicines, I looked at all of 'em. In each case, it was usually that person's belief in the remedy that was most important, rather than the remedy itself.

"Consequently, I put my faith in God and chemo, the conventional method. And I wouldn't change anything."

At five feet nine and 175 compact pounds, Mark had little fat.

"But I had to get in better shape to fight this," he said.

Somehow, he tuned himself more tightly. As miracles go, that probably outweighs his ability to prolong overtime for a year and a half.

"That competitiveness kept me alive these 18 months," he said. "And that 18 months supplied me with an opportunity to be with my family at a very tragic time."

Mark also realized a career goal when County Police Chief Ron Battelle promoted him to captain during that grace period. Shortly after his promotion, Mark took a U-turn for the worse. Cars lined the street in his subdivision as friends hurried to his side. Mark, of course, rallied again. An organizational fanatic, he put this latest overtime session to good use.

"I've been conducting a living wake here the past three weeks," he said wryly. "The other day, my eight pallbearers came in and we took a picture together. It sounds weird, but I couldn't thank them otherwise."

Mark was told he has one week left, maybe two. But he's still joking about the tubes that run fluids in and out of his body. Despite losing 60 pounds of muscle and gristle, he still looked fitter than his three pudgy visitors on a recent afternoon.

One of them, taking leave with a handshake, said, "I'll see you at the Showdown." Mark smiled. The boxing event is held on Thanksgiving Eve, more than four months away.

"That'd take a miracle," said Mark, an expert on the subject. "But one way or another, I'll be watching."

If it's the other way, someone else will have to present the Mark Gartland Award to the fighter showing the most courage. That recipient will have an impossible act to follow.

"I only have two sorrows," said Mark. "One is missing my family, the other is missing my friends. But I'm at peace with this. Although it may have gotten the best of me, it didn't do it without a fight. And I know that when the time comes, the first person I'll look for is Andy."

Meanwhile, the Great Scorer is tapping his pencil, on hold for another day. Mark Gartland, who never did know when he was beaten at anything, is still playing the game for all it's worth.

SHERMAN CURTIS

A Coach with Two Schools of Thought

In these days, when good teachers and coaches are hard to find, there is nothing unusual about working at one school and coaching at another. Unless the party of the first and second part is Sherman Curtis. In the 2001-2002 school year, he is working at Vashon and coaching at Gateway Tech, another Public High League school.

But he doesn't just work at Vashon. He is assistant principal. And he doesn't just coach the Gateway girls basketball team. He built it into a juggernaut that rolled in the 4-A Final Four from 1997 to 1999—placing first, third and fourth in the state.

And the girls' teams from Vashon and Gateway aren't just PHL rivals. Vashon KOed Gateway's Final Four streak last year with a rout in the 2001 district finals. This situation is unusual but not uneasy for Curtis. From his dual position of authority, he insists that the rivalry stays fierce, not ferocious.

"It's just a game," Curtis said by phone from his Vashon office. "I'm embracing that. I know with the wrong person that this can explode. And I still have some work to do in that area. But, hey, the girls on both teams know each other. They go to parties together. They go roller skating together. They go to the mall together. And a girl from Gateway might have a boyfriend over here."

He also knows that teens consider it a sacred duty to annoy their friends, and nearby adults, whenever possible.

"I try to keep it friendly," Curtis said. "The kids are always going to be trash talking. That's part of the game. But we want to keep it under control. Last year, some of the girls here at Vashon came up to me and said, 'We're going to beat you, Mr. Curtis!' And I said, 'Well, you're supposed to do that.'"

And if the taunting turns mean?

"I don't want that," Curtis growled in his masterly bass voice. "It's about these kids' lives. We're trying to teach sportsmanship."

Last season, he delivered that lesson from opposite vantage points. First, the two teams met to start the season. Gateway, in a rebuilding mode, barely escaped with a win.

"We got down by 15 points," Curtis said, "and we came back and won by two. But before districts I told my team, 'That was a long time ago. If you get down by 15 again, they won't let you back.'"

He was right twice. His team did fall behind early, and Vashon did not back off while winning by 20 points. Then Vashon students quickly saw—or heard, to be exact—that Curtis is a role model who walks what he talks.

"I congratulated them on the PA system the next day," he said. "My girls at Gateway had experienced that feeling three years in a row when they won districts. And I was happy for these girls at Vashon, who had been here for four years and finally had an opportunity to move on."

Sincere? Absolutely, according to Martin Jenkins, the rookie girls coach at Career Academy. Jenkins played junior college ball at Three Rivers, major college ball at Stetson and pro ball in Europe. He started his high school career at Roosevelt playing for a young junior varsity coach named Sherman Curtis.

"He's an educator," Jenkins said. "He cares about kids. Of course he wants his kids to experience state every year. But if they can't go, he's happy that another PHL team could advance and try to get that experience."

In fact, Curtis treated Gateway's elimination as education.

"It worked out fine," he said. "I had a young team last year. They weren't used to that playoff atmosphere. Hopefully, they're a little more focused now."

Talent, as usual, is not an issue at Gateway. Sophomore Mesha Williams, a six-foot-one forward, was All-PHL last year as a rookie. Her partner inside is six-foot junior Tracie Harris, a three-year starter. The playmaker is 5'3"Alicia Robinson, another sophomore who started last year as a rookie. The other likely starters are 5'3" junior guard Erica Raspberry, who is Robinson's cousin, and 5'10" senior Shaunessie Holmes. Workaholic guard Erica "Speedy" Anderson, a 5'4" sophomore, may have hustled her way into the lineup. The lynchpin is, or should be, Williams. She can dominate all over the court when the urge strikes.

"She can handle the ball on the outside," Curtis said, "and she probably led the area in blocked shots at about four per game. She's one of the better players I've had a chance to coach, but she's being a little lazy. I've talked to her already about it."

They also chatted last year about the need to curb freshman emotions.

"She was real nervous at first," Curtis said, "so I just gradually put her in there. Then when she was in, she didn't want to come out. So I had to change her attitude about 'team.' She's got a lot more positive attitude this year, but it depends on her mood."

That may sound cold. But Curtis, in his 10th year as Gateway's charter coach, has warmed up to new ways of making the game fun. He is hatching scavenger hunts, skating parties and other team-building antics that do not follow the bouncing ball.

"I'm not trying to corral all their time for basketball," he said. "I always tell the kids their family is first, and then their religion and health and academics. Then comes the basketball, fifth."

Walking with a foot in two competing schools, though, was not Curtis's first choice. A biology teacher at Gateway, he was passed over there for assistant principal before landing the same job at Vashon.

"At the time of my interview at Gateway, I had a prior commitment out of town," said Curtis matter-of-factly. "When I came back, they had already hired for that position."

Rescheduling an interview for a top employee is the usual way to do business. For some reason, it wasn't in this case. But this way, Sherman Curtis can work his unusual magic at two schools.

35

JACK LANE

Sharing Rick Ankiel's Pain

J ack Lane winces every time he thinks of Rick Ankiel bouncing the baseball and his career off the backstop. It's like looking into a mirror that runs 40 years deep.

Ankiel is the phenom who is trying to regain control of his pitches and his big-league career with the Cardinals. Jack, 59, never had a big-league career. He was never classified as a phenom. However, he did have a 15-8 record in 1961, his first year in the minor leagues, and an upbeat future. The next year, he started bouncing his curveball, got demoted from Class B to Class C and went 7-13 overall. His control mysteriously returned with the change of scenery, but a new affliction popped up the next year.

Jack pitched with a sore arm from Opening Day through the whole 1963 season, just as Ankiel recently added a sore arm to his troubles. Unless Ankiel enlists in the fight against terrorism, their parallel tracks will diverge at the point. Jack joined the army reserves in 1964 and missed that whole season while on active duty. When he went to spring training in 1965, his arm hurt too much to lob a baseball. He retired on the spot, rather than scuffle along on the injured list for $650 a month and no relief in sight.

"What can I say? I did what I wanted to do," Jack said. "It was fun. I played with Hall of Famers. And I played with guys you thought could never miss, and did."

Remnants of his career decorate his St. Charles home. A wonderful scrapbook compiled by his grownup children, John and Ashley. Framed photos on the wall of himself as a scrawny right-hander in the minor leagues. A Stan Musial jersey signed "To another Hall of Famer" in honor of Jack's place in the St. Louis Amateur Baseball Hall of Fame. And, for ceremonial and sentimental use only, an original Colt 45s warmup jacket. Jack said he "liberated" that garment in 1962 in spring training with the expansion Houston club, before it took the stage name Astros.

"When they hear I still have the coat," Jack said with a twinkle, "they might send me a bill."

His sense of humor survived his baseball career, along with many timeless memories and one eternal mystery.

"I don't know if anybody could examine my arm now," Jack said, "but I'd like to know what happened and why. Nobody ever took any X-rays. I never got any treatment. I was at Portsmouth, Virginia, in '63, and when my arm kept bothering me, the manager told me, 'Go downtown, and there are these guys at the YMCA who can give you a massage.'

"That was the treatment. And it was a good massage, I will say that. But then I went in the army the next year, and by the time I got back in '65 and talked to a doctor, it was a year and a half later. And it was too late."

Through the years, Jack has kept his regrets to a minimum. One is that as a youth, he ignored some fateful advice.

"We loved playing corkball," said Jack, a city kid who attended Roosevelt High. "People would say, 'Don't play corkball or you'll hurt your arm.' The ball was so light, there was no resistance when you threw it. And they were right. I hurt my arm."

He also wishes he had gone to college, but that was not a practical option. His mother was in poor health and his paycheck was needed at home, during and after his baseball career. Although not obsessed with the question, he still finds himself asking: What if?

"Sure I do," Jack said. "I often wonder if I hadn't had that problem with my control in '62, if I'd have had a shot at Triple A in Oklahoma City."

Unlike Ankiel, he was not a fireballer. His calling card was his curveball.

"Pitching is three things," Jack said. "Speed, location and movement. And speed is the least important. Look at John Tudor when he was with the Cardinals, or Greg Maddux in Atlanta now.

"They're moving the ball around. The hitter's eyes can't adjust. You want to have the guy hit it on the handle or the end of the bat. And you want to stay ahead in the count, so he can't guess as much."

Jack signed with Houston on January 26, 1961, an event documented by a story and photo in the *Post-Dispatch*. That clipping is preserved in his scrapbook, along with his various pro contracts. His signing bonus was $25,000, and his salary was $500 per month for a five-month season. Back then, Jack stretched only 135 pounds across his five-foot-11 physique. That explains how his liberated Colt 45s jacket can still fit some 40 years and 50 pounds later.

"It was the smallest jacket they had," Jack said, "but it was way too big for me then."

He started small in the Houston farm system: Class D ball in Salisbury, North Carolina. He went 11-3 and was promoted in midstream to Class A Jacksonville, Florida. Jack left there with a 3-4 record and a Hall of Fame memory.

"Willie Stargell played in that league for Asheville," Jack said. "A future Hall of Famer, and I struck him out twice."

After a moment's pause, Jack continued, "He also hit one over the palm trees off me in the same game in Jacksonville. It was a hanging curveball and he hit it with one hand. A pretty good poke."

The next year, 1962, Jack scored his only victory over a big-league team—the parent Colt 45s in an exhibition in Apache Junction, Arizona.

"I pitched three innings in relief for our Oklahoma City Triple A team," Jack said. "We took the lead while I was in there, so that's my big claim to fame. I was 1-0 against a big-league team in spring training."

He started the year in Class B with Durham, North Carolina, an outpost later immortalized in the movie *Bull Durham*.

"We played in that same little ballpark," said Jack, "and I played with Joe Morgan and Rusty Staub."

Both became big-league stars, with Morgan reaching the Hall of Fame.

"They were both good guys," Jack said. "Rusty had a perfect swing. He was just a phenom. Joe wasn't. Joe made himself what he is today. As he got promoted, he simply got better with the competition."

So did Jack, it seemed, as he won his first start with Durham.

"Then something just happened," he said. "I lost my release point on my curveball. I lost my control. I never threw the ball to the backstop like Ankiel did. But I'd bounce the ball in front of the batters. I'd walk 'em. I'd hit 'em. It was ugly.

"I had a major-league curveball. My plan was to have a pretty good year at Durham and move up to Oklahoma City. Instead, I went the other way."

He slid to Class C Modesto, California. But the major leagues were still reachable from there. Three of his teammates proved that—catcher John Bateman, pitcher Tom Burgmeier and outfielder Paul Runge, who made it as an umpire.

Modesto was the site of a minor miracle. Jack's career returned from the dead.

"I can't quite describe the change of feeling," he said. "It was a new uniform, a new city. I did know some of the guys, but my confidence just came back. I started throwing my curveball for strikes again. It was just a mental thing. It's hard to explain."

He wound up winning four games, losing seven and throwing well enough to earn another promotion in '63. He was back in Class B as the opening day starter for Portsmouth.

"The first pitch I threw was a high fastball," Jack said. "I felt a twinge in my shoulder, like something pulled away. It didn't really hurt so I finished the game. It was never right all year, but after I'd warm up the pain would go away. I'd pitch the whole game and the next day be a little sore. There was nothing to indicate there was a serious injury. And you didn't sit down. There weren't as many teams back then. Somebody'd take your job. I won 10 and lost 15 that year for a last-place team and threw a ton of innings. I came home in the fall of '63, and in November somebody shot President Kennedy."

Jack was 21, the same age as Ankiel, when he added a sore arm to painful control problems.

"I knew the draft age was 22 back then," Jack said, "but they lowered it to 21 after Kennedy was killed. Who knows why? So I got stuck. I could either get drafted and lose two years in the army, or join a reserve unit and miss six months on active duty."

He could have avoided service altogether by marrying his girlfriend.

"But we didn't think that was something you should do just to keep you out of the draft," said Jack, who eventually married someone else.

The Colt 45s asked the army to delay activating Jack until after the '64 season. Instead, he missed that campaign while learning the artillery racket at Fort Leonard Wood and Fort Sill, Oklahoma. When he finally threw at spring training in '65, the pain was unbearable. The team finally called a doctor.

Jack said the doctor gave him this diagnosis: "We'll call it adhesive tendinitis, for lack of a better term. Muscles grew together in your arm that normally don't grow together. As long as you were pitching, they didn't have a chance to grow together. When you didn't pitch for over a year, they did."

So Jack retired and came home. He started working in sales for a friend's supply company and then spent a decade with UPS. In 1979, he started work as an account manager for Dana Corporation, which makes auto parts. He thought he would retire from the firm but was recently swept out in the downsizing current. Now Jack, who is divorced, is looking for a new job. And he still finds himself looking back on his first job. Especially after finding that his old soupbone can throw batting practice without mishap for his son's adult team.

"I do miss it," Jack said. "There's nothing quite like the feel of a good baseball. It's a good feeling."

Until he thinks of young Ankiel.

"It's like pulling the golf club back and slicing the ball, no matter what you do," Jack said. "That's Ankiel's problem. He's lost his release point on his pitches, and it's all up here."

Jack taps his head.

"It's just an incredible mental block. It can go away. It did for me. But you just have to experience it. It's hard to describe."

And harder to accept. Even 40 years down the road.

36

SANSONE CLAN

SLUH Football is a Family Reunion

There are 2,345 seats at St. Louis University High Stadium. On any given football Friday in 2001, not all of them are filled by Sansones. Some clan members prefer to stand, such as brothers Chris and Joe Finley of Glendale and their cousins, Craig Schlapprizzi of Ladue and Tony "Boch" Sansone III of Kirkwood. They take the field on defense for the St. Louis U. High Junior Bills.

Several of their female cousins and sisters congregate with other teenagers on the track behind the home bench. Several of their preschool kin careen around the premises, with parents and older siblings in hasty pursuit. Don Schlapprizzi and Dan Finley, lawyers who married Sansone sisters, are railbirds at the top of the grandstand, watching their sons knock helmets. Tony Sansone Jr. often abandons his seat below his brothers-in-law to pace alone behind the end zone. Tony and his sisters, Deby Schlapprizzi and Cindy Finley, are joined by their five younger brothers, in turn accompanied by their wives and children. All told, the eight Sansone siblings have 39 offspring—seven each for Tony and Cindy, four for Deby. The weekly football reunion gives new meaning to the term Sansone Group, the family's commercial real estate business.

Crunchin' cousins: from left, Craig Schlapprizzi, Tony Sansone III and Chris Finney.
(Photo courtesy of the Sansone family)

"Everybody kind of finds their spot," said Deby Schlapprizzi, the eldest sibling who mother-hens the clan. "I would say at every given game we almost get 100 percent attendance, except for the itty bitty babies."

"We pack the house," said her husband Don, adding with a twinkle that marrying into the clan "is fun…for the most part."

Especially on football Fridays.

"The man won't leave work for anything," said Deby of her legal-beagle husband, "and he's here an hour before the game."

"I get my ankles taped at 3:30," said Don, who captained his football teams at Southwest High and Washington University.

When SLUH opened district play by beating Gateway Tech 34-14, the Sansone clan had two notable no-shows: Family partriarch Tony Sr. and matriarch Mary Anne.

"My dad was out of town or else he'd be here," said Deby. "And my mom doesn't come to all the games. She's not too crazy about it 'cause someone might get hurt."

Ditto for Deby and sister Cindy.

"They always worry that somebody on either team will go down," said Dan Finney, Cindy's husband, "or that everybody's not playing enough to feel good about themselves."

On this Senior Parents Night, Dan was wearing jersey No. 44, which belongs to son Joe, a junior. Dan started the game wearing No. 31, which belongs to son Chris, a senior.

"My wife made me change at halftime," said Dan, who takes heavy ribbing as an Irish interloper in this Italian family.

"You're talking to the John Madden of SLUH football," said Tony Jr. "That's why we saved him for the last five minutes of the fourth quarter, or he'd be talking to you all game."

It was Tony Sr., the family patriarch, who played a key role offstage for the unbeaten Junior Bills.

"This summer, all four of our boys were at their grandpa's house to lift weights," Deby said, "and a lot of their team members were, too. My dad had a gym built onto the house."

A fifth cousin also joined the workouts and could also be on the team. But Mike Sansone, Boch's kid brother, is a hockey standout who opted to focus on that sport at local power DeSmet.

"The cool thing about this family," Deby said, "is that all these kids are so close to one another."

Especially in the SLUH defensive huddle, where four cousins hang out. Craig Schlapprizzi is a six-foot-two, 202-pound linebacker and major college recruit. Chris Finney is a 5'11", 170-pound senior whippet who plays defensive back and running back. He is another major college prospect. Joe Finney, a six-foot, 180 pound junior, is currently out with a bruised knee. He shares his brother's all-around ability and hard nose for the ball. Then there is Boch Sansone, whose nickname came "because he looked like a little bocce ball when he was a baby," said his Aunt Deby. Boch, an undersized defensive end at 5'10", 178 pounds, lost his starting job in the season opener. He platoons now and is a special-teams commando. Despite playing less than his cousins—and less than any senior would like—he is the kind of gritty, gung-ho competitor needed to glue any winner together.

"Don't worry about Boch," said Tony Jr., eyes misting. "Boch is fine. He's the consummate teammate."

He has lots of company besides blood relatives.

"These seniors have never lost as a group," Tony Jr. said. "They were unbeaten as freshmen and unbeaten as sophomores. They lost some games last year on the varsity as juniors, when they were mixed in with other seniors, but now they're unbeaten so far as seniors."

Two weeks ago, the season took on a new urgency for coach Gary Kornfeld's team. Steve Pettit—whose son, Mike, is a senior defensive back—was diagnosed with a vicious cancer.

"In the game that week," Tony Sr. said, "Mike got an interception and raised the ball up to his dad in the stands. After the game, the entire team, on its own, told Steve to come down on the field. Then they gave him the game ball. He couldn't believe it."

The team's closeness goes far beyond the Sansone clan.

"That's my point," Tony Sr. said. "The whole team's unified. The whole team's a family."

PRESTON THOMAS & LEE WINFIELD

Stressing Books and B-Ball at Fo-Po

Preston Thomas and Lee Winfield have followed many a bouncing ball in their coaching careers. Now they have a new dual adventure as the tag-team coaches for men's basketball at Forest Park Community College.

Some of the ricochets they see these days are strange, even by their recent standards. Preston, the head coach, just came off a two-year hitch as co-coach for one of three Harlem Globetrotters travel teams. Lee, the associate coach, assisted the Swarm to a second championship despite the undertow that finally sank the International Basketball League.

"This is the hardest thing I've ever done," said Lee, a longtime assistant with Mizzou and St. Louis U. "But it's the most fun I've had in years. Working with 'Thom' is great."

"It's been crazy," said Preston, who spent 17 years building Cardinal Ritter into a high school power, "but we never stop laughing. When I got this job in August, I called Lee. Immediately. I didn't know anyone else more qualified. I can't believe he's not a head coach somewhere."

That's not all the longtime friends can't believe since they began sharing their closet of an office at Fo-Po.

"We were playing up at Olive Harvey College in Chicago," said Preston, "and they start warmups with seven guys, all little guys. Then all these big guys start walking in, one at a time, while warmups are going on.

"We go, 'Who are these guys?' There are no names in their scorebook. Just numbers. So I say to a ref, 'Hey, they've got to have some names there.' And the ref says, 'Hey, don't worry about it.'

"So we start the game, and one of their guys gets a foul. Our scorekeeper says, 'Coach, I don't have a name *or* a number for that guy.' So we tell a ref, 'Hey, this guy's nowhere in the book. That's a technical foul.' And the ref says, 'Hey, it's not important. We'll just go and play the game.'"

Lee, picking up the story, said, "We come out to start the second half, one ref—the only one with an official patch on his shirt—says, 'Okay, we'll shoot that technical now.' And we did. It was wild, man."

It was also a victory, a rarity in this 5-11 rebuilding year. Preston and Lee took the job on the fly, after Evan Pedersen left to pursue business interests. They had no time to recruit and no scholarships left. The scholarship problem then quickly solved itself.

"We started with 17 guys," Preston said. "Now we've got nine."

"But we didn't fire anybody," Lee said. "They all fired themselves."

The new coaches had some strict demands. The issues were matters like schoolbooks and discipline and work habits and responsibility.

"That's exactly why we hired them," said athletic director Darin Hendrickson.

"We have four rules and 30 laws," Preston said. "Rules are negotiable. Laws are not. And they were being broken. And then there's consequences."

That's the way it was at Ritter, when Preston was winning three small-school state titles in basketball and two more in track. Unlike many top high school coaches, he sacrificed team success at times to help groom his players for their next step in athletics and academics. The first basketball wave included Lee's son, Julian, now a State Farm Insurance agent here. Julian starred at SLU and then Mizzou, moving when his dad changed jobs after SLU submarined the Grawer regime.

Smokey Evans, who played with Julian at Ritter, went to Arkansas State. Then came Jahidi White (Georgetown and now the Washington Wizards), Loren Woods (Wake Forest, Arizona and the Minnesota Timberwolves), Chris Carrawell (Duke and the NBA Development

League), Brian Brown (William & Mary), Brandon Campbell (Cal-Ful-lerton for basketball and track), Corey Hill (Northern Iowa), Gerald Weatherspoon (Towson State) and Brandon Gilmore (walk-on at Duquesne). Almost all have their degrees or are on track to get them. At Ritter every player, from star to scrub, was expected to make good grades and pass the college entrance test.

Lee had even higher standards, as Julian learned at Ritter when his dad benched him until his grade point average made the Winfield Family eligibility cut. Lee, a St. Louis Public High League alum, played seven years in the NBA. His decade with Rich Grawer at SLU produced two trips to the NIT Finals and an NBA player, Anthony Bonner. Lee also spent seven years at Mizzou as a coach and academic support adviser. He helped Norm Stewart groom three NCAA Tourney teams, including a trip to the Elite Eight and an undefeated league champion.

At 54, Lee is a juco believer. He might not be here, or anywhere, if not for a scholarship to the old St. Louis Baptist Junior College in 1965. That kept him out of the Vietnam War and gave him some direction.

"That started it all for me," said Lee, who went on to star as a point guard at North Texas State. "People say I was lucky not to go to Vietnam, because the army had just ruled me 1-A. But what is luck? Luck is an opportunity. What happens if you're not prepared to take advantage of your opportunity . . . is it luck then?

"We often overlook junior college or don't respect what it can do for these kids. We have to train the kids that this is not high school. This is another level. And there's another level after this: A four year-institution. You can get that education, and get it paid for, and get a degree, and do something you like to do. Which is play basketball."

At Ritter, Preston always looked ahead to the college level. Critics ripped him for not planting his big kids near the basket with orders only to shoot bunny shots. Instead, White and Woods and Carrawell were told to handle the ball and shoot jump shots. The misses and missteps helped polish those three for big-time colleges and now the pros. If the critics didn't appreciate that, the players did.

White and Carrawell and several other local talents—including Larry Hughes of the Golden State Warriors—asked Thomas and Winfield to work them out in the summer of 2001, before their first Fo-Po school year began. A pro career is not the main goal at Fo-Po, where the hoops staff also included Jason James (Parkway West and Graceland College) and Earl Holloway (ex-McLuer North assistant).

"These opportunities we're talking about are so vast," said Lee, "you can't count them."

For example, Lee is looking for full-time work to augment his part-time coaching job. To do that, he is networking with Grawer, ex-SLU official Jim Velten of Kirkwood High and other old buddies.

"Kids don't realize that you meet other people at these institutions," Lee said. "You meet people when you travel and when you play against them.

"What happens with these new friends that you meet? They go out into the business world and they meet other people. These are the things I've learned along the way. And I'm still learning."

And, along with his coaching sidekick, still teaching.

38

THE PHILIPPIS

Like-Father, Like-Son Zebras

And now the cloning of zebras has begun.

Steve Philippi is one of the top high school basketball officials in the area. He is tall, erect, poised and respected. Ditto on all counts for Craig Philippi, his son. The dad is 26 years senior, an inch taller and sports hair a judicial shade of gray. Otherwise, watching father and son in tandem—as they were when the Oakville boys played at Seckman late in the 2001-2002 season—can cause double vision. In black and white.

"When they're together, it's something special," said Judi Phillipi, Steve's wife and Craig's mom. "They have such a great working relationship. I think it carries over from their relationship as father and son. It's a neat thing to watch."

The Philippis seldom get to work together for high school varsity games. But they are more than a curiosity. They are also excellent refs. Steve Siaus, the popular roly-poly veteran who completed the three-man crew at Seckman, said, "I'm just along for the ride tonight with the big boys."

Ray Cliffe, who observes boys' basketball officials for the Missouri State High School Activities Association, keeps a personal top 15 ranking of local refs.

"The Philippis are both on my list," Cliffe said.

Veteran ref Mike Winklemann, who assigns crews for the Metro Catholic Conference, said, "They both do a real nice job. Steve is cutting back some now, but Craig is one of the real up-and-coming guys. And as good as they are at officiating, they're even better as people."

Craig, 24, who lives in Dogtown, was named "Most Promising Official" by the St. Louis Officials Association. He is finishing work on a degree in business agriculture from Southeast Missouri State and hopes to become a golf course superintendent.

Steve, 50, is a postal worker who lives in Affton. This season he is reffing just two games per week, half his former load. That is partly due to his officiating odometer, which has 25 years' worth of miles on it. Family reasons are also a factor. With Craig and his older sister Amy out of the house, Steve wants to spend more evenings with his wife, Judi, who works at the Anheuser-Busch Employees Credit Union. Amy has already presented them with a grandson and has another child on the way.

"I'd like to spend more time with them," Steve said.

His officiating never came between him and his own family.

"I would take the kids to the games once in a while so they could see what he was doing," Judi said. "But somebody's always unhappy with every call. You'd have to sit there all night and explain to your children why somebody doesn't like their dad.

"Especially when they call technical fouls. You don't call technicals unless something is really intense."

For the record, Steve said, "I've only called one technical this year. And that was at a girls' game."

Craig also works girls' games, but said, "Boys' games are easier. Girls' games are too dirty. They really get rough."

He also takes junior varisty as well as varsity games if his schedule permits.

"I pretty much work anywhere and everywhere," Craig said. "The more basketball you see, the better your eyes get. The layoffs always seem to kill you."

He began officiating while still at St. Mary's, where he played on the varsity his last two years. He started reffing at Catholic Youth Council games when he was about 15.

"My first CYC game, the kids were fifth-grade boys," Craig said. "I still remember parts of it. It was rough, real rough. I found out that it's

Craig and Steve Philippi, like-father like-son whistleblowers at work.
(Photo by David Kennedy)

definitely easier to play the game than to go out there and actually think you can ref it.'"

Was he nervous or mistake-prone?

"Both," Craig said. "I was working with an older guy, and when we walked off the court, he said, 'Don't worry, the next night's always better.' What he meant was, 'After this, it can only get better.'

"My dad was there, and when it was over, he just said, 'There's many things we need to work on.'"

When Craig started college at Southwest Missouri State, he reffed intramurals for spending money.

"I had just gotten my patch from the state," Craig said, "so I was one of the few certified refs working intramurals. We got eight to 10 bucks an hour, and they had a running clock at the games.

"One time I threw a fraternity out of a Greek League game. Somebody mouthed off to me, so I called a technical. I called a second technical for an illegal substitution—a kid just ran out on the court, like changing on the fly in hockey. The third technical was when they all started yelling about the second one. I threw the team out, and I threw the whole crowd out."

His breakthrough game this year was working a two-man crew with veteran Bob Dunahue when No.1 DeSmet was upset at then-No. 2 Chaminade. The spillover crowd included his sister Amy, her husband Ken and their toddler, Kade.

"My sister had never seen me work before," Craig said. "She really had a good time. She couldn't wait to get home and watch the highlights on the news. She said, 'How do put yourself in front of all those people? Everyone's yelling at you.' I said, 'I don't hear it.'"

His dad also shares that hearing quirk, along with a similar biography. Steve also attended St. Mary's, although he didn't play basketball, and he got his start officiating in CYC games at St. Anthony's, his boyhood parish in south St. Louis.

"In high school, I was a short kid," Steve said. "Then at the end I grew six inches in one year. After high school, I played in a CYC men's league at the Cherokee Rec Center."

He started officiating by accident in his early 20s.

"I ran a basketball tournament at St. Anthony's for seventh and eighth grades," Steve said. "If an official didn't show up, you just stepped in. There was always a whistle lying around the gym."

Officiating wasn't the only turn his life just happened to take. Judi was the proverbial girl next door while they were growing up in the city.

As Judi recalled, "His dad said it was a marriage of convenience: We were too lazy to look for anybody else. We didn't have to ask what high school we went to. We knew."

Judi stands all of five feet tall, more than a foot shorter than her husband, but that's not the only opposite attraction at work.

"I read a variety of books," she said. "Steve reads rulebooks. He's always been a rules person. There isn't any game that he plays that he doesn't know the rules. I refuse to play Monopoly with him. It's ridiculous."

Sports were never her hobby, not even when her new groom was immersed in three or four softball and basketball leagues.

"For our first anniversary," Judi said, "he gave me a softball mitt. Do you believe that?"

"Hey," Steve said, "isn't leather the gift for the first year?"

Nice try.

"He just thought I'd like to play with the other wives on the team," Judi said. "That lasted a year. It was too much work. I'd rather not be a player. I'd rather watch and scream than have somebody screaming at me."

As for officiating, she said, "I ref at home."

Judi estimates that she has seen "thousands of basketball games. I just don't want anyone to know I'm the ref's wife. Or mom. Whichever."

She can't be too critical of critics in the crowd.

"When Craig played, I always yelled at the refs," she said. "I was really bad. I didn't know the rules, but who cares? He was my son. I was a mom. You don't have to know what you're yelling."

Her husband and son accept that as part of the job they love. That's why Craig constantly pumps his dad for feedback, such as during every timeout at Seckman.

"It's always a bonus to work with my dad," Craig said. "We worked together a lot when I was doing CYC games, and then we'd go home and talk about situations.

"I didn't always want to be a ref. But I got to stay in competition and make a little money, and I just fell in love with it."

That's also why his dad got started, but it's not why he keeps putting on the striped shirt.

"I can't talk myself into going to the gym," Steve said, "so it's a good way to keep in shape. And it's fun being with the kids. People talk about kids today, but I'd say 99 percent of the players are wonderful to deal with."

As for dealing with Craig, both parents offered words of wisdom when he began his career as a whistle blower.

His dad told him, "You can make a bad call, but if you look good doing it, it makes a big difference."

And his mom told him, "Wash your own uniform. I'm not doing it for you. Those things can really stink."

39

HIGH PERFORMANCE

They'd Rather Spike than Dunk

It was a double historical twist. At the 2002 USA Volleyball Junior Olympics in Louisville, the St. Louis High Performance Volleyball Club placed second in the Open Division for boys aged 18 and under. That matched the best finish by a non-California team in Boys 18 Open, the highest division.

The St. Louisans were a game away from upsetting the mighty Long Beach Club, but dropped the next two games and settled for the silver medal. In even more of an upset, the High Performance middle blockers—six-foot-10 Andrew Neff and 6'8" Joe Caruso—attended DeSmet High. The school is a magnet for tall basketball players. Yet neither one suited up for the Missouri 4-A basketball runnerup. Caruso can explain that shocking development.

"We don't like basketball," he said.

He and Neff helped make High Performance the tallest team in the Junior Olympic field. But the St. Louisans had more going for them than altitude. They also had aptitude. Three of them made the 15-man all-tournament team, and none of them were named Neff or Caruso. The High Performance honorees were 6'4" Mark Greaves and 6'1" Phil Goedeker, both of Vianney, and 6'5" Frank Masek of CBC. All are outside hitters.

High Performance coach Frank Buggs made good use of his entire roster, which also featured: Doug Cox, a 5'10" setter from Hazelwood Central; Michael Getz, 6'6" hitter-setter, Parkway North; Rico Lange, 5'11" defensive specialist, Vianney; and Drew Zabek, 6'5" hitter, Oakville. Four have committed to NCAA Division I volleyball schools.

Greaves, the *Post-Dispatch* Metro Player of the Year, is off to Ohio State. Caruso and Masek will play at Quincy. Getz is headed to Findlay in Ohio. Neff is uncommitted but is being wooed by Ohio State and California-Irvine. Goedeker turned down Quincy—to the dismay of Caruso and Masek—to stay home at Missouri Baptist, which plays an NAIA small-college schedule. And Zabek, the team's only junior, will be a D-I recruit next year.

The team drew from volleyball bloodlines. Neff's older sister, Katie, starred at Cor Jesu and just finished her sophomore year at Notre Dame as a 6'4" middle blocker. Getz is the cousin of Jeff Getz, who starred on the Missouri Thunder 18s that placed fifth five years ago—and plastered St. Louis boys volleyball onto the national map. The Thunder team was brimming with D-I players such as Getz, Tim O'Connell, Rob Steinkhuler, Tom Tegethoff and Marty Zambo. That group looked like a rugby team. Steinkhuler, a 270-pound lineman at Mehlville, turned down a football scholarship to Southwest Mizzouri State. Zambo, built like a 6'5" a tight end, once broke a volleyball with a monstrous spike.

By contrast, this High Performance bunch fits the stereotype of the gangly, jangly, California beach player. That's why this crew bounced into the finals with no sense of awe for Long Beach Club, or LBC, as the volleyball dynasty is known. That's also why the St. Louisans did little celebrating at a post-tourney party at Cox's house in North County. They gathered almost grimly, more than a week after the finale, to mutter about what might have been. Or should have been.

"I keep telling myself that second is good," Caruso said. "But first would have been better."

And sweeter. The St. Louisans were long shots, seeded fifth among the 40 teams. The top seed was LBC, with its hotshot roster, storied history and corporate sponsors to pick up the travel tabs.

"But they were scared of us," said Caruso. "They knew we were the only team in the gym that could beat them. Before the match, they'd always run around doing a cheer. But they quit that when they got to us."

They're No. 2…High Performance teammates from left, Drew Zabak, Joe Caruso, Andrew Neff, Doug Cox, Michael Getz and Frank Masek Jr.
(Photo by Trisha L. Siddens)

"They'd stare at us in warmups," Cox said. "I think they were staring in awe."

"We were the best team there," said Scott Niebruer, the High Performance club director who assisted Buggs on the bench.

All of that is more than runner-up bluster. Two years ago, Caruso, Cox, Goedeker, Greaves and Masek played for Missouri Thunder, the Open champ at 16 and under.

"But it's a huge jump to 18s," said Zabek, the team's lone 17-year-old.

"It's always California then," Cox said.

For many reasons.

"They recruit all over the state," Zabek said, "and they have a much bigger area. They have a ton of guys playing volleyball out there, and they play 'sand' all the time. When they come indoors, the best guys all combine. Here in St. Louis, you have the 10 to 15 guys you know who play volleyball, and they're a team."

Not always. Sometimes positions overlap and personalities collide. Then the top St. Louis boys split into two or three camps.

"The year that Tommy Tegethoff and Marty Zambo played, they had the best players in St. Louis on that team," Niebruer said. "This year, we had the best players in St. Louis."

They looked like the best team in the country as the finals match began. The setup is best of three games. Teams play to 25 points in the first two games, win by two points or more, and to 15 points if a third game is needed. The St. Louisans were in control in the first game, winning 26-24 after leading 24-19.

"That's the best game we ever played," Cox said.

At that point, the team was 19-3 in Louisville and a game away from the gold medal and a perfect 8-0 match record. Their momentum got a big push from the crowd in Louisville. Even though Long Beach Club, with several entries in the younger age groups, had a formidable cheering section.

"That first game, all the parents from LBC were stunned," said Sandy Zabek, Drew's mother. "Their fans are always so loud. Kids on the other teams in the stands were chanting, 'Why are you so quiet? Why are you so quiet?'"

The St. Louisans had the vocal support of Midwest rivals like Sports Performance in Chicago and North Shore in Milwaukee, rooting against the California monopoly.

"But even other California teams were cheering for us," Neff said. "They hate LBC because they win all the time."

The St. Louisans had other appealing qualities.

"They're very nice young men," said Sandy Zabek, Drew's mom. "Even the ones who aren't my children."

To be fair, so was the Long Beach Club.

"They were a good bunch of guys," Caruso said.

And a great bunch of players. LBC, whose middles were nearly as tall as Caruso and Neff, took Game 2 in a 25-16 breeze.

"They block," Cox said. "We got blocked like eight times."

The St. Louisans bounced back in Game 3, the 15-point rubber game. The score was dead even at the halfway mark when the favorites caught a break.

"It's 8-8," Cox said, "and I set Joe. He threw the ball off this kid's hand for LBC, but the refs didn't see it. They said we hit it out. So now we're down 9-8 instead of being up 9-8. That was a big point."

"There was a stoppage of play," Neff said. "The fans were yelling. We were yelling. We argued about it, but it didn't do any good."

When play resumed, they lost two quick points to go down 11-8. Did they lose the momentum because they lost concentration?

"Basically," Masek said.

LBC took four of the next seven points to win the game, 15-11, and the gold.

"Rematch!" Neff said.

That's all the team could think about on the safari back from Louisville.

"It was an especially long ride," Caruso said, "when we were stuck in a traffic jam for three hours. There was a wreck on the interstate and we couldn't move."

Once home, no one has moved to pop in the finals video. The next time most of them see each other in person on a court, they'll be across a college net. Ohio State, Quincy and Findlay are all in the same volleyball conference. For Neff and Caruso, those facedowns will be stressless compared to the glares of some DeSmet basketball backers.

"I played two years," said Neff, whose father played college basketball. "I guess I was decent. My sophomore year, I broke my ankle during the season. And then I just lost interest."

Club volleyball season kicks in after January 1, overlapping the last half of basketball season.

"I started feeling more comfortable with volleyball," said Neff, who lists his exact height at 6'9½". "People would say, 'You've got to play basketball because you're so tall.' One of the teachers came up to me once and asked if I was lost. He said, 'The weight room's over there.'"

Caruso bailed out of basketball a year earlier.

"I dislocated my knee freshman year—playing volleyball," said Caruso, who was then 6'4". "The dislocation gave me an excuse not to play basketball. To be honest, I didn't really like the basketball program at DeSmet.

"I had fun for a little bit, but I don't think the coaches liked me. I didn't really have any plans to play it. I liked water polo and swimming, which is in the winter, too."

As a senior, DeSmet won the state swim meet as Caruso won four medals, a silver in the 50 freestyle and a gold and two silvers in relays. He was first team All-Metro in the pool. He was also first-team All-Metro on the volleyball court, alongside Greaves, Getz and Goedeker. Zabek was second team All-Metro along with Masek, who turned down a personal appeal from CBC basketball coach Bob McCormack.

"Coach McCormack was nice about it," Masek said. "He talked to me outside the weight room and asked if I was interested. They were small this year. I wanted to swim instead."

Masek laughed and said, "But I was injured this year, so I couldn't beat Joe."

Without Neff and Caruso, DeSmet couldn't beat Vashon in the state basketball finals, losing in a record rout. And what if DeSmet had its two big boys in the middle of the basketball, instead of the volleyball, court?

"Yeah, it would have been different," Caruso said. "If we were on the floor, it would have been 40 points, maybe, not the 50 they lost by."

40

DAN ROGERS

Dream Come True on Hockey Stats Crew

Thirty years ago in South County, all that little Danny Rogers thought about was hockey. He learned to read by paging through Blues programs. He listened to every game on the radio. His room was painted Blues blue. His mom made him NHL curtains by stitching team logos onto plain material. Slapshot practice in the driveway forced his dad to replace two battered garage doors.

In the 1970s, youth hockey was still a fledgling sport here. Teams, rinks and ice time were not so prevalent. The only team with a spot for young Dan practiced on Sunday mornings at the Affton Ice Rink. Both of his parents taught Sunday school when practice was scheduled. They were willing to let him miss class, but they could not break away to ferry him to and from practice. They gently asked him if would consider dropping out, and so he did. Thirty years later, Dan is part of the 2002 Olympic hockey tournament in Salt Lake City. Not on the ice, but far above it.

"My husband laughs at me," said Nelda Rogers, Dan's mom, "but I like to think that Dan's reward for not playing hockey on Sunday morning was to go to Salt Lake City. And my reward is that he's there as a statistician and not as a player."

There was no danger of him being in harm's way on the ice. Even though Dan, now 37, eventually wound up making the Mehville High varsity as a defenseman.

"I played three years, and not very well," he said by phone from Provo, Utah, during the Olympics. "My dad accused me of spending more time tripping over the blue line than anything else. And my mom wouldn't come to the games. She just hated it. She thought it was too rough."

Call it divine intervention, his own initiative or dumb luck. But Dan is among just eight off-ice officials chosen by the National Hockey League to help the local minor-league and college crews for Olympic men's and women's hockey. The eight-man NHL roster includes Tom Hoy, 62, of South County, and Brian Varady, 28, of Mascoutah. Both are off-ice officials for Blues games at Savvis Center.

"It's the chance of a lifetime," said Tom, who served as an official scorekeeper at ice level at the E Center in Salt Lake.

"It's been incredible, just awesome," said Brian, a hockey novice until his Blues internship with then-publicity director Jeff Trammel, a fellow McKendree College grad.

"It certainly has been the experience of a lifetime," rasped Dan.

His job was to log shots on goal, blocked shots and missed shots for 17 men's and women's games in Provo, as Varady did in Salt Lake. But Dan also had to bark out the faceoff winners to a non-savvy member of his crew. He almost lost his voice from shouting over the crowd at The Peaks, a 6,000-seat barn.

Dan, by the way, is not part of the crew from his beloved Blues. He reached the Olympics—and the NHL—by way of Nashville, of all places. He had quit playing organized hockey when he left to attend William Jewell College near Kansas City. He then got his business degree and returned to work in St. Louis, where he spectated at 15 to 20 Blues games per season. Then Dan was transferred south four and a half years ago by State Auto Insurance, where he is a policy underwriter. He and his wife, Monica, a Parkway North graduate, have no children. So when he learned that the minor-league Ice Flyers were coming to Nashville, she encouraged him to call the club, sound unseen.

"I was too dumb to know any better," Dan said. "I got some secretary and told her, 'Hey, I played several years of hockey up north, and I know the game very well, so if you need off-ice officials…'"

Two days before the season opener, he got a callback. The expansion Predators hit town the next year, and Rogers applied. Again, he heard nothing until just before camp began. Even though he is not "a true computer geek," as he put it, the club chose him as its computer "trainer." This high-tech foreman helps each crew record the expanded, "real-time" stats package that the NHL premiered in 1998.

Then in November 2000, NHL chief statistician Benny Ercolani needed volunteers for a week-long international tourney in Salt Lake. Their job was to snap in minor-league and college crews from Utah on the NHL real-time system, which would be used in the Olympics. Ercolani wanted no slippage in his NHL game stats. So he only recruited from crews that had no NHL home games for that November week in Salt Lake. This bit of luck—or divine intervention, as Dan's mom would say—is why recruits were pulled only from crews in Nashville, St. Louis, Calgary, New Jersey and San Jose. Obviously, the Salt Lake locals wanted to fill as many seats as possible on the Olympic stat crews. Members of the SLOC, the Salt Lake Organizing Committee, spelled that out to the NHL arrivals that November.

As Tom put it, "We were told by the Salt Lake organizers, 'Keep your mouth shut about being from the NHL.'"

And the NHL crews were, in fact, resented.

"But that was before they knew us," Hoy said. "The guys on the crews here are the ones who went to the SLOC people and said, 'We want these NHL guys back.' Hey, we've made some great friends here. I invited my crew chief and his wife out to St. Louis for a Blues game and a barbecue."

The eight NHL gurus brought more than expertise.

Ercolani, the NHL stats meister, gushed, "The SLOC people said to me, 'We'd really like to use these people of yours for the Olympics. Not only for their qualifications, but also for the type of people they are.'

"They care about their job, but they're good people, too. Like Danny Rogers. He called me the other day from the Olympics just to say, 'Benny, I don't know how to thank you. We're having a blast.'"

Dan switched to the E Center, the main hockey venue in Salt Lake, for the Canada-Belarus men's semifinal on Friday and the bronze medal game on Saturday. That rink is where Brian, a software engineer for Mitek Industries in Chesterfield, witnessed the miracle of this Olympiad. Top-seeded Sweden lost 4-3 to tiny Belarus in possibly the greatest upset in the history of frozen water. The winning goal came on a shot from center ice that clanked off the noggin of goalie Tommy Salo, an NHL All-Star with the Edmonton Oilers.

"That was incredible," said Brian. "Two minutes before that happened, one of the guys on our crew said, 'Belarus just needs a freak goal, just bounce one in off someone's head.' He was as shocked as I was when it actually happened."

As hockey miracles go, that probably outranks the 30-year odyssey of Dan Rogers to the Salt Lake Olympics. His own vote for divine intervention does involve Sunday school, but not the one that seemed to end his hockey career at the Affton Ice Rink.

"I met my wife at Parkway Baptist Church," Dan said. "My sister went there and said they had a big singles department in Sunday School. So I went...and it worked!"

41

NICK VOGT

Grappling with the Loss of a Friend

Wrestling is supposed to be an individual sport. But not for Nick Vogt. Not in the 2002 season. Not with boyhood sidekick Tyler Wolk with him in spirit for what should have been their freshman season in the flesh at Meramec Community College.

Nick was wrestling for two, all the way to a No. 2 finish at the National Junior College Athletic Association tournament. Nick lost 8-5 in the 125-pound finals to James Rollins of Gloucester County (N.J.) College. By placing in the top eight of the 32-man field, Nick made Juco All-America.

"I do think he was on a mission this year," said Meramec coach Ron Mirikitani. "Tyler would have been very proud of how he performed."

Nick figured that Tyler would have been wrestling right there beside him at nationals.

"I think he would have had a shot," Nick said, "just from the way he liked to work and the way he liked to win."

They did a lot of both at Ste. Genevieve High School, winning individual state championships as seniors on a team that placed second in Class 3-A. To help balance the team, Tyler wrestled up at 215 pounds, giving away more than 25 pounds and still winning the heavyweight title.

They were headed to Meramec to team up again, as they had since Tyler first talked Nick onto the mat in seventh grade. Mirikitani still chuckles at the sight of the big extrovert and little introvert on their odd-couple recruiting visit.

"Tyler did all the talking and laughing," Mirikitani said. "He was a really, really neat kid. Nick is a neat, neat young man, too. He doesn't say a lot, but he's really smart. He's a brilliant math student. He's very, very intense. And he does not like to lose."

But life is not a game to be beaten, a lesson Nick had shoved at him on June 2, 2001. Just past 4 a.m. that day, Tyler was riding south on Interstate 55 with friends. They were making the hour-long trip from St. Louis, where he was fixing up an apartment for college, to Ste. Gen, where he would be graduating that night with Nick and the rest of the class of '01. The car crashed on Interstate 55 after the driver apparently fell asleep. The other boys escaped serious injury. Tyler was killed.

"There was no drinking involved," said Mirikitani. "There was no foul play or anything. They just had an accident."

John Buffington, then a first-year assistant on the Ste. Gen wresting team, phoned with the grim news for Nick and younger brother Adam, also a top wrestler on the team.

"They both got on the line," Buffington said, "and I told them what happened. I could hear them both crying."

"He was talking to me and my brother," Nick said, "and he asked us if we were okay. I don't even remember what happened after that."

Graduation night turned from a celebration into a wake for Tyler.

"I remember that his cousin had a picture of him and a couple of other guys out having fun," Nick said. "That's all I remember from graduation. Except for everybody crying."

Nick and Tyler had always been good friends, not best friends. But they had always been the best of teammates.

"I was actually better friends with his cousin, Derrick Wolk," said Nick. "But if Tyler and me bumped into each other at the movies or the bowling alley, we'd always talk and have a good time.

"And when we were at wrestling meets, when we weren't wrestling, Tyler was always goofing around, making everyone laugh. He always had some story, some little weird thing he'd do to keep everybody loose.

"You never knew what he was going to do. I was the serious one on the team. When I won state last year, he gave me a real big hug. And he

Nick Vogt, shown here controlling his opponent on the mat, is on his own but not alone.
(Photo by Bob Frischmann)

whispered, 'We beat Helias!' That was the first time we had ever beaten them."

While out-pointing the Jefferson City rival, Ste. Gen placed second in the team standings.

Then Tyler and Nick chose Meramec instead of a four-year school in part because of the scholarship money and chance to compete as freshmen.

"But he was probably the reason I was coming here," Nick said. "So I had somebody to wrestle with that I knew."

As the numbness from Tyler's loss began to fade, Nick could not see himself at Meramec as a solo act.

"I sat down for just a couple days, thinking," he said. "But I knew I had to keep moving. I knew I had to come up here anyway. That's what he'd want me to do, I think. I'm really close to his family, and his dad wanted me to come up here and wrestle."

In fact, Jeff Wolk had specific marching orders for his son's partner. "His dad told me, 'Go up there and show them what Ste. Gen is all about,'" Nick said softly.

He also drew on the support of his own wrestling family. Nick's dad, Norman Vogt, was a state qualifier at Fox High School. Kid brother Adam, as a Ste. Gen senior, succeeded Nick as the Class 3-A champ at 125 pounds. Youngest brother Jonathan has also started wrestling. And an uncle, Mickey Wright, was a two-time All-American at Meramec in the late 1980s. Nick hit the Meramec wrestling room with a vengeance. Mirikitani, accustomed to hard workers in his 32-year reign at the school, was impressed.

"Nick was a very dedicated young man," he said. "He trained very, very hard."

Others might call it self-motivation. Nick felt Tyler's invisible hand pushing him onward.

"I like to think of him when I'm out there working out," Nick said. "Sometimes when I feel like stopping, or when I get little bumps and bruises, I just work through them. I can't let them get in my way. That's what he used to say when we were working out back home."

Nick wrestled in seven tournaments, including the postseason, and placed in the top six every time. That does not mean his young career was a straight arrow to the national finals. His first setback came in the second week of the season.

"It was an open tournament at Central Missouri State," said Mirikitani, "and they had this Russian who was world-class. Nick got beat 17-nothing. Most kids would have been devastated. I had a kid last year, a three-time state tourney champ, who got pinned in his first tournament and quit. He couldn't handle losing.

"Nick got beat 17-nothing, and he went and won his next six matches in a row. And he pinned five of them. And he took third in the tournament. That's how tough this kid is. That's the kind of kid I'm looking for."

All Nick said about that reversal was, "I figured if I could win six matches in a row at a tournament like that, I could do pretty good."

And he did. Until he derailed in a late-season dual meet in Ellsworth, Iowa.

"I was 2-2," Nick said, "and I wrestled really bad. I wasn't even coachable. I was scared after that, because the season was almost over."

Assistant coach David Mirikitani, Ron's son, snapped Nick out of his funk.

"David just told me that he hoped that was my bad tournament, and that it was better to get it out that weekend than at zones or nationals," Nick said.

All the while, he knew Tyler Wolk was in his corner.

"I thought about him when I go to sleep and stuff," Nick said. "He gets me more fired up for the next day."

Nick was on fire at the Central Zone Qualifying Tournament at Meramec. He was seeded third, with only the top two guaranteed a trip to nationals. First, he surprised the defending national runner-up. Then in the finals, he surprised a wrestler who had beaten him twice this season. Both times, Nick trailed in the second period. Both times, he gutted out an 8-6 victory. Both times, all the extra nudges from Tyler's spirit in the workout room gave Nick the extra oomph to pull an upset. Nick also had more tangible support that day from Ste. Gen. In the stands were his brother Adam, Derrick Wolk—on his way to third place at state—and Ste. Gen coach Chris Werner.

Then came nationals. Nick opened with a bye. Then he won his next two matches by pins to reach the Final Four and secure All-America honors, his season-long goal. The next day, he scored a 13-4 victory over Derek Jones of Colby (Kansas) College. Then came the finals against Rollins.

"I was nervous," Nick said. "I gave up a takedown early in the first period and let him get riding time. I got down by five points, and the rest of the match I was trying to catch up. At one time it was 6-5."

The rookie who lost 17-0 in Week 2 had shown everyone what Ste. Gen was all about.

"Well," said Nick, "I tried."

He was disappointed at falling short in the finals. But the pain was squeezed away by the friend who had never left his side.

"Yeah," said Nick, "he was giving me hugs."

And did Tyler Wolk whisper anything in his ear at these championships?

"No," Nick said. "But I think he would have thought I did a great job."

VALERIE BEESON

Harris-Stowe's Backstage Hall of Famer

n sports, the folks who work behind the scenes seldom get to take a bow. For 32 quietly exceptional years at Harris-Stowe College, Valerie Beeson was no exception. And then in the spring of 2002 in Kansas City, her cover was blown. The NAIA, formally known as the National Association of Intercollegiate Athletics, enshrined her in its Hall of Fame.

"My middle daughter, Aimee, came with me," said Valerie, who lives in University City. "She told me, 'All these people kept coming up to me after the presentation and talking about you. The reason I knew it wasn't your funeral is that they were saying *your mother is* and not *your mother was.*'"

There is no need for a funeral, at least in the athletic sense. As a Hall of Famer, Valerie is now immortal. Her citation was for meritorious service to the 332 NAIA small colleges, who still resist the heavy gravitational pull of the NCAA (National Collegiate Athletic Association). Her Hall of Fame plaque will hang in the new NAIA offices in Kansas City.

Jim Velten, a former Harris-Stowe athletic director, said no Hall of Famer is worthier than his gentle mentor.

"Fabulous. The best. Absolutely," said Velten, now athletic director at Kirkwood High. "Valerie is *the* source authority for NAIA rules and

regulations. And not just at Harris-Stowe. Everyone around the country would call her when they had a question. Hey, people from the NAIA office would call her when *they* didn't know something."

A year before her induction, NAIA headquarters called with the most flattering request of all.

"She was running the NAIA for several weeks as acting director," Velten said. "They wanted her to take over full-time, but she's retired now. She doesn't need that aggravation."

Most of all, Valerie is too beholden to her beloved Harris-Stowe. Even in retirement. She officially stepped down last year from her day job as director of admissions and advisement. She also stepped aside from her non-paying job as faculty representative to the NAIA. At age 61, she still reports daily to Harris-Stowe as a consultant to students, coaches and colleagues. She is proud of her award, not for her sake but because it highlights Harris-Stowe. Even though the school was an NAIA founding member in 1937, she is its first Hall of Famer. She hopes to see her framed copy displayed in Harris-Stowe's new Physical Education and Performing Arts Center, a jewel on the cozy campus on Market Street not far from Union Station.

"I hope our students can see this," she said, taking her award out of its wrapping, "and know that anything is possible."

They may also sense that the best competitors don't always wear sneakers and sweatshirts and snarl in the line of duty. Well, she actually has done her share of polite snarling in the best interests of Harris-Stowe students.

"Boy, she will defend her kids to the death," Velten said. "She is so good for the kids. Black or white, boys or girls, she is indiscriminate. The kids just love her. And she loves athletes and athletics."

So much so that Velten, stumped on eligibility issues for his volleyball team, once had Valerie check his paperwork from her hospital room. She had just left intensive care after major surgery. He then sent her flowers with a note that said, "The eligible athletes of Harris-Stowe thank you."

To which she said, "What about the ineligible athletes?"

In fact, the ineligibles were always kept to a minimum with Valerie on the prowl as faculty athletic rep. She originally was dragooned in 1978 for temporary duty.

Valerie Beeson (right) with Harris-Stowe colleagues Mary Jones (left) and Kathie Kinderfather.
(Photo courtesy of Harris-Stowe State College)

As she recalled, "One of our vice presidents called and said, 'We need somebody to fill in these forms for our athletics. You go to all the games. You know all the kids. And you can add 12 and 12.'

"I said, 'Oh, sure, I can do that.' Then he dropped this big book on my desk. I said, 'What's this?' He said, 'A book of rules.' I said, 'You need rules to add 12 and 12?' He said, 'Well, it's a little more than that.'"

It was also more than temporary, unless that term can stretch to cover 23 years. Along the way, she chaired the Eligibility Committee for the America Midwest Conference, the former Show-Me Conference, where Harris-Stowe competes. At the NAIA she served in a half-dozen major roles, including the chair of the Conduct and Ethics Committee, plus the Faculty Athletic Representative Association. Those jobs sound deadly dull.

"Yes, there's paper involved," Valerie said, "but 99 percent of it is people. It's a way to stay involved with people. Good people."

Her job went far beyond telling coaches which players could suit up for the next game.

As Valerie put it, "Somebody told me once, 'Students won't care how much you know unless they know how much you care.' I always felt it was necessary to learn the whole student, not just what each one did in class or on a team.

"It's not, 'You are eligible, hooray!' Or, 'You are not eligible, boo!' It's, 'You are not eligible this semester, so let's see what we can do to get your grades up and get you eligible next semester.'"

This is clearly one New Yorker—her accent is a dead giveaway—who can never be accused of being cold and aloof. Valerie was in fact born in Brooklyn, raised on Long Island and educated at the College of New Rochelle in Westchester County, New York. She ventured across the Mississippi River to attend graduate school at the University of Arkansas. She then migrated north to St. Louis because of "a spouse who is no longer a spouse."

Her then-husband had a job waiting. So did Valerie, as it turned out.

"I saw in the *Post-Dispatch* that there was a math opening at Harris Teachers College, due to the death of a professor," she recalled. "So I called the school, innocently, and asked if they had a vacancy in the math department. They said, 'You won't believe this, but one of our professors just died.'"

Valerie managed to suppress her shock long enough to join the faculty in September of '69. Her marriage dissolved, but her bond to her little college did not.

"The last 32 years have been a labor of love between me and Harris-Stowe College," Valerie said. "I would like for us to get more respect as an institution, because I think we deserve it. If I didn't, I wouldn't have stayed 32 years. It's the best-kept secret in town. It just sounds so platitudinous, but Harris-Stowe has a purpose and a mission that can't be beat. And our mission keeps expanding in the metropolitan area here."

She proudly traced the school's evolution from a teacher's college, to an option for black students in a once-segregated world, to an outlet now for adults to widen or sharpen their workday skills.

"We have over 1,900 students," Val said, "and their average age is 28. A lot of them are non-traditional. We have business people, accountants, health-care professionals who want to add to their professional skills. The challenge is making sure that their class schedules can accommodate their work and their families. And a lot of our younger students have part-time jobs, too."

Velten put the issue more bluntly:

"Harris-Stowe has kids who couldn't make it anywhere else. Not because they're not capable. They just have other issues, like money or family situations. At Harris-Stowe, Valerie and a lot of other great people like her can give these kids the attention they need."

Valerie, by the way, was no math nerd. She played field hockey and basketball as a schoolgirl, back when female perspiration was frowned upon in this country.

"We played six-on-six basketball in high school," she said, "where only three players on each team could cross midcourt."

She and Kathie Kinderfather, a longtime colleague at Harris-Stowe, once described those quaint times in a seminar on the history of sports. "This was in the 1970s," said Val, "and the kids looked at us like we were from the 1600s."

That is no indictment of kids in the '70s. Or of today, for that matter.

"They want to get better," Val said. "They want a quality education. They want to graduate. And they want to be productive citizens."

She can see beyond the skin-deep changes in the student body, with its tattoos and piercings on males and females.

"Hey, I went through the 1960s," Val said with a laugh. "If you see the kids all the time, you sort of mellow with them. If I'd been in a cocoon for 10 years and suddenly burst out, I'd be surprised. When you take it day by day, it's a little easier to adjust. And it's easier when they're somebody else's children!"

For the record, Valerie found time to raise three successful daughters: Audra, Aimee and Adrienne, who range from 31 to 24 years old. She also has one grandchild, Audra's daughter, Olivia. Her extended family starts with Harris-Stowe but stretches far beyond.

"She embraces everybody who ever works there or goes to school there," Velten said. "You should see the people who come to her office, who left Harris-Stowe and come back just to talk and get a hug.

"She could walk into any police station or firehouse in St. Louis and have former students coming up to talk to her. Hey, not everyone who goes to college becomes a professional person."

And, needless to say, not every math teacher goes on to become an athletic immortal.

43

BRUCE COOK

From Figure Skates to Football Cleats

Bruce Cook, Vianney's carnivorous linebacker, was born to be a football player. His great-grandfather, Jimmy Cook, from Dundee, Illinois, lettered in football at the University of Illinois from 1898 to 1902. Then he veered into big-league baseball in 1903 as a backup infielder with the Tinkers-to-Evers-to-Chance Chicago Cubs. Bruce's grandfather, David Cook, played quarterback at Soldan High (for his father, Jimmy Cook), then starred at fullback for the University of Illinois from 1931 to 1933 and joined the NFL's Chicago Cardinals from 1934 to 1936. Bruce's dad, Dave, starred at Southwest High and lettered as a backup nose tackle for Darrell Royal at the University of Texas. Dave, who still wears his Cotton Bowl watch, also was a standout wrestler at UT and later coached football, track and wrestling at Southwest High.

So 15 years ago, when David Bruce Cook toddled out to play at age three, he instinctively tackled the harshest sport in the family tree: Figure skating. Bruce decided to follow in the skates of his sister Beth, then aged eight and already a veteran at the Brentwood Ice Arena.

"Beth was in all the skating shows," recalled June Cook, their mom. "Bruce thought they looked like fun. Plus, Beth was getting all the attention. Bruce always did like to show off."

Bruce Cook on skates at age six, foreshadowing his football future.
(Photo courtesy of Cook family)

And so an impish tyke wobbled onto the ice in rental skates. He left a decade later, groomed to become the light-footed, heavy-hitting lynchpin of Vianney's first Metro Catholic Conference champions.

"Figure skating did help me," Bruce said. "It made me a better athlete all around."

"I really think Bruce developed his leg and butt muscles from figure skating," said June. "And his balance. Hockey players and football players don't have that center of gravity."

Bruce was a six-foot-one, 217-pound driving force at Vianney, which won its first outright M.C.C. title in 2002. Quick to the ball, he led

Vianney in solo tackles, total tackles and interceptions. Bruce also pitched in at fullback, his grandfather's position. Heading into districts, he rushed 30 times for 106 yards and two touchdowns and is a first-down machine on third-and-short situations. This fourth-generation football player is not just good for an ex-skater. He's good, period.

"There aren't many linebackers around here better than Bruce Cook," said Vianney coach Gene Gladstone. "He has great footwork. The figure skating definitely helped him with that."

Bruce also inherits athletic ability from his mother's family. Herman Giesecke, June's grandfather, was a half-miler at the 1904 Olympics in St. Louis. But June, a nurse, is resigned to the over-riding football gene. She is thrilled that her only son tried at least one sport that stressed grace over grunting. Dave, now coordinator of athletics for the Public High League, had no qualms about his only son starting off in a predominantly female sport.

"I was just glad he was wanting to do something," said Dave.

Both parents applaud the lessons that both of their children learned on ice. The learning curve arched far beyond coordination.

"It teaches them a lot of discipline," June said. "And learning to win and lose with dignity."

It also bred toughness.

"There were 10 little boys in Bruce's learn-to-skate class at Brentwood," June said. "That first day, the minute they stepped onto the ice they went in 10 different directions. It was like a beehive had dispersed. They were on their ankles, on their faces, on their butts."

Bruce quickly got his feet under him. The falls came harder when he began practicing the various jumps. He stuck with it. Along with freestyle skating against other boys, Bruce and a girl partner competed in pairs events.

"People say that football is so rough," said June. "But when Bruce started playing he always said, 'This isn't as rough as figure skating. When you fall in football, you have pads on. When you fall in figure skating, you have nylon pants on.'"

The roughest stuff about skating was not physical. It was the razzing Bruce took. But the toughest guff didn't come from boys outside the rink.

"My friends didn't care, once they saw how I played football and soccer," said Bruce.

"The girl skaters were actually more abusive," said June.

"I guess I just had better-looking legs than they did," Bruce said.

Actually, June said, "A lot of them were upset because he started getting better than they were. They couldn't accept that. The girls were always better than most boys who came out there."

At about age 10, Bruce decided to outfox his female detractors. At a competition, he finished his pairs routine and hustled off to change for a freestyle event. A female freestyle event.

"I dressed as a girl and put a wig on with a pony tail," he said. "I put my name in as Jennifer Cook. My coach, Jennifer Thompson, was the only one who knew."

The unsuspecting judges ranked him first. He stood atop the podium with the other medalists, grinning for a photo that went straight to his scrapbook.

"Then I took the wig off," Bruce said. "Everyone was shocked. My pairs partner didn't even know who I was."

Finally, at age 13, Bruce swapped his figure skates for hockey skates. By that time, he was most smitten by his youth football league at Jefferson Barracks.

"I've enjoyed it ever since I started," he said. "I was five years old, playing in the eight-year-old division. We have a picture of me smiling in my uniform."

He was even happier in a uniform than in a skating costume. Two years ago at Vianney, he was the only sophomore promoted to the varsity. Strangely, he is not the only ex-figure skater on the team. Or even in the backfield. Steve Walther, another rugged senior fullback, skated for four years at the South County Rec Center.

"It's something my mom got me started with," said Walther, a solid six-foot 208-pounder. "She just wanted me to do as many things as possible when I was little."

Gladstone, built more like a Zamboni than a Scotty Hamilton, is a true believer.

"Given the quality of these two kids," said the coach, "I'm going to recruit figure skaters. They're both tough as nails."

44

BOB HAIDA

The Prosecutor Holds Court

On a good day, half of the people that Bob Haida serves are mad at him. And that's a good day. Haida is the State's Attorney for St. Clair County. In other jurisdictions, his job is called prosecuting attorney, circuit attorney or district attorney.

"Sometimes in my job, you don't make anybody happy," said Bob. "One side, they think the sentence should be higher. And the other side, the defendant's family, they don't think you should give any time to their loved one."

So what does he do for relaxation? Another activity where he has a chance to alienate everybody. He just finished his third year as volunteer coach of the sixth-grade boys' basketball team at Emge School in Belleville.

Coaching youth sports is often a thankless job. As Abe Lincoln would say if given a whistle and clipboard: You can make some of the people—kids and parents—happy some of the time. But you are most likely to make most, if not all, of the people unhappy most, if not all, of the time. That's why Bob started coaching on a trial basis, so to speak. That, and being leery of coaching his older son, Tyler, in his second year with the team. Instead of more worries, Bob wound up with the experience of his basketball lifetime. And that includes his playing days as a six-foot-four star at Belleville East High and at McKendree College.

"I'm getting a huge kick out of it," said Bob, who planned to return for the next season, when younger son Brian will be a sixth grader.

Bob agreed to be interviewed not as a know-it-all, but as a novice whose experiences might help other apprehensive new coaches.

"I've found that most kids, if you treat them with respect and you're fair, they'll give that back," Bob said. "I don't want to sound trite, but at this level kids aren't spoiled. They want to learn. They try hard.

"It's that old saying: The coach says 'Jump!' and they say 'How high?' At the pro level, you read about all the misdeeds of sport. At this level, a lot of that is eliminated. It's all about the kids having fun and playing a game."

It was less fun his first season. Bob could not break away from his day job to practice right after school. So the team had to work out after dinner.

"That was unsatisfactory from every aspect," he said. "I was zapped at the end of a work day. The kids were zapped at the end of a school day."

Bob, always an early riser, found the solution in the late start of the school day at Emge, where the first bell rings at 9 a.m. Why not practice before school, from 7:00 to 8:30? However, school officials were dubious.

"I understood that," Bob said. "It requires a lot of parental support. Parents have to get up around 6 a.m. and get the kids up and then drive them to practice."

He surveyed the parents to gauge their resistance. "There was none," he said. "Absolutely zero."

So any day that no game was scheduled, Bob held an early-bird practice. The best thing about a predawn start is that only motivated players show up. And some kids cut themselves during tryouts by refusing to set their alarms. Even so, 28 boys competed for 14 spots.

"That's was the hardest thing, to tell half the kids they didn't make the team," Bob said. "I have four or five days of tryouts, but I'm not perfect. I always use the Michael Jordan example, that he didn't make his freshman team in high school.

"I tell them, 'If you really want to be a basketball player, you can do it. Work hard. Prove that I made a mistake. Use the ability that's there.'"

Bob learned quickly that with preteen boys, the best athletes are often just the ones who won the race with puberty. They are not always the best when the rest of the class catches up. He fought the urge to separate the young men from the boys prematurely and permanently.

"I learned through my job," he said, "that it can be harmful to a case that you're working on if you draw too quick a conclusion about what a witness is thinking. Just because a kid's not the best player on the team in the tryouts, you don't want to jump to conclusions about how he'll do over the course of a season.

"The more time you spend with the kids, the more you can find out that some first impressions are mis-impressions. And even the most skilled players are still only 11 or 12. They're not ready for the NBA yet."

That was a tough sell to boys who could simply overpower their peers.

As Bob wryly recalled, "I would say, 'You guys have got a lot of work to do: free throws, footwork, boxing out.' And occasionally I'd get the hint back that, 'We're *already* pretty good...Hey, I just made that shot.'"

The novice coach had other battles to fight.

"In my opinion, the scourge of grade school basketball is the three-point line," Bob said. "So I had a rule. I said, 'You guys don't make 30 percent of your free throws. So if you launch one from back there, you'll have a seat next to me.'

"I found out later that one of the other coaches used it against me. We were talking after the game and I said we don't shoot three-pointers. And he said, 'Oh, I know. We told our players that you don't have to guard them at the three-point line. Make them drive.'"

Walking the tightrope between discipline and fun was a constant challenge.

"I had a rule that every minute you're late after seven o'clock, you have to run a lap," Bob said. "It was so cute. If it was 7:08, a boy would run in and say, 'How many, Coach?'

"One kid never wanted to be late. So guess what time he had his parents bring him...20 minutes of! So then I had to be there at 6:30 and get the gym lights on. It was a hilarious."

So was the pre-workout ritual.

"Before the practice officially started," Bob said, "they could do whatever they wanted, as long as they weren't hurting somebody or climbing on the backboards. They could shoot balls from half-court.

"Ideally, I'd want them to shoot free throws, but they're sixth graders. They need some time to be kids. Eventually, you'd see two kids playing one-on-one, and another group playing '21,' and another group playing 'knockout.' It was neat to see their personalities on who was getting along with who that morning."

One non-negotiable rule came from a higher authority. And Bob was a gung-ho supporter.

"At our school, grades are important," he said. "In our conference, even at the fifth and sixth grade level, kids can't participate in sports if their grades aren't up to a certain level. Every Friday during the season they run a grade check. We lost our best player for a week in the middle of the season because of a minor problem in one class."

His second season brought another stress test. His son, Tyler, moved into sixth grade and made the team.

"We survived the father-son thing," Bob said with a laugh. "I was probably more sensitive to that than anything else about coaching. I've seen situations where it hasn't been too positive. I did a lot of talking to parents who'd been through it, and I got a varied response. I had parents tell me, 'We've had some of our greatest success coaching our own kids.' And I had parents tell me it was a big mistake. So my son and I had discussions in advance. I told him, 'If we have disagreements, I'm a coach when I'm out there and you're a player.'"

Unlike many coaching dads, Bob was secure enough not to make points with his team by making life tougher on his own son. The coach stuck to a simple rule for playing time.

"In the first half, we used a rotation system," Bob said. "In the second half, whoever hustles and listens to my instructions gets to play. We never said we're playing to win. And you know what? We almost always ended up playing everyone the same in the second half. They all did such a good job."

And what about the win-loss record?

Bob never raised the topic until the end of the interview.

"Our first team was like 8-6," he said. "The second team was about the same. This year, we lost two games. But this year's team was undefeated the year before. They came in with full expectations. Winning is important to the kids."

To the coach of such young players, the major victory was the cooperation of players and parents.

"The thing that I learned," said Bob, "is that through your communication and your actions, you make it clear that everybody's treated the same."

Hear ye, hear ye.

KEITH PICKETT

Shootout Playmaker Hasn't Lost a Step

Young Keith Pickett was hoop-happy. Growing up in rural Council Grove, Kansas, he shot constantly at his driveway basket. By day, even in winter, after shoveling snow off the court and taking timeouts as needed to thaw his hands at the kitchen sink. By night, by the light he placed by climbing high in the elm tree overlooking midcourt. He made the high school varsity his last two years, a sometime starter at point guard.

Young Keith was fundamentally sound in anything he could practice in the driveway—passing, dribbling, shooting. A natural non-athlete, he was fundamentally lacking in physical gifts—running, jumping, heavy lifting.

Which is why, despite turning 54 just before the 2002 Shootout, the ex-kid can honestly say, "My game is the same as it was in high school. I haven't lost a step."

Neither has his love of high school basketball and the annual token of his affection—the Shootout. The 22nd annual event was cranking up, as usual, on the first week of December at Savvis Center. The lineup featured one girls' game and eight boys' games. As always, the field is split between area teams and national powers.

"The High Holy Day of Hoops," Blues president Mark Sauer reverently dubbed it. And he's not alone.

Fans making the annual pilgrimage range from Blues owner Bill Laurie of Columbia, Missouri, to Illinois State Senators Frank Watson (R-Greenville) and Dave Luechtefeld (R-Okawville), who once coached in the event. Joining them were 10 NBA scouts, college coaches like Quin Snyder of Missouri, Bill Self of Kansas and Roy Williams of North Carolina, and over 11,000 fans.

Pickett, who claims to be five foot nine, is coldly honest about his athletic limitations and all other matters. He is quick to note that he is the Shootout organizer, not its founder. He deflects that honor to Greg Rensinger, a 7-Up official, and Randy Albrecht, the men's basketball coach at Meramec Community College. They started the event in 1981 as a tripleheader for local teams. When attendance sagged in '84 they turned to Pickett, then in corporate communication at 7-Up. He coaxed his bosses to invest in high school hoops and used those extra bucks to fancy up the event. In came the most recognizable program in the country, Morgan Wootten's DeMatha behemoth from Washington, D.C. With it came star player Danny Ferry, son of former SLU great Bob Ferry, whose jersey hangs from the Savvis Center rafters. In came Chicago power Providence St. Mel. Suddenly, the Shootout had gone national, and fans savored the spicy new flavor.

Pickett charged ahead with that formula. He showcased local teams and their stars along with nationally ranked teams and stars. He works almost a full year ahead, scouting most Missouri and Illinois candidates himself and relying on a network of fellow hoop-a-holics for leads on national invitees. His lineup is set by May or June, with one opening kept in reserve. That way, if an unheralded player lights up the summer camp circuits, Pickett can bring the team in for a national coming-out party. Pickett makes his pairings according to interest...mainly his, because he has a fan's sense in these matters.

He loves regional Missouri-Illinois showdowns. He is always on the lookout for a local power to match with a national power. And he is on the alert for head-to-head billings, such as the celebrated "Alonzo-LaPhonso" duel between future NBAers Alonzo Mourning of Indian River, Va., and LaPhonso Ellis of East St. Louis Lincoln. The novelty act in 2002 was the first time Mizzou recruits ever squared off: Thomas Gardner of Portland (Oregon) Jefferson against Spencer Laurie, Bill Laurie's nephew, of Springfield (Missouri) Kickapoo. Pickett added a girls' game in '93 so that local fans could see Kristin Folkl of St. Joseph on her way to the WNBA. And, due to fan demand, at least one game matches two "long-distance" powers, as Pickett calls the best of the 48 other states.

For all of that, in modern sports lingo, the Shootout is year to year. One down year, from bad weather or bad karma, would not kill the event.

"But it would definitely affect us," he said. "That's why it's important to have other sponsors involved."

Shop 'N' Save and KMOX Radio are solid financial backers. But this is the event's fifth sponsorship group. The event has run the soft drink gamut from 7-Up to Coca-Cola to Pepsi, now a silent partner in the operation. Pickett has charged on through good economic times and bad. He absorbed rent hikes at Savvis, paid all expenses for long-distance teams, made do with Thursday dates when the Blues and Billikens got dibs on Saturdays, fended off a challenge from a local promoter and competed with the Rams—this town's 900-pound, ticket-gorging gorilla.

Until 1988, running the Shootout was Pickett's job for 7-Up. When the company was sold and moved to Dallas, he took over the Shootout himself. He won't reveal his financial take, except to say it varies from year to year. In some years, the event barely breaks even.

"Let me put it this way," he said. "Everybody else gets paid before I do."

His take-home shrinks because he insists on "doing everything first-class." That includes renting Savvis, which he calls the finest venue of any high school tournament. He also continues to pay airfare for any team with a drive over five hours. He also springs for lodging and meals at a major hotel, like this year's headquarters at the Drury Inn by the Arch.

"Some of these tournaments put teams up in cheap hotels and feed them fast food," Pickett said.

Other than expenses, long distance teams are not paid to play. The one out-of-town coach who asked to have his palm greased found his team quietly scratched from the lineup. Local teams do get a stipend equal to their average home gate.

"That's what the Missouri State High School Activities Association put in their guidelines," Pickett said, "so that's what we pay."

But teams that sell tickets beyond their stipend can keep the difference.

Pickett craves a Saturday date. But the Blues don't release their schedule until July and the Billikens follow a month or two later.

"We can't wait that long," he said.

He refuses to consider a Friday, because that night belongs to local boys' games. He designed the Shootout to promote local basketball, not compete against it. Besides, he loves to see the school and community spirit that comes when busloads of students and adult fans take the school day off to support their team.

"O'Fallon, Illinois, has sold 800 to 900 student tickets alone," Pickett said. "McCluer sold 600 or so. Troy is bringing a lot of kids, too. That wouldn't happen at night time. You wouldn't get that many kids."

He weathered the main storm, a frontal assault by St. Louis sports promoter Earl Wilson, who signed six top local programs to exclusive contracts for his own one-day tournament in December. That challenge lasted just three years. If Pickett is bitter about that, it doesn't show. But he is sad that local fans—not to mention his cash register—missed out on NBA lottery pick Darius Miles of East St. Louis and at least two years of Jimmy McKinney-led Vashon. But, as Pickett pointed out, the Shootout wasn't the only loser.

"Vashon would have played Lincoln High of Dallas, which went on to be voted the national champion," Pickett said. "If Vashon had beaten them here, then they might have won the national title.

"Also, about half of the voters for the McDonald's All-Star Game come in every year for the Shootout. If Jimmy McKinney had played and had a great game, he might have been a McDonald's All-Star."

Wilson still has exclusive contracts with several schools, including Vashon, for a Martin Luther King Day tourney in January at Savvis.

"I don't know of anybody else in the country who signs teams to exclusive contracts," Pickett said. "We'd never do that. The more exposure the kids get, the better."

The Shootout is also at the mercy of various state associations.

"We can never have teams from Georgia, Iowa or Ohio," Pickett said. "They can't go out of state during the week. That's why we couldn't get LeBron James. He'll be the No. 1 pick in the NBA draft this year, and his coach really wanted to come, but his school is in Akron, Ohio.

"Michigan has a 300-mile travel limit, and New Jersey doesn't start until the 15th of December. Those states have some great teams, and we can't ever get them."

But the Shootout does get the best of much of the rest. In the first 21 years, the event showcased 64 future NBA draft picks, including 25 first-rounders. A whopping 61 Shootout teams have ended their season with a state title. And in the last 10 years, five Shootout teams wound up No. 1 in the *USA Today* rankings.

After 22 years of practice, Pickett's stewardship is fundamentally sound. And his step is actually livelier when he hears the atta-boy comments from grateful fans.

"I have people tell me all the time that it's their favorite sports event, that they come every year with their kid or their buddies," Pickett said.

His favorite line was from a guy who, like most casual fans, can't keep up with the latest crop of schoolboy sensations around the country.

The fan told Pickett: "Going to the Shootout is like opening a big Christmas present. You don't know what it is till you open it up. But you know you're going to be surprised. And you know it's going to be good."

CAM JANSSEN

A Hockey Hit from Eureka

C am Janssen is a teen hockey sensation.

The latest of bloomers, he was virtually anonymous in his hometown of St. Louis. A 17-year-old from Eureka, Cam took his act north of the border to the cradle of hockey in 2001. The rookie right wing became an instant folk hero with the Windsor Spitfires of the Ontario Hockey League, usually considered the world's top junior loop. The Spits plucked him in the third round of the OHL draft. Local hockey watchers can't remember a local boy being chosen that high by any of Canada's three major-junior leagues.

Through his first 38 games in Windsor, Cam had two goals and seven assists. His minus-12 rating was the team's worst. He stands just five foot 11 and 190 pounds. He is a third-liner at best on a team with five National Hockey League draftees, including three first-round picks. Yet Cam is either Windsor's most popular player or in the top two, alongside Steve Ott, a Dallas Stars No. 1 pick. Folks in Windsor are smitten with this grinning import. From coach Tom Webster, to boys seeking autographs, men wearing Janssen jerseys, to girls leaving mash notes. What gives? It has something to do with Cam's robust play, namely a team-high 158 penalty minutes and 18 fights against all comers. It has more to do with his gung-ho approach to games, practices, public appearances and everyday life in a Canadian hockey town. It has everything to do with a happy, likeable, appreciative, sincere kid who—for lack of a more sophisticated term—is an original piece of work.

"He brings infectious, positive energy," said Bob Duff, sports columnist for the *Windsor Star*. "He's like a bowling ball on ice. He goes out of his way to crash into somebody. He's like a less refined Kelly Chase, if there is such a thing."

Cam is flattered to remind anyone of Chase, the popular ex-Blues enforcer, or any NHL player living or dead. The lad is bent on hammering out a name for himself. For now, the Spits and the OHL office still spell his surname with one "s" on all stats and literature. Cam would never gripe about that. Or anything else. He's had no worries since camp opened last summer and Spits officials blanched at his klunky skating. Was the rookie hurt? Sick? Overrated?

"No," Cam told them. "My skates don't fit. My agent gave me a new pair to take to camp. They were a gift, so I didn't want to tell him they were two sizes too big."

When asked about that yarn, Cam laughingly confirmed it with a plea to avoid embarrassment. But not his.

"My agent still doesn't know," he said. "You don't need to tell him, do you?"

Early in camp, the team asked the players for their equipment preferences. In Canada, junior stars have endorsement tie-ins, and even lesser lights have quirky requests for specific brands. But not Cam.

When the equipment manager came asking for stick choices, Cam chirped, "Right."

As in right-handed. Never mind the brand, or if it's made of wood or metal. That pond-hockey attitude has endeared him to blue-collar Windsor, located just across the border from Detroit. Webster, a grizzled former NHL head coach, found it refreshing.

"Absolutely, it is," Webster said. "He's just a great kid, very enthusiastic. He loves coming to the rink. He has a great time playing. He brings a lot of energy into our dressing room, and I love that. No matter how much he plays or how little he plays, he always gives you that energy.

"And he's got very good skills. He's strong on his skates"—after the club found him a pair that fit—"and he's got good hands. It's happening so quick for him. At times, I think it's a little overwhelming. There's a lot

NHL draftees on ice: from left, Jason Kostadine, Mike McKenna and Cam Janssen. (Photo by Don Adams Jr.)

to be done. He's trying to absorb it all and learn from it. You can see how intense he is."

That intensity has not been contagious enough. The highly touted Spits are light on results. With just 39 points in 42 games, they were 16th among 20 teams overall in the OHL and last in the West Division. To shake things up, the team recently sent center Jason Spezza, drafted second overall by the Ottawa Senators, to Belleville for forward Kyle Wellwood, the OHL's top scorer the previous year.

Cam stands out as a rising overachiever.

"Things are going really good," he said by phone from the Windsor home where he is billeted. "It's a big change. I've never really been away from home for more than a couple of weeks. But I'm having fun.

"The family I live with, Louis and Arlene Deschamps, are really great. At first it was kind of weird. My family at home was kind of lenient, and here I have to clean up after myself."

The new lodgings at first seemed to have compensations.

"They have five daughters," Cam said, "but they're all like 35 years old and married. It's too bad. But I go to Riverside High School here with two or three other guys from the team. The other kids kind of look up to us. We pretty much rule the roost. And the girls at school are great. They all like us."

Sound like a typical, self-absorbed teen? His parents, Dennis and Amy Janssen, were stunned when a reporter relayed the following testimonial. "If I get a pro contract," Cam said, "I'm going to buy them a house. My mom had her dream house, in the middle of the woods, with a cliff in the back and a creek, just a great setup. But it cost too much to keep me in Triple A hockey. So they gave it up and moved to a littler house. That's the only reason I'm up here. Because my dad spent all his money on me in Triple A, flying me up to a league in Michigan every weekend with the Junior Blues. That's where the OHL scouts saw me."

Dennis works in the family construction business. Amy said education, not finances, concerned her the most about her hockey son. Their other child, Jonathan, is a freshman at Southwest Missouri State leaning toward law.

"I fought with Cam for two years about his grades here," Amy said. "But if you love them, you have to support them. So I said, 'Go for your dream, but be ready for the consequences.'"

Meaning that if hockey fails, there is no college degree to fall back on.

"I told him, 'If you give it your all, it's okay,'" she said. "And he is just passionate about it. We never pushed him. How can it possibly happen to a kid who started skating at 10 or 11? I still have pictures of Jonathan and Cam, with these little feety pajamas and these little hockey sticks."

She is happy that the Spitfires combine hockey with high school: "They watch them like a hawk with their grades. And his billet family are just wonderful people."

As a mom, Amy worries about his ruffian role.

"You have coping mechanisms," she said. "You just cross your fingers and say a little prayer. I still won't watch his fights. I'm like, 'Do you have to do that?' And my older son says, 'Mom, that's how he has to get recognition, starting late and coming from the Midwest.'"

Where does he get that pugilistic skill?

"My dad's a tough character," Cam said, "and my mom's dad was a tough character, and it all mixes in the genes and comes down to me. That's what my dad says. Basically, you just have to be fearless and don't back down from anybody."

Dennis knows his son can handle himself: "I can't believe he hasn't broken his knuckles, punching those helmets. His agent said he's got a brick in both hands. Undoubtedly, he's got a brick in his helmet, too."

The family keeps it light, but Cam's career is no joke. Even if some local critics think so.

"You hear people say that he's just a goon," said Amy.

Those folks may be chomping on their words. Cam turns 18 in April and is eligible for the 2002 NHL Entry Draft in June. His name—with one "s" or two—could be on the board. His agent, Scott Norton of Kitchener, Ontario, is hearing good things from NHL scouts.

"I could go in the fifth or sixth round," said Janssen. "That's what my agent says."

As it turned out, Cam did better than that. He was taken in the fourth round, 117th overall, by the New Jersey Devils. They were impressed by his five goals and 17 assists...or by his league-high "34 or 35" fights and league-high 268 penalty minutes in just 64 games. Three other St. Louisans were drafted in 2002: Goalie Mike McKenna of Ballwin and St. Lawrence U., by the Nashville Predators in round six, 172nd overall; right wing Jason Kostadine of Manchester and Hull in the Quebec Major Junior League, by the Chicago Blackhawks in round eight, 251st overall; and center Yan Stastny of Chesterfield and Notre Dame U., by the Boston Bruins, round eight, 259th overall. Before that draft, only four St. Louisans had ever been drafted. The highest choice was defenseman Neil Komadoski of Chesterfield and Notre Dame, by the Ottawa Senators in 2001 in round three, 81st overall.

That makes Cam the second highest NHL draftee from St. Louis. Not bad for a teen hockey sensation from Windsor by way of Eureka.

47

JIM THOMPSON

From Tragedy to Coaching Hope

J im Thompson is a basketball coach of a different stripe. In the spring of 2002, he finished his rookie year as a head coach with the girls' varsity at Roosevelt High. Before that, he spent 12 years on the other side of the sideline as a high school referee in Illinois.

"There were some real changes for me this year," said Thompson.

Only some of them involved yelling at those in stripes instead of donning the stripes. Most of all, this season was a big step in the long process of moving past the loss of his wife, Peggy. She was murdered eight and a half years ago in a shooting while working at the couple's newly opened shop, 1st Lady Antiques, on Cherokee Street, not far from the Roosevelt campus in south St. Louis.

"It was August 14, 1993," said Thompson. "It took them four and a half years to solve the crime. The two guys are in jail now. She was only 33 when they killed her."

Thompson, 53, has not remarried.

"I can't say I've ever really dated again." He smiled and said, "I guess you'd say I'm still in love with my wife."

He is the single parent of two sons now at Lindenwood College. Adam is a baseball player and Blake is a golfer. They have no sisters.

"We were trying to adopt a girl when Peggy was killed," Thompson said. "We were in the process."

All of a sudden, eight years later, he was in charge of a dozen teenage girls on the Roosevelt varsity.

"My wife would have helped out a lot," Thompson said. "And I think she would have really enjoyed it."

He knows he did. Even though his girls managed just one victory in a season that ended with a 74-29 loss to Beaumont in the district opener.

"It was a learning experience for all of us," he said. "I've grown from it and I think they've grown, too. A lot of the girls had never played basketball before. But we didn't cut anybody, because we only had 20 to 22 girls for the A team and the B team together.

"Obviously, we didn't have a winning season, as far as wins and losses. But we had a winning season in other ways. The girls really played hard every game, and they played as a team.

"On the bus back from our last game, when we got beat by 40 points in districts, several of the girls said, 'We feel like we won the game, because we did as well as we could. We really had fun out there.'"

There was another measuring stick.

"We still had 12 to 15 girls left in the program," said Thompson. "Usually, most of them quit if they're not winning."

The attrition came from personal problems. "Outside influences take girls away from the sport," said Thompson, who would not elaborate.

The deck was stacked in other ways.

The Roosevelt girls practice on a small floor. Their "home" games are at Gateway Tech and attendance is sparse.

"If more people came out to girls' games," Thompson said, "they'd see how entertaining it is. Because it is entertaining."

On the plus side, most of his players want him to coach them in spring and summer leagues. And the school administration has been gung-ho.

"Steve Warmack, our principal, and Sam Dunlap, our athletic director, are the reason I'm here," Thompson said. "They really do care about the total development of the students at Roosevelt High School, both academics and athletics.

"Sports here had really fallen off, but now all the programs are on the upswing. It all starts with the commitment of the school. That makes a big difference to a coach."

Jim Thompson is starting over at Roosevelt High.
(Photo by David Kennedy)

Thompson, 53, came on board a year ago to teach special education. That move was another change of pace in a life that had been forcibly changed. He still lives in the same house in Cahokia, within perfect view of fireworks displays at the Arch. He had spent the previous 19 years watching other people's money in a small accounting firm he ran with his wife. In his first year at Roosevelt, he continued to ref boys and girls games in Illinois. His only coaching had been coaching his sons' summer baseball teams for seven years before they reached high school. But last summer, a bum knee ended his officiating career. And so he said yes when his bosses asked him to step across in basketball season and fill the vacancy on the girls' bench. He was in for a few shocks.

"So many times when you're reffing a game," Thompson said, "you'd see a team making mistakes and say, 'If only I could coach that team!' Well, this year I learned a tremendous amount about looking at both sides and about being a little more humble.

"The hardest adjustment is sitting there and being helpless. When I was reffing, I would talk to the players out there on the court if they were doing things I didn't like—pushing and hand checks and things like that. As a coach, you're just not as active when the game is going on."

The biggest shocker?

"Some of the refereeing at these girls games was just atrocious," Thompson said. "We also had some of the best officiating I've ever seen. Danita Moore, Cathy Wietfeldt, Charles Kensler—their crews were great.

"I don't want to generalize about some of these other refs, but I think it's an attitude thing more than talent. They feel that the girls make more mistakes than boys, and if they called everything they'd be there all night."

And would that cause marathons?

"Sometimes," Thompson said. "But the calls still need to be made. If the girls start fouling out, they'll get the message. As a ref, I've done hundreds of girls' games, and when there was a foul, I called it. Before the game, I always said, 'Coach, I hope your girls know the rules, because we will be playing by them.' The rules are the same for the boys and girls. The only difference is the size of the basketball."

Style of play is another matter.

"The boys are bigger and stronger and faster," Thompson said, "but believe me, girls' games are rougher than boys'. These girls slap and hack each other like crazy. You can't let the girls get hurt. And they get angry when they get fouled hard. Things will never change if the refs allow it to happen. You want to run out there and blow your whistle and say, 'Ladies, come on! Let's clean this up and play basketball and not kill each other.'"

Thompson also can't believe that Missouri, alone among neighboring states, does not use the three-referee system. "With two refs," he said, "you just have too many blind spots."

For the record, the rookie coach drew just one technical foul. And, no shocker here, he claimed it was a bad rap.

"Only one referee showed up for a girls' varsity game," Thompson said. "Granted, it's just one person out there, but he was positioned wrong. With one person, you referee from the middle, not one side. So I asked him, 'Can you call them on both sides of the floor?' He looked at me and went, 'T.' I said, 'Okay.'"

He found that most of his chats with officials followed a familiar script.

"It's really funny," Thompson said. "You know exactly what they're going to tell you. 'You coach and we'll referee'—that's one cliché I heard all the time. Another one was, 'You take care of your team, and I'll take care of the game.'"

"But I will say this. The calls do look different on the bench than they do from the floor. It's like going from student to teacher. Or putting on a reversible coat. Or looking at mirror. I just want to thank Steve Warmack and Sam Dunlap for giving me an opportunity to jump through that mirror and see that reflection."

His bosses let him run the program his way, which meant ignoring a common suggestion from friends.

"A lot of people told me, 'You need to be hard on these girls,'" Thompson said. "But I did what Peggy would have told me: 'You have to be honest with them, and trust them, and let them trust you.'

"And that's what I think we did."

48

MARNIE TRIEFENBACH

Volleyball Ace Digs In After New Start

I t's the triple dilemma for all top athletes. How do you know when to quit playing kids' games? How do you deal with the expectations of others who can only envision you in a sports uniform? And how do you channel your competitive edge into your new life as a civilian non-combatant? For five years, those questions consumed Marnie Triefenbach, one of this area's most elite multisport athletes.

Marnie, who turned 28 in this summer of 2002, has just moved on to her third job since getting her degree from Stanford University in 1996. She is doing research and field work for Cambria Environmental Technologies, testing soil and ground water around gasoline tanks at 148 service stations and other spots in the San Francisco Bay Area. That's a long way from dental surgery, her aim during two years of premed at Stanford. And it seems to do little with her eventual degree in psychology.

"Oh, it has nothing to do with it," she said with a laugh.

As for sports, she still plays pickup basketball after work. "But my favorite thing that I do," she said, "is Sports for Kids."

The non-profit group works with youngsters whose grade schools have no sports teams, due to budget cuts.

Marnie is her third year of coaching girls' basketball and volleyball for Sports for Kids and serving on the eight-person board of directors.

She plunged in with her typical championship passion. She was recently chosen as one of the Bay Area's Top 25 volunteers.

It may be hard for St. Louis sports fans to think of Marnie on the sidelines.

She won two state volleyball titles in her last two years at Belleville West, was the Illinois girls' Player of the Year in both seasons and was named the national Player of the Year as a senior in '91.

She also starred in basketball on conference champions that "didn't quite make it to state," as she put it. Her bigger claim to basketball fame here was her select team, which featured five big-time college recruits. Marnie, Kristin Folkl and Charmin Smith all went west to Stanford. Molly Pierick stayed in the Midwest at Notre Dame and Carri Walker went east to Wake Forest. Marnie also played club volleyball with Folkl, who was two years younger. Folkl did the recruiting while Marnie, a high school sophomore, tried out for their summer basketball team.

"I watched her play for about a minute, " Folkl said, "and then I yelled, 'Hey, Dad, I think we found our outside hitter!'"

And that was before ever seeing Marnie hit a volleyball.

"But she was athletic, tall and lanky," Folkl said. "I thought, 'This is probably a no-brainer.'"

It was. And so Marnie trekked from Belleville to join the St. Charles Volleyball Club. And ended up trekking a lot farther west than St. Charles.

"Stanford people were already looking at Kristin when she was in eighth grade," said Cheryl Triefenbach, Marnie's mom. "And when they came to see Kristin, they saw Marnie."

They also saw both girls and Smith on their club basketball team. Marnie, a six-foot-one forward and outside hitter, was the eldest. Smith followed her to Stanford the next year and Folkl the year after that. Marnie meant to play both sports at Stanford but quickly focused on volleyball. She won two NCAA championship rings in three Final Four trips and made second-team All-America. She had dropped basketball partly because of her rugged premed studies.

"I didn't sleep much for two years," she said. "And I wanted to try to be the best volleyball player I could be."

She dropped premed because of the long apprenticeship for dental surgery.

"I didn't want to be in school for 10 years," she said.

She did want to play volleyball for a living, but fate dropped that option.

"It's one of those 'woulda, coulda, shoulda' things," Marnie said.

First, a leg injury cost her a starting spot as a senior.

"I lost 15 pounds and wasn't at full strength," she said. "It was pretty disappointing having to watch, especially losing to Texas in the Final Four. We should have beaten them."

After graduation, she planned to move to Los Angeles and hit the beach as a volleyball pro. That career, as she put it, "didn't go at all."

The culprit was another injury.

"When I was in college," Marnie said, "we weren't allowed to go skiing or sky diving or bungee jumping. They were paying for our education, and they didn't want the liability if we got hurt."

But after her eligibility ended, some friends invited her to go snowboarding at Lake Tahoe. She quickly mastered the beginner courses. Then someone suggested she step up to the ultimate slope.

"They took me five chair lifts up to the Double Diamond," Marnie said, "which is the craziest thing you can do when you don't know what you're doing. My claim to fame is that I actually made it halfway down the hill. Then I hit an icy patch and went head over board. The problem was, one boot didn't release and my ankle stayed in the boot. I ended up with my ankle on one side of the board and my body on the other.

"But the worst part was being skied down the mountain on this little sled. They put a tarp over you like you're dead. It was hysterical, but it was so embarrassing."

For awhile, embarrassment seemed like the worst result. Marnie could walk on the ankle with no more pain than a sprain, and an X-ray was negative.

"I spent January to June working out on it, playing on it, training in the sand," said Marnie, who had moved to L.A. "I told myself, 'I've just got to suck it up, and tape it up, and get back to what I need to do to get ready for the beach.' But it was just excruciating."

So she finally flew back to San Francisco to see her college orthopedist. He ordered the more sophisticated MRI test and then gave her the grim news: A bone chip, multiple tiny fractures, torn ligaments throughout the ankle and surgery scheduled for the next day. After the operation, she returned to L.A. for an eight-month recovery. After two months on crutches, the cast came off and she continued chasing her dream in the sand.

"I started some pretty aggressive rehab," she said, "but some underlying things were happening in my life. I looked around at the women playing beach volleyball, and one thing they all had in common was a life outside of volleyball. You don't make a lot of money on the beach.

"I'd been a volleyball player my whole life. That's what everybody thought I would do. But I was really burned out. Six months after the surgery, I just got bored. I knew I didn't want to play any more. The injury kind of gave me an out. I could save a little face and do something else."

That something was a job as marketing director for the San Jose Lasers of the ABL, then the women's pro basketball rival of the WNBA. The team's husband-wife owners had been fans of Stanford volleyball. So Marnie moved back north to San Mateo, near the Stanford campus in Palo Alto, about a 45-minute drive from San Jose.

"I was happy as a cat," Marnie said. "I was getting out of the house, learning something new, meeting new people, still involved with sports but on the business side. To see a different side of sports, it really sparked me."

And then the ABL folded.

"I no longer had a job," she said. "I thought, 'You know what? I've got to get a life.' I wanted to be on my own and prove to myself I could do whatever I wanted to do."

That proof came with Title 9 Sports, a women's apparel company across the bay in Berkeley. Marnie was familiar with the fledgling company through its catalog.

"I walked in off the street," she recalled, "and said, 'I'd like to work here.' And they hired me in customer service."

That was in 1998. Six months later, the company asked Marnie to hatch a web site.

"I had no idea what I was doing," she said, "but it was the best year and a half of my life, business-wise. It was day after day a challenge, and I was using my brain. And it was a big success. Last year, our web site sales were 30 percent of our total sales. But after a year and a half, I wanted to get out from in front of the computer. I wanted to make the deals. I had an opportunity to work in the merchandising department and help produce photo shoots. I got to travel to places like Hawaii and Tahoe. Then we needed somebody to do our recruiting and public relations, so I did that for a year."

By then, she had run through every major position but chief executive, which was not vacant. It was time to move on. Marnie promptly violated the No.1 rule of every job search: Don't quit the old one until you find a new one.

"But I knew I wouldn't devote as much time looking for a new job if I still had my old job," Marnie said. "Looking for it part-time and looking for it full-time, to me that was the difference in getting a job."

She got moral support from her sister, Tara, who is three years older and working in the Bay Area.

"She's kicking some butt at Veritas Software, one of the biggest software companies in the Bay Area," Marnie said. "She's a manager for sales and training."

Marnie, though, did not apply at her sister's company.

"No, no!" Marnie yelled in mock horror. "I love her, but *no!* We're very close and she's one of my best friends, but we've got to draw the line somewhere."

While hustling up her new post with Cambria Environmental, Marnie filled the job void with Sports for Kids.

"I work with fourth- and fifth-grade girls," she said, "and it's incredible."

So was the recognition as a top 25 volunteer in the Bay Area. Even for someone with a crowded trophy case.

"It's such a huge honor for me," she said. "It's one of the most rewarding awards I could earn. I know from when I was going to camps, you remember the great counselors. You remember the fun ones. When I joined Sports for Kids, I thought, 'I want to be the one who gets them fired up and infuses them with energy.'

"When I worked at the Stanford volleyball camp, it cost 600 bucks for three days. Kids want to be there. The kids I'm working with now aren't like that at all. Because of budget cuts, they don't have organized sports at the grade school and the junior high level."

While helping the young girls, they have helped her recognize some things about life...hers and theirs.

"I think every kid has the right to go out and just play for the sake of playing," Marnie said. "But many of these kids come from single-parent homes. They have to cook the meals and take care of brothers and sisters.

I am where I am today because of family and sports. But it's heartbreaking to see some of these kids. They come to school every day, and they're loners, and they don't have any self-confidence.

"In school, people are always saying, 'You're not smart enough, you don't dress right, you're not good enough.' But sports made me what I am. I felt I could do anything I wanted to."

Three nights a week, 10 weeks a season, Marnie coaches self-confidence and self-worth into her girls.

"On my fifth-grade team, my quietest player was my best player," Marnie said. "The shift in her attitude from the beginning of the year was incredible. Not just the way she looked at herself, but also the way the other kids looked at her.

"Certainly some of these kids have a family. But many of them don't have an adult in their lives to tell them that they can do it. I tell them that I believe in them and to take a sense of ownership in what you do. They see that, 'I am in control of what I can and cannot do, not what other kids say I should be able to do.'"

Or, for that matter, what other adults tell the coach what she should be able to do.

49

GRAHAM BENSINGER

Teen Sounds Off with Own Internet Station Show

G raham Bensinger of Ladue is 15 years old, fresh-faced and as eager as any beaver in the forest. When he dreams up a project, he doesn't just jaw about it. He starts gnawing. As an eighth grader, Graham thought it would be fun to interview sports celebrities on the radio. Never mind that radio stations do not hire cub reporters still in grade school. That was just a technicality.

Graham upped and started his own station—on the internet, without the need for a frequency, transmitter or FCC approval. Then he put himself to work as the one-man staff of GsportRadio.com. In one year's time, Graham was a grizzled freshman at Mary Institute-Country Day School, and his station was up and running with one new interview per week. The lineup was built around All-Stars of every ilk.

On this particular week, the headliner was Monte Irvin, who left the Negro Leagues to help break baseball's color line en route to the Hall of Fame. Previous heavy hitters include baseball greats Ernie Banks and Harmon Killebrew, football greats Jackie Smith and Ron Yary and broadcrasting greats—or near greats—John Madden and Tim McCarver. Graham's interview archives also feature active players, such as Scott Mellanby and Brent Johnson of the Blues. On deck was Tim Forneris, the

Graham Bensinger gets Tim Forneris on the record.
(Photo by David Kennedy)

law student and part-time groundskeeper who returned Mark McGwire's record 62nd home run ball. After just a year, Graham figured that GsportRadio.com was drawing 75 to 100 hits per day. The interviews run just as Graham taped them over the phone or in person. Transcripts are not available, so visitors to the site must use a computer wired for sound.

Graham gears the operation to his peer group, 12- to 19-year-olds, and approaches his guest stars accordingly.

"I usually start off by asking them what it feels like to be in their position," he said, "and what the influences were on them growing up. Just stuff that kids would be more interested in."

In that respect, Graham could best serve his audience, young or old, by interviewing himself each week and posting the latest installment of what he's been up to and how he did it. He is resourceful, resilient and relentless. Granted, Graham has some personal advantages over most teenagers. He attends a ritzy prep school, lives in a ritzy zip code and has a father, Scott, who runs his own company, Plaza Financial Group in Clayton. But Graham leans on almost none of the above in his interview project. The Web site costs about $300 per year to run. Graham pays for that from his home business: selling packs of baseball cards on another internet site, Grahamscards.com. He started his card-collecting business in the summer before seventh grade, when he was 12, and now averages about 1,000 packs sold per month. His dad did give that project a little push at the start.

"He fronted me some money for the hosting of that web site," Graham said. "It was a little bit at a time, maybe a hundred or two hundred dollars overall. But I paid him back. Most of my money I save and put into inventory. I don't spend much money at all."

His dad did foot the bill for high school, but going to Country Day was not a birthright. One day, when Graham was in fifth grade at the local public school, he announced that he would be attending MICDS the next year.

"He said he thought that was the best way to get into Harvard," said his dad. "I told him, 'It's not that easy. I don't know anybody there. Your mom and I didn't go there. They require applications and interviews and tests to get in. If you do all of that, and keep a 3.0 average when you get there, I'll pay your tuition.' Well, he did everything he needed to do."

As for the sports interviews, Graham is on his own, aside from his mom, Vicki, ferrying him to appointments until he's old enough to drive.

"I haven't read a sports page in almost 20 years," said his dad. "That's his deal."

In the line of that duty, Graham hoped to land a press credential to Cardinals games. He did wrangle a one-day pass last year, parlaying that into interviews with Colorado Rockies stars Larry Walker, Mike Hampton and Denny Neagle, plus bench coach Fred Kendall.

"I have the press pass on my bulletin board. It was April 12, 2001," Graham said. "I just sent them a fax a week earlier, and they told me to come down the day of the game. So I just left school early. I'm not sure what I told them at school, but I had to convince my mom to pick me up. It took a lot of convincing."

It took even more at Busch Stadium when he met with Brad Hainje, the team's assistant public relations director.

"I had about five minutes to convince him," Graham said. "I'm not sure what I said, actually."

Graham was admitted only for that day. A season's pass wasn't in the cards for obvious logistical reasons. The ballpark isn't big enough to hold every teenager with a tape recorder and an itch to be the next Joe Buck or

Bob Costas. Graham's auditory system does not easily process the word "No." So he took the next logical step, to his teenaged mind, and went straight to the top.

"I just called one of the owners, Drew Baur, at his bank," Graham said. "I was surprised when he actually answered the phone. My throat locked up. I could barely get anything out."

Graham croaked out his name, his mission and his Country Day connection, knowing that Baur and his fellow owners were proud alumni. That ace card got instant results.

"He laughed," Graham said. "And he referred me to Fred Hanser, another owner. And when I called Mr. Hanser, he referred me to Bill DeWitt."

Graham thought he had reached Bill DeWitt Jr. In fact, it was the chairman's son, Bill DeWitt III, a Cardinals official who promised to look into the matter. Young DeWitt did, referring Graham by email to Hainje. At the end of that rollercoaster loop, Graham was still frustrated but wiser when it came to talking to grownups.

"The last time I was shy about it was when I called Drew Baur. I said to myself, 'Look, this guy's just a normal person like me . . . except he's got millions.'"

Graham was willing to scuffle for interviews but did not want to invade anyone's privacy. So he writes letters. He hands an introductory letter to players at public functions. And he's gotten a big lift from Dave Jackson, who runs St. Louis Sports Collectibles in the Metro East and promotes card shows across the St. Louis area. Graham got Jackson's permission to interview some of the autograph guests at the shows, such as Irvin.

"At first I was pretty apprehensive because of his age," Jackson said. "But he works really hard. He is so focused. I didn't know that Monte Irvin stole home once in the World Series, but Graham did, and Monte really enjoyed talking about it. This kid really does his homework."

At the Bensinger home, the parents are no longer annoyed when fielding calls for their son.

"It is kind of interesting when the phone rings now," Scott said. "One time someone asked for Graham and I asked who was calling. And a guy yelled, 'Will Clark!' Several days later my wife picked up the phone, and it was Ernie Banks."

Graham, meanwhile, is busier than ever as the center fielder on his junior varsity baseball team. He also enjoys mountain climbing and hopes to scale the tallest mountain on each continent, a goal almost as tough as getting a Cardinals credential. Graham was filling mail orders for his card business the other day when he took a break to ponder the training he's giving himself.

"I'm getting good broadcast experience, sort of," he said. "And business experience with the web site. And experience with the internet."

Through it all, his biggest fan base may be the Cardinals' media office.

"We're rooting for him," Hainje said. "Like I told him, we have no doubt that he'll succeed, and that he'll be back here one day as a full-time member of the media."

Or maybe as a future owner of the ball club.

50

CAROLYN & LAUREN COPELAND

Viz Twins Mix Assault and Battery

They don't claim to have the most talent. Their high school team is not exactly a district contender. So what's so special about the pitcher-catcher combo from Visitation High? More than just their surname, Copeland, and their adjacent mugshots in the school yearbook. These two seniors, Carolyn and Lauren, share a special spark missing from most softball batteries—as innocent bystanders keep learning.

"We got on the elevator at my dad's building," said Lauren, "and this guy looked at us and said, 'Are you two sisters?' We said, 'Oh, noooo.' And he said, 'Oh, my God! You know what they say about everyone having a twin somewhere in the world? You really look like twins.'"

Astute point. The Copeland girls are twins.

And when they play games, be it on elevators or softball fields, they could be joined at the lip. They are best friends and bitter competitors—with each other, as well as the opposition. That can be a double eye opener for strangers, like first-year Viz coach John Guyre and new pitching coach Barb Krus.

"They really go at each other sometimes," said Krus, a former head coach at St. Louis U. "You should have heard them in our game with Nerinx. We had a rough inning, and when they came into the dugout,

Lauren yelled, 'You can't pitch!' And Carolyn yelled, 'If you could catch better, I could pitch better!'

"Lauren was ready to yell something back, but then she said, real calmly, 'You know, I can't be doing this. I'm the oldest. I was born 10 minutes before you were. I have to be the mature one,' and she walked away. And it was like nothing had ever happened."

Assistant coach Gayle Lund, who is Guyre's older sister, said, "They were having a good little tiff. John was told by Carolyn that she never wanted Lauren to catch her again. But she got over it fast."

Guyre was stunned, by the sudden eruption and the sudden solution.

"This was just our second game of the year," he said. "I still didn't know the twins that well. So I did what any coach would do. I called in their mom and said, 'How do you handle them when they're like that?' She just laughed and said, 'I don't. There's nothing you can do. That's just the way they are.'"

Krus sees this as the perfect pairing.

"It's a pitcher's dream to be pitching to your twin," Krus insisted. "If you make a mistake, she knows what you meant to do." Krus paused and then smiled. "Of course, if you make a mistake, you're in trouble with your sister."

When Lauren gloves a bad pitch, she is apt to fire it back even harder to the mound. That stunt can sting a pitcher, especially since only the catcher wears a padded mitt. Lauren doesn't always wait for trouble. She prefers preemptive action when her twin finishes her warmup tosses from the mound each inning.

"When I throw the ball down to second," Lauren said tenderly, "I love it when she forgets to duck."

Once, Krus looked out in the middle of an inning to see the twins confronting each other between the mound and home plate.

"I can't see your signals," Carolyn barked at her catcher.

"How can you not see the signs?" Lauren barked at her pitcher. "I put tape on my fingers."

So the Copeland family started a new tradition. The pitcher flashes the signs to the catcher for each pitch, instead of the other way around.

Other disputes are variations on endless themes.

Krus, the pitching guru, said, "Lauren will come out to the mound and say, 'Your boyfriend's ugly…Throw harder.' Carolyn will say, 'Oh, yeah? Your hair looks ugly.' That's how they fire each other up to play better."

They and their teammates are playing better than expected. Still, that effort produced only three wins in the first 11 games. It could be much worse, if not for the Viz twins.

"The whole team is fueled by their energy," Krus said.

They make up the core of a program struggling to switch from spring to fall softball in 2002. Most of their teammates dropped out because of conflicts with their preferred fall sports. The move was supposed to happen last year. The twins put posters in the school halls to drum up interest, but only five other girls signed up. Undaunted, the Viz twins spent last season helping their dad, David, coach the school's team seventh- and eighth-grade teams. This fall, they helped round up 10 other varsity hopefuls for tryouts.

Before a ball was thrown or batted, Guyre assembled his prospects and said, "Congratulations! You *all* made the team."

They number five seniors, two juniors, two sophomores and three freshmen. They hustle at practice, are much improved and never say die in games—even when losing to some of the jayvee squads on their light schedule. But the Viz kids remain in high spirits, largely because of the intensity and antics of the Viz Twins.

"They're entertainment even when we lose," said Krus.

And not just by their public displays of sisterly non-affection.

"One time, they came in from a rough inning," said Krus, "and I asked Carolyn, 'What were we throwing out there?' She told me, and I said, 'Let's try something else.' I started making suggestions, and I looked and saw the number on her back, and it was Lauren."

Lauren wears No. 22 in honor of fellow catcher Mike Matheny of the Cardinals. Carolyn sports No. 43 in tribute to ex-Cardinals reliever Dave Veres.

"I said to Lauren, 'Hey, you're the catcher! Why didn't you say something when I was talking?' And she said, 'I was just having some fun with you.'"

The twins insist they are not identical, in any sense of the word. Lauren claims to be sturdier. She makes her point by hoisting her younger half and lurching around the bullpen. Lauren answers to "Lou," which should probably be spelled Lu since it's derived from Lulu. Carolyn's hair is a tad lighter than her older half. She is a slightly less rabid competitor and knows it. That's why she actually welcomes her twin's rude motivational ploys. When softball is over, Carolyn is a Viz cheerleader. And she cheerfully answers to "Girly Girl," her sister's pet name for her.

To the untrained eye, their differences vanish when one has a cap covering her hair, the catcher's gear is off and the jerseys have numbers only on the back. When those optical conditions are met, the Viz twins could be clones. Fortunately, the team has a trained expert who can separate the twins. Visually and vocally, if need be. Second baseman Laura Cherre is on call for emergencies, foreign and domestic. Her last name is pronounced "Cherry," and her teammates apply it like a nickname. The twins consider her the triplet they never had.

"I have a room at their house," Laura said. "I just tell their mom, 'I'm staying here tonight.' She thinks I'm her third daughter."

Laura, in fact, is the daughter of C.J. Cherre, the noted raconteur and traveling secretary for the Cardinals. Laura inherited his wit and wisdom, which makes her the ideal foil when the twins are dueling.

As Guyre put it, "Laura's like the referee in a boxing match."

"They're the worst people I've ever seen," Laura said, almost keeping her face straight. "I just come in and slap 'em both, and then I separate 'em and put in 'em in a timeout."

Actually, the twins plan to separate themselves at college, one in Ohio and the other in Nebraska. Even then, they'll be easy to confuse. One likes Dayton, the other prefers Creighton. The look-alikes at sound-alike schools? Good luck trying to remember which twin is where.

PAT McSHEEHY

Two Heart Surgeries, Too Busy to Slow Down

P at McSheehy, new college graduate, has a plan for his future.

"I've got a lot of time to think about what my life's goals are," he said. "The first one is to slow down."

Isn't that just what you'd expect from this younger generation? How tired can a 23-year-old be after four—or five, in Pat's case—years of college? Light schedule. Late mornings. Parties. A couple of classes a day, a cameo appearance in the library, the odd all-nighter before a test. Those were the days, eh?

Well, they weren't Pat McSheehy's days at Webster University. He hardly cruised through, unless that reference is to the pace of a cruise missile. Just reading about his athletic feats might wear out the average couch potato. Factor in his staggering workload off the field and out of class, and exhaustion sets in. Then figure in his three surgeries on major organs—one on a kidney, two on his heart—in his sophomore year. Now you can see why Pat—high on a rooftop, installing siding in blazing heat in one of his many side jobs—might think about decelerating. Think about it, yes. Actually throttle back, no.

"It was kind of scary, with all his operations," said his younger sister Joyce. "Especially the second heart surgery. But the worst thing about that was, he couldn't be active for six weeks. He was cranky. He's the most active person I know."

Unless she knows Martha Stewart, that's no exaggeration.

That's why Pat, gaunt at five feet 11 and maybe 155 pounds dripping wet with sweat, said, "I don't look like a whole lot of anything. But I do what I can."

For starters, he was a four-year starter in soccer and baseball at Webster. He was also voted the conference player of the year in each sport. And he was twice named the school's Student Athlete of the Year.

"He was a throwback to the old days," said Webster soccer coach Marty Todt. "We had him in every position but goalie, and he never complained about anything. Never. And he never had an alibi on a bad day. No matter what the adversity, he'd say, 'Hey, let's move on.'"

"There's no one ever who even compares to what he did in the program," said Webster baseball coach Marty Hunsucker. "And he wound up playing every position except first base. You'd watch him play the outfield, and you'd want to tell the other two kids just to get out of his way and let him do it."

In soccer alone, he was first-team All-Region (11 players chosen from 53 schools), a three-year captain, and leader of the school's first two berths in the NCAA Division III tournament. In baseball, he was All-Region twice and All-Conference three times, holds Webster season records in batting average (.466), slugging percentage (.767), runs (51), hits (63) and at-bats (115), and career records in batting average (.403), hits (214), runs (156), runs batted in (117) and at-bats (530).

Much of that rundown is news to Pat. He has no down time to collect scrapbook items.

"I don't care about all that stuff," he said. "I just do what I do because it's what I like to do."

He doesn't mind studying either, carrying a 3.8 average on a 4.0 scale at McCluer North High. That dipped to 3.0 at Webster, a solid B average that displeased him. To be sure, it's not like Pat spent his mornings with video games, his afternoons tuned to soap operas and his nights at toga parties. Despite the demands of two-sport stardom, he holds Webster's unofficial record for most jobs worked in a season and a career.

As Hunsucker put it, "He probably made more money last semester than I did. I've had some ballplayers who sleep as much as Pat works in a day."

Pat's work-study deal at Webster involved odd jobs throughout the athletic department.

"I did just about everything in the gym for basketball and volleyball," he said. "Fix the shot clocks. Hang banners. Set up for the game. I did stuff outside, too, like keep score for women's soccer."

He grinned and said, "They made out real well with me, yes they did."

And that was just the campus workload. When he went back to his Marlborough apartment, he would bounce back out to install home siding in his own branch of the family company, McSheehy Properties, where he hired and supervises one employee of his own, a college buddy. He also has a regular gig as handyman at Midwest Soccer Academy in south St. Louis, run by Todt's brother-in-law.

"Mechanically, Pat's extremely gifted," said Todt, meaning more than athletic mechanics. "He can fix anything, from plumbing problems to electrical problems."

Pat also works as a landscaper, and he's manned a fireworks stand since he was 10. His spot work included a bid to rebuild a chimney box, a job that he underestimated but still completed. In his idle seconds, he restores vintage trucks, currently working on a '54 Chevy pickup and a '49 Ford flatbed.

"I just bought a '90 Chevy flatbed," Pat said, "but that one actually runs already. So that'll be my work truck."

Remember, this go-getter went in for three major repairs of his own less than four years ago.

"I was having a lot of back problems toward the end of high school and beginning of college," said Pat. "They found out that my left kidney swelled up because of a blocked tube. It was the size of a cantaloupe, and it's supposed to be the size of your fist. The doctor said, 'That's the biggest one I've ever seen. We'll cut it out, filet it and put it back in.'"

Pat got a kick out of that humor from the surgery, which finally came before his sophomore year in August, 1998. He was less amused by an old heart condition that butted in.

For Pat McSheehy, it's time to excel, not dwell on heart-stopping surgery.
(Photo by Bob Frischmann)

"It started out as an irregular heartbeat," Pat said. "They found out about it through my eighth-grade physical to go to high school. So it's like five years later, and they're going to fix the kidney problem, and I go for a routine physical, and the heart condition has become almost constant."

His resting pulse was 140 beats per minute, double the normal rate. The kidney surgery was delayed until his pulse was calmed down through medication. Pat missed only a couple days of sophomore classes and eventually returned to soccer practice.

"My doctor told me my heart was getting weaker from overwork, because it was beating too fast," Pat said. "There's an electrical current that runs through your heart and tells it when to beat. Mine had extra connections, so it didn't turn off when it was supposed to."

Pat's options were a lifetime of medication—"and that's no fun," he said—or an operation. The first attempt came in January, 2000, and did not involve open-heart surgery. Fiber optics were threaded through an artery to Pat's heart to burn the extra connections. And it flopped.

"I knew it about four hours after I woke up in the hospital," Pat said. "I was talking on the phone with a friend, and my heart monitor started going beep-beep-beep! It was right back to where it was."

He had decided to sit out Webster's soccer season, saving that year of eligibility, but he could not just sit around.

"They did the procedure on a Friday," Pat said, "and I was playing indoor soccer the next Wednesday."

The next option was a full-blown surgery that was risky, to say the least. One skeptical doctor told Pat he faced four possible results: "It'll work, or you'll have a stroke, or you'll have a heart attack, or you'll die."

Pat opted to take the risk rather than have to slow his pace for the rest of his life. The doctor who did the first procedure here recommended a surgeon at Georgetown Hospital in Washington, D.C. But there was another hitch.

"When I was five," Pat said, "I had an inverted breastbone. They fixed that, but they had to break my breastbone. When I got to Georgetown, the doctor didn't want to open that up, which they do in a regular open-heart surgery.

"So he decided to go through the back right side of the heart. He said, 'I've never done it this way before, but I think it'll work.'"

This news did not exactly inspire Pat's family—parents Carol and Patrick and kid sisters Joyce and Jennifer.

"My mom was a wreck," said Pat.

This surgery, on April 3, 2000, lasted three and a half hours, less than expected.

"They separated the atrium and the ventricle with a scalpel," Pat said. "They had sensors in the heart, and they just started cutting away until it slowed down, I guess. I wasn't awake for that part."

When he woke up this time, the problem was fixed. So much so that he planned to join Todt's soccer team for practice in July, as it prepared for a tour of Holland.

"He's out there three months after major heart surgery," Todt said. "I'm thinking, 'How long will it take him to be at full speed? Six weeks? Six months?'"

The answer?

"Two practices," Todt said. "He was dragging a little those first two days. It was extremely hot in July. But then he started scoring goals, and he had an excellent trip to Holland. That year, we came back and went 16-1-2, won our conference and went to the NCAA Tournament for the first time. It was amazing."

In fact, all of Pat's finest two-sport hours at Webster came after that major heart surgery.

"His first couple years," said Hunsucker, "the kid had like a sugar fetish. He always had a huge bag of candy with him. When he was sitting, his heart was working like other people do when they're running full-out on a treadmill. I kidded him that when they fixed that thing, he might have to slow down and be like a normal person.

"Then he goes out and puts up the numbers he did for us the next three years. And he probably didn't tell you that he was hitting over .500 this year until he got hurt and couldn't swing without pain. He started hitting like a human being after that."

Pat, though, thinks he is still not up to snuff.

"I actually had a little more zip before I had the heart surgery," he said.

He is saying this on Monday, after picking up lumber in South St. Louis on his way to a condo job in North County. And after a Sunday spent painting condo ceilings in the afternoon, playing sandlot baseball at 7:30 p.m. and indoor soccer at 10:30 p.m.

"Hey, I'll still go all day," Pat said. "I don't like letting people down. I don't know what their expectations are, but they're probably not as high as mine are anyway."

"He's a unique cat," Hunsucker said. "I will miss him, just having him around."

Actually, he won't. Pat will be back on campus as Todt's paid assistant on the soccer team. Along with all his other jobs, Pat also plans to enroll in a junior college industrial arts program. He thinks he might want to teach shop class one day, which is why he hopes to substitute teach wherever possible this term. So what was that noise about slowing down?

"My parents are trying to put together a family vacation in late July," Pat said. "Hopefully a cruise. That'll be my getaway. Five nights and four days, or five days and four nights, whatever."

Pat McSheehy, trapped aboard ship and bouncing off bulkheads? Some getaway.

52

ACE BAILEY

The Ex-Blues Nice Guy and 9-11

With no personal connection, an outsider could be left numb by the September 11 terrorist attacks. For hockey folks, the general sense of grief gave way to stabbing pain as the passenger lists were released from the four planes airliners that were hijacked and crashed. Ex-Blues wing Ace Bailey, the pro scouting director for the Los Angeles Kings, was aboard United Flight 175 from Boston to Los Angeles. His was the second plane flown into the World Trade Center towers, as captured on live television. He was 53. A native of Lloydminster, Saskatchewan, he lived in the Boston suburb of Lynnefield with his wife, Kathy. The couple had one son.

Ace was travelling with his young protégé, Kings amateur scout Mark Bavis. Ace was flying west for his 32nd year as a big-league player or scout. He played 22 games for the Blues in 1973-74 and 49 more in 1974-75. In those 71 games, he scored 22 goals, 29 assists and totaled 51 points. To hockey folks, having Ace's face superimposed on this outrage is doubly cruel. Nobody had more fun in a too-short life than this big, tanned, smiling lug, whose given name was Garnet.

"God, it really hits home when that happens," said Blues sales director Bruce Affleck, who played here with Ace. "It's scary, unbelievable."

A continent away in Anchorage, Alaska, the Blues canceled the opening of training camp as the 9-11 tragedies unfolded. And pro scout Bob Plager had an uneasy premonition.

"We were all watching on the television," said Plager, a teammate for both of Ace's years here, "and somebody said some hockey scouts were on a plane. You think, 'Boston . . . Los Angeles . . . training camp . . . It may be Ace.' Then you find out.

"It's been rough. I've known him for 35, 36 years. We played against each other in junior and in the minors, and you fight and you stick each other, and then you're on the same team. We were roommates for awhile. And then we did the same job, so I'd run into him on the road.

"There are certain people around that everybody knew up in the press box, and Ace was one of them."

Doug Palazzari, who runs USA Hockey in Colorado Springs, was a rookie forward in Ace's last Blues season.

"It's awful," said Palazzari the day after the attacks. "I don't even know what to say. What an awful, awful thing. He was such a fun-loving guy, and a great practical joker."

Evidence of that will not be found in the public record.

"There are some great stories about Ace," said ex-Blues defenseman Bob Hess of Chesterfield, "but nothing that can go in the paper!"

"It's all locker room stuff that I can't let out," said ex-Blues winger John Wensink, now a contractor in St. Charles, forcing a laugh. "He was one of my first roommates, and he was a character. He was always upbeat. If you're going to hang out with somebody, he'd be the guy to hang with."

And to help you learn hockey.

"He was great in the dressing room," said Hess, chain manager for liquor wholesaler Glazers Midwest. "Me and Bruce and Pallazari were all rookies, and Ace was a great influence on us. He had been through the experience of winning the Stanley Cup in Boston."

Ace won two rings playing for the Bruins in the early '70s, plus five more as a scout for the Edmonton Oilers dynasty of the '80s. He also played two years with Detroit, the two here and three more with Washington. His playing career ended in 1980 with the Oilers, when he was a linemate and big brother to a skinny teen named Wayne Gretzky. But Ace did not just befriend famous phenoms.

"I was a rookie when I played in St. Louis," said the five-foot-five Palazzari, "and he did the same thing for me."

"He came to play every night," said Plager, "and he'd get in your face every night. He wasn't the superstar in Boston, but you need other players to do the battling."

Ace, at 5'11", had bulked up through the years from his 192-pound playing weight. That's why his buddies believe that the thugs on United Flight 175 had their knife-wielding hands full.

"You wonder what was going down," Hess said. "If you know Ace, he's not the type of guy who would sit quietly."

As Gretzky, the former Blues captain, told the *Edmonton Sun*, "I'm going to imagine Ace up out of his seat fighting those guys. I'm going to imagine Ace fighting to the end."

53

BOB ZAMBO

Heart 'n' Soul of Guns 'n' Hoses

B ob Zambo has been in the Guns 'n' Hoses corner since the slug-a-thon began in 1987.

"The first year I was a spectator," said Bob, a St. Louis Police Department major who lives in South County. "Like a lot of people I sat there and said, 'Hey, I can do that.' And the next year a lot of people reminded me of that."

So Bob, a former Cleveland High football player, laced on a pair of boxing gloves in the annual charity bash between local firefighters and police. He then became coordinator and co-coach of the city police boxers. The 14th annual event in 2001 was set, as always, for Thanksgiving Eve at Savvis Center.

The 13 previous shows netted $668,000, with all proceeds going to the St. Louis Backstoppers, which supports families of area police and firefighters killed on duty.

Then came the daylight nightmare of September 11 and the four terrorist hijackings in the northeast. In New York City, some 300 firefighters and 50 police officers died in a fearless rescue effort at the doomed World Trade Center.

Bob had initially joined the Guns 'n' Hoses cause for personal reasons. A fellow cop and boyhood friend, Greg Erson, was murdered in 1980 on a special detail in South St. Louis.

"We were grew up together," Bob said. "We were like brothers."

He felt the same way about his anonymous colleagues buried in the rubble in New York. And he had an idea.

"I thought we should send all our proceeds this year to New York," Bob said. "It was time for us to step up and help our brothers and sisters who made the ultimate sacrifice.

"It'll never change the circumstances of what happened. But it'd help give a lifestyle to their families as if they still had a head of household."

He broached the idea to the 20 city cops, including three women, training with him and co-coach Roger Engelhardt.

"I said, 'If anybody has an objection, speak up,'" Bob recalled. "And there were no objections whatsoever."

When he surveyed local firefighters, he got the same reaction, as expected. After all, these men and women in uniform know that their jobs could some day bring sorrow to their families.

But as Bob put it, "I've yet to meet anyone in this field, first responders, who went on a risky call and said, 'I'll never do this again.' They will respond. They will save lives. And they will put their lives on the line."

So Bob took his mandate to tournament director Myrl Taylor, who consulted with Jerry Clinton of Grey Eagle Distributors, the event's founder and sponsor. Clinton was already on the same wavelength about New York's fallen public servants. St. Louis Fire Department chief Sherman George, University City fire chief Bob Metcalf and Tim Fitch of the St. Louis County Police Department joined Clinton and Zambo in announcing the new mission for Guns 'n' Hoses. Clinton then donated $25,000, which Blues owners Bill and Nancy Laurie quickly matched. The Lauries also made Savvis available rent-free, chopping $40,000 off the Guns 'n' Hoses overhead.

"That basically puts us up $90,000 before the show starts," said Bob.

Last year's show netted $121,330 and drew 13,388 fans, both records. With a similar response on Thanksgiving Eve and the extra $90,000 up front, this year's take would top $210,000.

"But what our guys wanted to know," Zambo said, "was what can we do to raise more?"

For starters, Zambo said, they could hustle to sell out the 20,000-seat building. Tickets are $25, $20 and $15. Organizers are asking local companies to become major sponsors. The goal: $500,000 for the New York relief effort. Meanwhile, the cupboard will not be bare for the local Backstoppers, who cover St. Louis City, the Missouri counties of St. Louis, St. Charles, Jefferson and Franklin, plus the Illinois counties of St. Clair and Madison. Cardinals broadcaster Jack Buck, a Guns 'n' Hoses fan, recently raised $500,000 through the sale of autographed prints of Redbird greats. Cardinals co-owner David Pratt matched that total, giving the Backstoppers a $1 million windfall.

Guns 'n' Hoses raises more than money. It lifts the mystique from the men and women in uniform who step into the ring.

"The average person, when you see a firefighter or a police officer on the news, you don't relate to their family," Bob said. "We think of someone in a uniform as almost in a robot-like situation. But we're not. We're real people. We all have families. Now you see on TV that several of the police wives and firefighters' wives in New York were expecting babies. And the fathers will never be there to see their babies.

"Now, for the average person, it's almost a personal situation."

KEN BRADEN

The John Wayne of Officials

Nowadays in Missouri high school sports, it's hard to find game officials of any stripe, much less good ones.

The search just got a lot harder. Ken Braden of Oakville died on November 15, 2002, of complications from a stroke. He was 65 and, before he was afflicted, still looked like he could break a train. He was stricken in the hospital, barely two hours from bypass heart surgery that would have prevented the lethal stroke.

In a time when three-sport stars are almost extinct, Ken did more than just officiate baseball, basketball and football. He was at the top of the class in each. He officiated the Final Four twice in basketball, four times in baseball and did three football title games. In 1998, he completed the Triple Crown by working the finals of all three sports. Those striped honors, in a career that began belatedly at age 40, aren't what made Ken Braden an original.

"He was one of those unforgettable characters you read about in *Reader's Digest* or somewhere," said Bob Wagner, a longtime officiating buddy. "He was a grizzly bear on the outside and a teddy bear on the inside."

Ken covered his barrel chest in T-shirts that read "Awesome" or "Hard Rock Café: Lemay" or "Heine Meine Lounge: Catch a Cold One." He sported a driving cap, thought his 200,000-mile van was a luxury car, blasted patriotic marches on the van stereo and serenaded Peggy, his wife of 37 years, with showtunes from the Muny. He was more impressed with sportsmanship than championships. If a team showed class, win or lose, he would dash off a letter of praise to the athletic director—unbeknownst to the happily startled coach.

"He was a man among men," said Ray Cliffe, 79, a longtime friend, mentor and officiating supervisor. "I admired him, I respected him and I laughed with him. He was a good plateman in baseball. He was even better in basketball and football, probably 50-50 between them.

"I don't know about the best, but Ken Braden was the most fearless official in those three sports. He was like John Wayne, riding in the saddle. He's irreplaceable. I called him The Adonis. He was a Greek statue. He had that charismatic approach to disarm you with a quip. Witty things just fell off of him."

Truth be told, Ken's rugged mug does not fit the classic mold of Adonis, the pretty boy of the pantheon. A better handle is "Sergeant Slaughter," as one basketball lad called him—out of earshot, of course.

Make no mistake, Ken was godlike in a wonderfully earthy way. With his blunt toughness and sharp tongue—"he was clever but not a wise guy," Cliffe said—there was no better sidekick at a game or a watering hole. After a game, Ken always recommended imbibing a few "adult beverages" for curative purposes. "Just replenishing the fluids," he would say, ordering another round of "medicine" or "blood thinner." In fact, his blood was not thin enough to pass through three clogged arteries. They were detected after he contracted pneumonia, probably from working a recent game in a chilly downpour. The pneumonia was only detected because of a sharp pain in his side, caused by a collision with a player two weeks before his death. Ken accepted, even relished, such accidental contact as part of the job. A football umpire must set up in the middle of the defense.

"I see these guys 10 or 15 yards from the line of scrimmage," Cliffe snorted. "Then the ball's snapped and they start backpedaling. I tell them to buy a ticket. Kenny would be five to seven yards back, and then he'd step into the play. He wanted to see the holding and all the dirty sneaky stuff."

Ken Braden: an arbiter without peer.
(Photo courtesy of the Braden family)

Occasionally, a player plowed into him. Usually, the player hit the deck—not Ken, who would help the lad up while chirping, "C'mon, you can do better than that!" Cliffe rates officials for the Missouri State High School Activities Association. Shortly before Ken's death, Cliffe watched a district game and wrote what would be his last evaluation of his friend: "The greatest football umpire. *Ever.*"

"I broke him in in basketball," Cliffe said, "and we'd get into a tense situation. People would be yelling and screaming at us. And all that uproar just rolled right off his back, like a rainstorm. He'd just smile and say, 'Isn't this a beautiful thing?'"

Even with a blown call, Ken never lost control of himself or the situation.

"He knew how to unlock that tension," Wagner said. "One time we're working a basketball game at Wash U. and a player drives down the key. There's nobody around him, but Kenny blows his whistle. The kid doesn't even get to shoot the layup. He just stops. Everything stops. The place gets real quiet. Everyone's waiting to see what the call is.

"Kenny nonchalantly walks into the key with his arms folded. And then he says real loud, 'I think that's what they call an inadvertent whistle!' Everybody just starts laughing. The coaches. The players. The fans. Me. It was a hoot."

Ken never willingly pulled the spotlight onto himself. He was a law-and-order man whose politics were slightly to the right of his hero, Rush Limbaugh. But he scoffed at Barney Fife types, insecure and self-important, strutting around to show who's the boss. Ken never forgot that players are kids and coaches get emotional because they care. Better to keep them out of trouble than wait for a chance to penalize them.

"He had a good way of control without intimidation," said Don Meyer, a football crewmate. "He could deal with the problem athlete and get him out of the game without getting him out of the game, if you know what I mean."

Wagner elaborated: "If a kid was mouthing off, Ken wouldn't throw him out. He'd walk him over to the coach and say, 'You better rest him awhile. He's got an injured mouth.' Or he'd say, 'Coach, better take Number 50 out and check him. I think he broke his brain.'"

Ken could also massage coaches who were bent out of shape. Once when Cliffe coached junior varsity football at Affton, an opposing runner barely made a first down. Cliffe asked for a measurement. The referee refused and ordered the first-down chains to be moved.

"So I stood on the chains," Cliffe said. "I asked Kenny to ask the guy again if he'd measure. Kenny came back and said, 'He said he doesn't need to. It's a first down.'

"I said I wasn't moving. Kenny said, 'Get off the chains,' real low so no one else could hear. I said no. He said, 'Get off the chains.' I still wouldn't do it. Kenny said 'Get off the chains…Pleeeeeeez?'

"I broke up. What could I do? I got off the chains."

Ken was a star catcher at Roosevelt High, class of '55, and played two years at Southern Illinois University-Carbondale. A sandlot standout, he was inducted into the St. Louis Amateur Baseball Hall of Fame, his proudest honor. He also proudly served two years in the Air National Guard and was stationed in Europe during the Berlin Crisis in the early '60s. He came home, went to work for a bank and married Peggy in 1965. They raised two strapping sons: Tim, 36, and Dan, 35.

Ken was always up for back yard sports, but always under his rules. After catching the boys with "accidental" elbows, their dad would coo: "Old age and treachery will always defeat youth and skill."

Both boys played Division I college baseball. Dan, a star pitcher at Memphis State, once earned a game ball and presented it to his delighted dad. Tim caught for St. Louis University, where a makeup game with Missouri-St. Louis sticks in his mind.

"Dad came to watch me," Tim said, "and the umpires didn't show up. The coaches asked him if he had his gear in the car. I thought that was a big compliment. They knew he'd be fair even if his kid was playing.

"So Dad got behind the plate. My first time up, I walked on four pitches. The next time I came up, he said, 'Get out of the box.' I said, 'Yes, sir.' And he said, 'You're making me look bad. Swing the bat!' "

Both boys are now married and dads themselves. Tim has two young daughters, Dan a young daughter and a son on the way. Ken was a doting grandpa. No "accidental" elbows occurred when the little girls came to visit. More than ever, Tim and Dan appreciate their tough-love dad. And only they knew him in all of his favorite haunts—the back yard, the ballfield and the bar.

"He was more than our dad," said Dan. "As we got older, he was our friend. We could go golfing together or just hang out and have a beer together."

Ken's kids weren't the only ones in awe of him. So were the neighbor kids.

"As soon as you walked in the room you respected this guy," said Dan Ernst, now a St. Louis City policeman. "The way he carried himself. The way he treated people. As a kid, it was nice to have someone like that to look up to."

Bruce Hook, another football official, saw the same response when the crew would wind down after a game.

"We'd be out socializing," Hook said, "and some young man would stop by the table and start up a conversation with Kenny. The young man would say something like, 'You worked my game back in '94, when I was a defensive tackle for Pattonville…' It happened so many times, it finally wasn't surprising. But years later, how many high school players remember an official who worked their game?"

As Meyer said, "Ken was good because he treated players with respect—until they failed to return that respect or abused the privilege of playing."

At the bank, Ken's specialty was credit card fraud. That meant teaming with police in their squad cars.

"Respect and discipline, those where his things," said Tim. "That's why he loved the military. And the cops."

And officiating. His one fear in the hospital was not death itself, but the thought of never working another game.

At the six-hour wake, mourners waited 90 minutes to pay respects to this most respected official. Ken Braden was buried with his riding cap, Dan's game ball, a sleeve of golfballs, a photo of his granddaughters…and his eyeglass case, which he was forever losing.

That's right. The most outstanding official of them all had imperfect vision. Good thing he knew the job by heart.

Ken Braden's Ruling on Fairness

Here is an excerpt from a letter that Ken wrote to his younger son, Dan, then a promising left-handed pitcher having arm trouble at Memphis State University:

"I compare life to sports in the fact that you can do your best but you cannot dictate how the game is ultimately called. Ball-strike, safe-out is not in your control as a player. What you have to do is adjust to the umpire's zone and throw to it. If you think you should be getting a strike on the corner but the umpire is not calling it, you had better adjust or you will not win the game.

"In your case, if your life does not revolve around throwing a baseball, so be it. Who knows what good thing is right around the corner for you? What you cannot do is sit around, all melancholy, complaining about 'This situation is so unfair.' Buddy, no one said it would be anything but.

"We do not dictate the hand that God deals us. What you have to do is adjust. If you cannot adjust, you will not achieve."

AP/WWP

SPECIAL THANKS TO THE FOLLOWING FOR THEIR SUPPORT OF THIS BOOK.